Medicine and Medical Ethics in Nazi Germany

D1566704

MEDICINE AND MEDICAL ETHICS IN NAZI GERMANY

Origins, Practices, Legacies

Edited by
Francis R. Nicosia
and
Jonathan Huener

Berghahn Books
NEW YORK • OXFORD

Published in 2002 by
Berghahn Books
First reprint published in 2004

www.berghahnbooks.com

Library of Congress Cataloging-in-Publication Data
Medicine and medical ethics in Nazi Germany : origins, practices, legacies /
edited by Francis R. Nicosia and Jonathan Huener.
    p. cm.
Includes bibliographical references and index.
ISBN 1-57181-386-1 (alk. paper) ISBN 1-57181-387-X
    (alk. paper: pbk.)
    1. Medicine—Germany—History—1933–1945. 2. Medical
ethics—Germany—History—1933–1945. 3. World War, 1939–
1945—Atrocities. 4. National socialism—Moral and ethical aspects.
I. Nicosia, Francis R., 1944– II. Huener, Jonathan.

R510 .M385 2001
610'.943'09043–dc21

                                                            2001037996

British Library Cataloguing in Publication Data
A catalogue record for this book is available from
the British Library.

Printed in the United States on acid-free paper.

CONTENTS

Preface   vi

Introduction: Nazi Medicine in Historiographical Context   1
   Francis R. Nicosia and Jonathan Huener

1. The Ideology of Elimination: American and German
   Eugenics, 1900–1945   13
   Garland E. Allen

2. The Nazi Campaign against Tobacco: Science in a
   Totalitarian State   40
   Robert N. Proctor

3. Physicians as Killers in Nazi Germany: Hadamar,
   Treblinka, and Auschwitz   59
   Henry Friedlander

4. Criminal Physicians in the Third Reich: Toward a
   Group Portrait   77
   Michael H. Kater

5. Pathology of Memory: German Medical Science and
   the Crimes of the Third Reich   93
   William E. Seidelman

6. The Legacy of Nazi Medicine in Context   112
   Michael Burleigh

Appendix   128
Contributors   140
Selected Bibliography   142
Index   151

PREFACE

THE FIRST FIVE ESSAYS in this volume are based on the lectures given by five internationally renowned scholars at the Miller Symposium on the theme of "German Medicine and Ethics under National Socialism," held at the University of Vermont in April 2000. In the fall of 1998, several members of the advisory board of the Center for Holocaust Studies at the University of Vermont, most prominently Professor Emeritus Arthur Kunin, M.D., initiated plans for a symposium centered on issues and controversies related to the practice of medicine, the medical profession, and medical ethics in the years of the Third Reich.

Established with the goal of honoring the scholarly and pedagogical contributions of Professor Raul Hilberg, who served on the faculty of the University of Vermont for more than three decades, the Center for Holocaust Studies remains committed to furthering the cause of Holocaust education and serving as a forum for the presentation and discussion of new perspectives on the history of Nazi Germany and its crimes. As is so often the case, our exploration of controversial and insufficiently charted territory in the history of National Socialism and its crimes begins, and returns to, the orientation and compass that Professor Hilberg's pioneering work in the field provides.

The Miller Symposium was one such effort and, with the support and cooperation of the University of Vermont College of Medicine, was designed to address several of the most critical issues in the study of Nazi Germany and the Holocaust. Among these issues are the place of the Holocaust in the larger context of eugenic and racial research; the motivations and roles of some of the most important perpetrators of Nazi crimes, namely, the German scientific and medical establishment; the forms of racial and medical research undertaken with the support of and in the name of the Nazi state; the multiplicity of victims of Nazi persecution and murder; and the impact and legacy of the eugenics movement and Nazi medicine on physicians and the practice of medicine since World War II.

Confronting these issues from a variety of disciplinary and methodological perspectives, the individual essays contained herein are based on the authors' original scholarship. They introduce the reader to the foundations of Nazi medicine in racial and eugenic research in Germany and elsewhere, and ground German medical practice and research in the regime's racial ideology. Moreover, they describe some of the murderous forms that medical practice took, accounting all the while for the motivations and complicity of the medical establishment in the crimes of National Socialism. Finally, these essays confront the complex and troubling legacy of medicine in the Third Reich, as they direct our attention to current debates over the nature and course of research in genetics and biotechnology. In its entirety, this volume is intended to offer the reader a brief, yet focused introduction to this controversial subject area, and is suitable for undergraduate and graduate students; for students in the fields of history, medicine, philosophy, ethics, and the sciences; and for the general reader interested in the history of the Third Reich and the Holocaust.

Neither the symposium itself nor this volume would have been possible without Leonard and Carolyn Miller, whose generous support and engagement have helped to sustain and expand the programming of the Center for Holocaust Studies in recent years. It is therefore only fitting that this symposium bears their name. Recognition and thanks are also due to the College of Medicine at the University of Vermont, the University of Vermont Department of History Nelson Grant for Faculty Development, Kathy Johnson of the Center for Holocaust Studies, Wolfgang Mieder, and the symposium's organizing committee, which included Nancy Gallagher, Martin Koplewitz, Roy Korson, Arthur Kunin, David Scrase, and the editors of this volume. Finally, the editors especially wish to thank Michael Burleigh of Cardiff University for his concluding essay. His path-breaking scholarly works on this topic are well known, and his observations here, the reader will undoubtedly agree, are both provocative and synthetic. They serve to guide and challenge us as we consider the historiographical relevance and moral implications of the issues raised in this volume.

INTRODUCTION

Nazi Medicine in Historiographical Context

Francis R. Nicosia and Jonathan Huener

IN THE HISTORIOGRAPHY of the Third Reich and the Holocaust, the category of perpetrators of Nazi crimes against Jews and other victims has evolved and expanded considerably during the decades since the end of World War II. Gerald Reitlinger's *The Final Solution: The Attempt to Exterminate the Jews of Europe, 1939–1945*,[1] published in 1953 and based largely on the documents used by Allied prosecutors against major Nazi war criminals in Nuremberg in 1945 and 1946, naturally identified Hitler and top officials of the Nazi Party and the state during the Third Reich as the perpetrators of Nazi crimes. Raul Hilberg's groundbreaking work *The Destruction of the European Jews*,[2] published in 1961, was the first comprehensive history of the Holocaust based on the massive documentation available to Western scholars beginning in the 1950s. Its focus on the administrative and bureaucratic process of genocide came at a time when the trial of Adolf Eichmann in Jerusalem and the subsequent publication of Hannah Arendt's *Eichmann in Jerusalem*[3] focused attention on this quintessential SS bureaucrat.

These events expanded the definition of perpetrators to include those in the Nazi state apparatus who, like Eichmann, operated just below the top military, civilian, and SS officials named and prosecuted just after the war. This redefinition was followed by trials before a West German court in Frankfurt from 1963 to 1965 of SS personnel who had worked at Auschwitz during World War II. For almost twenty years thereafter, perpetrators of Nazi crimes were typically considered to be Hitler, his top military and civilian lieutenants, and some of their subordinates in the party, state, and police bureaucracy, all motivated more or less by Nazi ideology and anti-Semitism on the one hand, career opportunities presented by the regime and its policies on the other, or some combination of both.

Since the late 1970s and early 1980s, the concept of Nazi perpetrators has expanded considerably. Historians have endeavored increasingly to write history "from the bottom up," within a context of sociological, economic, and psychological analysis of "ordinary Germans," their opinions and attitudes under Nazi rule, and their role in the persecution and extermination of Jews and other victims. Interest has turned to the extent to which ordinary and not so ordinary citizens—people who were not Nazi ideologues or true believers, or individuals with positions of authority in the bureaucracy, the party, or the military—were complicit in Nazi crimes. The effort over the past twenty years has produced a wealth of scholarship that has greatly expanded our understanding of the human catastrophe that was the Third Reich.

Addressing trends and opinions in the German population at large, Marlis Steinert's *Hitler's War and the Germans: Public Mood and Attitude during the Second World War*, published in 1977, was followed in the 1980s by Ian Kershaw's *Popular Opinion and Political Dissent in the Third Reich: Bavaria* and Sarah Gordon's *Hitler, Germans and the "Jewish Question,"* which considered the popular reactions of ordinary Germans to anti-Semitism and Nazi policies toward the Jews.[4] Detlev Peukert's *Inside Nazi Germany: Conformity, Opposition and Racism in Everyday Life* characterized everyday life in Nazi Germany as running the gamut from consent to accommodation to nonconformity.[5] In the 1990s, consideration of "ordinary Germans" was focused more on their attitudes and role in the "final solution" with the publication of several works important both for their scholarly contributions and their controversial nature. David Bankier's *The Germans and the Final Solution: Public Opinion under Nazism* concluded that indifference rather than a lust for murder characterized the German public attitude toward the Jews and the Jewish policy of the Nazi regime.[6] This focus on the attitudes and actions of ordinary people climaxed with the publication of Christopher Browning's *Ordinary Men: Reserve Police Battalion 101 and the Final Solution in Poland*[7] in 1992, followed four years later by the appearance of Daniel Jonah Goldhagen's *Hitler's Willing Executioners: Ordinary Germans and the Holocaust.*[8] Omer Bartov's *Hitler's Army: Soldiers, Nazis and War in the Third Reich* appeared in 1991, and the controversial touring exhibition of the Hamburg Institute for Social Research on the German army's role in the Nazi genocide was published in book form in English translation in 1999.[9] Browning's microhistory of one reserve police battalion and both the Bartov book and the Hamburg exhibit on the German army demonstrate the capacity of "ordinary men"—in the Order Police and in the regular army, respectively—to commit mass murder. Goldhagen goes so far as to claim that this capacity was typical of virtually all Germans because it was inherent in a broadly accepted, annihilationist German anti-Semitism.

Somewhere between Hitler and high-ranking officials of the Nazi state and party on the one hand, and ordinary German citizens inside and outside the police and the military on the other, we confront the thousands of perpetrators in the professions: industrialists and businessmen, scholars and teachers, lawyers and judges, artists, and scientists and physicians. Of course, these people were not "ordinary" in the same sense that most police and soldiers may have been; the professionals were, after all, the best-educated members of German society. Many occupied positions of enormous prestige and influence in the life of the nation, and some even had access to high offices of the state. But like those more commonly considered "ordinary" in the literature, professionals generally did not formulate state policy; rather, they were often co-opted by the state to implement policy, first in Germany and later throughout Europe.

Over the past generation, scholars have considered the attitudes and roles of Germany's most educated and talented citizens, its professionals in the worlds of business and industry, the arts, education and academia, science, and medicine. Certainly, an early exception to this time line is Max Weinreich's *Hitler's Professors: The Part of Scholarship in Germany's Crimes against the Jewish People*.[10] Published in 1946, it is a study that faults German scholarship for providing the ideas, techniques, and justification for Nazi Germany's crimes against humanity. But it was not until the last two decades of the twentieth century that scholars turned their full attention to the subject of the professions and their role in the crimes of the Third Reich. Studies of German industry in the Third Reich during these years range from Joseph Borkin's *The Crime and Punishment of IG Farben: The Unholy Alliance of Adolf Hitler and Germany's Great Chemical Combine*, to Peter Hayes's *Industry and Ideology: IG Farben in the Nazi Era*, to Neil Gregor's recent *Daimler Benz in the Third Reich*.[11] Most recently, the arts and the role of artists and historians in Nazi Germany have became the subject of scrutiny by scholars with the publication of works such as Alan Steinweis's *Art, Ideology and Economics in Nazi Germany: The Reich Chambers of Music, Theater and the Visual Arts*; Michael Kater's *The Twisted Muse: Musicians and Their Music in the Third Reich*; and the collection of papers on German historians in the Third Reich edited by Winfried Schulze and Otto Gerhard Oexle, *Deutsche Historiker im Nationalsozialismus*.[12] Important studies on science and the role of scientists in the Nazi state and society have included Alan Beyerchen's *Scientists under Hitler: Politics and the Physics Community in the Third Reich*; Kristie Macrakis's *Surviving the Swastika: Scientific Research in Nazi Germany*; and Ute Deichmann's *Biologists under Hitler*.[13]

Complicity in or indifference to the crimes of the Nazi state by some of the most educated people in German society is unquestionably one of the most disturbing issues that students of Nazi Germany and the Holocaust must confront. The most troubling example of highly educated professionals acting as perpetrators in this context is certainly the medical establishment. Trained to care for the sick, relieve suffering, and save lives, some physicians withheld care, inflicted pain by experimenting on human subjects, and committed murder. Of those who did not participate in such crimes, most were indifferent or acquiescent to the behavior of their colleagues and the suffering of their colleagues' victims. Physicians and others in the medical professions became some of the most lethal perpetrators of Nazi crimes.

The 1980s and 1990s saw the publication of major studies of the German medical profession during the Nazi period. Robert Jay Lifton published *The Nazi Doctors: Medical Killing and the Psychology of Genocide*, the first in-depth study of the complicity of leading German physicians in systematic mass murder.[14] This was followed in quick succession by Benno Müller-Hill's *Murderous Science: Elimination by Scientific Selection of Jews, Gypsies and Others, Germany 1933–1945*; Robert Proctor's *Racial Hygiene: Medicine under the Nazis*; Michael Kater's *Doctors under Hitler*; and Hugh Gallagher's *By Trust Betrayed: Patients, Physicians, and the License to Kill in the Third Reich*.[15] Michael Burleigh's *Death and Deliverance: "Euthanasia" in Germany, c. 1900–1945* and Henry Friedlander's *The Origins of Nazi Genocide: From Euthanasia to the Final Solution* expose the role of the medical establishment in the forced sterilization and eventual mass murder of the handicapped in Germany as preparation for its larger role in the extermination of Jews and Gypsies, while Robert Proctor's recent book, *The Nazi War on Cancer*, demonstrates that Nazi Germany's positive health activism in some areas ultimately came from the same roots as its medical crimes against humanity.[16]

Of course, German physicians during the 1930s and 1940s did not respond to Nazi racial ideology and the career opportunities it offered as if they existed in a scientific and philosophical vacuum. The first three decades of the twentieth century witnessed the growth of the eugenics movement in Europe, North America, and elsewhere. This movement provides a necessary context for understanding the role of German science and medicine in Nazi crimes against humanity.[17] The term "eugenics" was coined in the 1880s by Francis Galton, an English aristocrat and a nephew of Charles Darwin. Although eugenics meant different things to different people, eugenicists generally believed that human progress could be ensured only through national breeding programs designed to increase the number of children born to the educated, intelligent, and accomplished upper classes, and to discourage the birth of children among the poor and handicapped lower classes.[18] Science, not religion or philosophy, would direct humanity toward a biological, social, and moral utopia.

The Nazis translated eugenic principles into a program for the racial purification and moral improvement of the German nation. The program resulted in the forced sterilization and murder of the physically and mentally handicapped in Germany; the segregation and enslavement of Slavic peoples in the east; the expulsion, ghettoization, and extermination of "alien races," such as the Jews and Gypsies; and medical experimentation on all of these victims. Michael Burleigh's nine essays in his *Ethics and Extermination: Reflections on Nazi Genocide* ponder these separate but interconnected examples of Nazi genocide, the motivations of the perpetrators behind them, and the scholarly debates that in recent years have swirled around the study of Nazi Germany and the Holocaust.[19] Not all German eugenicists were Nazis who believed in notions of "Aryan" racial supremacy, nor were all German physicians eugenicists or adherents of the eugenics movement before and after 1933. But eugenicists in Nazi Germany were complicit in crimes of the state because their support for Hitler's regime rested on the regime's support for their work.[20] German physicians, moreover, whether they actually used and mutilated humans as subjects for medical experiments, murdered them, or simply acquiesced in the crimes of their colleagues, knowingly practiced their profession in a medical system that pursued racist goals based in large measure on eugenic theory and practice.

* * * *

THE ESSAYS ASSEMBLED in this volume are authored by some of the most important authorities in the world today on the history and legacy of eugenics, Nazi racial theory and medical practice, and the Holocaust. Garland E. Allen's essay, "The Ideology of Elimination: American and German Eugenics, 1900–1945," surveys the international eugenics movement in the early twentieth century, focusing on the growth of eugenic research in the United States and its links to the German scientific and medical establishment. Introducing the reader to eugenic research programs and the political action programs associated with them, Allen emphasizes the necessity of understanding these initiatives in their social and economic context, noting that the growth of eugenic research and programs for racial "betterment," whether in the U.S. or Europe, arose in a period of great social upheaval. Given these factors, it is clear that the study and application of eugenic principles did not begin with National Socialism, although it was with the rise of the Nazi state that eugenics became central to state policy. A historical analysis of the eugenics movement, Allen argues, "provides some important parameters for comparison to and understanding of the genetic claims that abound today and suggests how current claims are being or might be used. Nowhere," the author continues, "is this history more dramatic and disturbingly relevant than in the case of Nazi Germany, where genetics and its associated eugenic claims became the centerpiece of an economic and a racial ideology that ultimately led to the Holocaust and the deaths of millions of people." Like all of the essays in this volume, this analysis prompts the reader to consider more carefully the current process of "medicalization and geneticization," for "[w]hen genetic arguments are extended to all facets of our behavior and personality, as they were during the old eugenics movement and as they are today, we need to take a critical look at both the science being presented and the social environment calling it forth."

Addressing the concrete application of medical research within the larger eugenic and racialist context of Nazi medicine, Robert N. Proctor's provocative essay, "The Nazi Campaign against Tobacco: Science in a Totalitarian State," locates the motivations for "good" science in the Third Reich, such as innovative cancer research, within the broader goals of the Nazi medical establishment that led to the systematic murder of the handicapped, Jews, and Gypsies. Although historians of medicine have generally regarded the 1950s as the starting point of tobacco health research, Proctor notes that in the 1930s and 1940s, under National Socialism, German epidemiology was the most advanced in the world and was the leading force in establishing the relationship between tobacco use and lung cancer. This culminated in the establishment of the Jena Institute for Tobacco Hazards Research in 1941. Yet Proctor reminds the reader that research on the hazardous effects of tobacco was in line with the regime's larger principle of *Gesundheitsführung* (leadership in health) in the service of public health and racial hygiene. Indeed, there existed a symbiotic relationship between science and politics, according to which "[p]ublic health initiatives were launched in the name of National Socialism," while "Nazi ideals informed the practice and popularization of science, motivating it and reorienting it in subtle and complex ways." Although Nazi efforts to combat tobacco use met with only limited success, the legacy of the campaign provides the reader with a compelling, and ultimately more precise, view into the complexity of the regime's racialized public health initiatives, responsible as they were for both better nutrition and forced sterilizations, antismoking campaigns and mass murder. A more rigorous investigation of the issue lends the genocidal elements in Nazi science a certain tangibility that might otherwise be lacking. As Proctor concludes: "The exclusive focus on the heinous aspect of Nazi medical practice makes it easy for us to relegate the events of this era to the monstrous or other-worldly, but there is more to the story than 'medicine gone mad.'"

Henry Friedlander's analysis in "Physicians as Killers in Nazi Germany: Hadamar, Treblinka, and Auschwitz" leads the reader directly to the murderous application of the eugenic and racial principles and motivations outlined in the previous two essays. He sets out to demystify German physicians and their profession, arguing at the outset that their motivations can, in large part, be understood as those of any other profession, namely, the desire for career advancement, higher incomes, and recognition from their peers. While these general pursuits may have been rather mundane, the means to the end were extraordinary, as Friedlander makes clear in his discussion of the "euthanasia" practices of the T4 wards and killing centers, the gassings at Treblinka, and the experimentation on human subjects and "mass murder on the assembly line" at Auschwitz. Friedlander offers a concise examination of both the process and the perpetrators of these crimes, giving the reader a view into the biographies, character, and motivations of medical killers such as Hermann Pfannmüller, Irmfried Eberl, Johann Kremer, and

Josef Mengele. Motives certainly varied, and the author leaves no doubt that these physicians subscribed to Nazi ideology and its racist elements. But ideology, he contends, was not the primary motivation for most physician-murderers, though it offered them a rationalization for their actions. Recognizing this, it is perhaps the "ordinariness" of the physician-killers that the reader finds most unsettling.

In his essay "Criminal Physicians in the Third Reich: Toward a Group Portrait," Michael Kater aims to examine the profession as a whole according to two categories of analysis: the level of physicians' political association with organizations of the Nazi state, and the physicians' professional-ethical conduct. Kater's findings are most disturbing as he describes German physicians' high level of voluntary association with the National Socialist Physicians' League, the Nazi Party itself, the SA, and the SS. Some one-third of all physicians were members of the Physicians' League, and by 1939 nearly 45 percent of all physicians were members of the Nazi Party. This figure becomes all the more significant when it is compared to percentages for other professions, such as lawyers (25 percent) and teachers (24 percent), and the population as a whole (9 percent). Moreover, physicians were greatly overrepresented among the ranks of the SS: while only 0.4 percent of teachers were in the ranks of Himmler's black shirts, 7 percent of all physicians became members. The SS, as Kater argues, held a particular attraction for these medical professionals who, "initially not quite at ease with the political change portended by the Nazis, craved enduring professional and socioeconomic security and desired recognition—even in a 'revolutionized' polity such as that which Hitler's new regime claimed to represent." In addition, the "SS's seemingly limitless control over life and death" held out a certain attraction to those who already exercised such power in their professions. Having illustrated through specific examples the forms and levels of physicians' participation in the "euthanasia" program, in disabling or deadly experiments on human subjects, and in "selections" at Auschwitz, Kater's provisional conclusion is that a significant number of these men and women were seeking career advancement in the form of new research opportunities, increased salaries, or more prestigious titles or ranks in the profession or state hierarchy. Unwilling to dismiss ideology as a motivation, he argues that the goal of eliminating those perceived as racially inferior "turned into a mandate actually believed in by a plurality of Nazi doctors, to the extent that they took Nazi ideology at all seriously." Finally, Kater's findings direct our attention to more current considerations of postwar medical training and practice in Germany and beyond. "All this means," he concludes, "that the negative paradigm of Nazi medicine must be circumscribed and the facts sought with greater accuracy than in the past, so that on both sides of the Atlantic, and wherever else medicine is being taught and practiced, further salutary lessons may be learned."

It is the failure to heed such lessons and learn from the past that is the focus of William E. Seidelman's essay, "Pathology of Memory: German Medical Science and the Crimes of the Third Reich." In detailing the background and development of academic psychiatry, he forges a link between National Socialist ideology, the institutionalized and exploitative research conducted on human specimens in service of that discipline, and the sterilization, "euthanasia," and extermination practices of the Nazi regime. His analysis leads us to a broader consideration of the legacy of Nazi medicine and the "amnesia" that has plagued the German and Austrian medical establishment since the end of the Third Reich, particularly with respect to the continued use of the results of Nazi medical experiments and medical practice. As Seidelman argues: "[T]he same academic and research institutions that gave birth to modern medicine and medical science and medical education also fostered what was to become the greatest program of human destruction in the history of humankind." German and Austrian researchers and institutions may have been at the forefront of work on memory disorders, but "the memory of their own role in the terror and tragedies of the Third Reich is itself disordered." Moreover, a tragic irony emerges from Seidelman's own work with patients who have Alzheimer's disease: although many academic institutions have forgotten or repressed the memories of their criminal research programs in the 1930s and 1940s, many survivors of the Shoah who suffer from Alzheimer's disease and have experienced the loss of recent memory nevertheless retain clear memories of their persecutors, their suffering in the camps, and their lost loved ones. Seidelman's strongest indictment is directed at the extensive and well-funded Kaiser Wilhelm Society and its postwar successor, the Max Planck Society. Here he emphasizes the paradox that "the pathology of institutional memory is also exemplified by the very organization responsible for the momentous advances in the pathology of memory and behavior."

Michael Burleigh seeks in his concluding essay to integrate the five essays above, and in doing so offers us a number of cautionary observations as we seek to apply some of the lessons learned here to issues of medical practice and ethics today. Although in no way suggesting that the claims and agendas of German eugenicists should be taken lightly, he issues a warning against "the danger of taking the scientific pretensions of eugenics at their face value. After all, eugenics was a gigantic leap of faith, which, by its very ambition, raised its devotees way above ordinary mortals." Burleigh also advises us to consider seriously the importance of the "blank spaces," that is, those contexts in which eugenics was unsuccessful, and why. At the same time, as we assess the ethical and political issues surrounding genetic research in our own societies, we are encouraged to consider the appeal and legitimacy of eugenic research and programs within democratic liberal and progressive circles, not least in Weimar Germany. "Perhaps we need to know more," Professor Burleigh writes, "about why eugenics appealed so much to the Social Democratic Party as well as the National Socialist German Workers Party to find idioms appropriate to discussions in contemporary North America or Europe regarding the new genetics." And as we search for the proper idioms and modes of discourse, we are cautioned against the deployment of "forced analogies" and all-too-facile comparisons between the murderous policies of the Nazis in the past and the current genetic research and practices of voluntary euthanasia in the present, for even as we are compelled to demystify and demythologize the Nazi past, so too are we called upon to consider the applicability of controversies and policies in past and present democratic societies.

Regardless of our own national or institutional contexts, the questions raised in this volume bear an immediate relevance to current controversies over the nature and course of research in human genetics and biotechnology. Are we in danger of witnessing the evolution of a new eugenics that could have similar or even more murderous consequences than those effected by eugenic thinking and its co-optation of science and medicine in the Third Reich? Does a reflexive and restrictive focus on the evils of medicine under the Nazi regime eclipse our view of the history and practice of eugenics in our own societies, and if so, what are the potential outcomes? The answers to those questions no doubt depend on the nature and goals of the political, economic, and social culture and institutions that govern our world today, and on the ends and means of scientific research that society mandates for those engaged in genetic research and biotechnology. We have the advantage today of learning from the experience of Germany and, indeed, from the experience of the United States. In these and other instances we can observe the extent to which science and medicine have been put to cruel and even murderous uses in modern, technologically advanced societies when an immoral political culture rather easily co-opts its citizens, especially the best educated and most highly skilled, for these purposes. As Saul Friedländer has concluded in his study of the Jews in Nazi Germany: "Nazi persecutions and exterminations were perpetrated by ordinary people who lived and acted within a modern society not unlike our own, a society that had produced them as well as the methods and instruments for the implementation of their actions; the goals of these actions, however, were formulated by a regime, an ideology, and a political culture that were anything but commonplace."[21]

Notes

1. Gerald Reitlinger, *The Final Solution: The Attempt to Exterminate the Jews of Europe, 1939–1945* (New York: A.S. Barnes, 1961).
2. Raul Hilberg, *The Destruction of the European Jews*, 3 vols. (New York: Holmes & Meier, 1985).
3. Hannah Arendt, *Eichmann in Jerusalem: A Report on the Banality of Evil* (New York: Penguin, 1994).
4. Marlis Steinert, *Hitler's War and the Germans: Public Mood and Attitude during the Second World War* (Athens, OH: Ohio University Press, 1977); Ian Kershaw, *Popular Opinion and Political Dissent in the Third Reich: Bavaria* (Oxford: Clarendon Press, 1984); and Sarah Gordon, *Hitler, Germans and the "Jewish Question"* (Princeton, NJ: Princeton University Press, 1984).
5. Detlev Peukert, *Inside Nazi Germany: Conformity, Opposition and Racism in Everyday Life* (New Haven, CT: Yale University Press, 1987).
6. David Bankier, *The Germans and the Final Solution: Public Opinion under Nazism* (Oxford: Basil Blackwell, 1992).
7. Christopher Browning, *Ordinary Men: Reserve Police Battalion 101 and the Final Solution in Poland* (New York: Harper Collins, 1992).
8. Daniel Goldhagen, *Hitler's Willing Executioners: Ordinary Germans and the Holocaust* (New York: Alfred A. Knopf, 1996).
9. Omer Bartov, *Hitler's Army: Soldiers, Nazis and War in the Third Reich* (New York: Oxford University Press, 1991); Hamburg Institute for Social Research, ed., *The German Army and Genocide: Crimes Against War Prisoners, Jews, and Other Civilians in the East, 1939–1944*, trans. Scott Abbott (New York: New Press, 1999).
10. Max Weinreich, *Hitler's Professors: The Part of Scholarship in Germany's Crimes against the Jewish People* (New Haven, CT: Yale University Press, 1999).
11. Joseph Borkin, *The Crime and Punishment of IG Farben: The Unholy Alliance of Adolf Hitler and Germany's Great Chemical Combine* (New York: Free Press, 1978); Peter Hayes, *Industry and Ideology: IG Farben in the Nazi Era* (Cambridge: Cambridge University Press, 1987); Neil Gregor, *Daimler Benz in the Third Reich* (New Haven, CT: Yale University Press, 1998).

12. Alan Steinweis, *Art, Ideology and Economics in Nazi Germany: The Reich Chambers of Music, Theater and the Visual Arts* (Chapel Hill, NC: University of North Carolina Press, 1996); Michael Kater, *The Twisted Muse: Musicians and Their Music in the Third Reich* (New York: Oxford University Press, 1997); Winfried Schulze and Otto Gerhard Oexle, eds., *Deutsche Historiker im Nationalsozialismus* (Frankfurt am Main: Fischer Taschenbuch, 1999).

13. Alan Beyerchen, *Scientists under Hitler: Politics and the Physics Community in the Third Reich* (New Haven, CT: Yale University Press, 1977); Kristie Macrakis, *Surviving the Swastika: Scientific Research in Nazi Germany* (New York: Oxford University Press, 1993); Ute Deichmann, *Biologists under Hitler*, trans. Thomas Dunlap (Cambridge, MA: Harvard University Press, 1996).

14. Robert Jay Lifton, *The Nazi Doctors: Medical Killing and the Psychology of Genocide* (New York: Basic Books, 1986).

15. Benno Müller-Hill, *Murderous Science: Elimination by Scientific Selection of Jews, Gypsies and Others, Germany 1933–1945* (New York: Oxford University Press, 1988); Robert Proctor, *Racial Hygiene: Medicine under the Nazis* (Cambridge, MA: Harvard University Press, 1988); Michael Kater, *Doctors under Hitler* (Chapel Hill, NC: University of North Carolina Press, 1989); Hugh Gallagher, *By Trust Betrayed: Patients, Physicians, and the License to Kill in the Third Reich* (New York: Henry Holt, 1990).

16. Michael Burleigh, *Death and Deliverance: "Euthanasia" in Germany, c. 1900–1945* (Cambridge: Cambridge University Press, 1994); Henry Friedlander, *The Origins of Nazi Genocide: From Euthanasia to the Final Solution* (Chapel Hill, NC: University of North Carolina Press, 1995); Robert Proctor, *The Nazi War on Cancer* (Princeton, NJ: Princeton University Press, 1999).

17. For a history of the eugenics movement and its legacy, see Diane B. Paul, *Controlling Human Heredity, 1865 to the Present* (Atlantic Highlands, NJ: Humanities Press, 1995). For the links between eugenics and racism in Germany, Great Britain, and the United States, see Sheila Weiss, *Race Hygiene and National Efficiency: The Eugenics of William Schallmayer* (Berkeley, CA: University of California Press, 1987); and Elazar Barkan, *The Retreat of Scientific Racism: Changing Concepts of Race in Britain and the United States between the World Wars* (Cambridge: Cambridge University Press, 1992).

18. Nancy Gallagher, *Breeding Better Vermonters: The Eugenics Project in the Green Mountain State* (Hanover, NH: University Press of New England, 1999), 1.

19. Michael Burleigh, *Ethics and Extermination: Reflections on Nazi Genocide* (Cambridge: Cambridge University Press, 1997).

20. Sheila Weiss, "The Race Hygiene Movement in Germany," *Osiris* 3 (1987): 193–236.

21. Saul Friedländer, *Nazi Germany and the Jews: The Years of Persecution* (New York: Harper Collins, 1997), 6.

Chapter One

THE IDEOLOGY OF ELIMINATION
American and German Eugenics, 1900–1945

———— ∽∾∾ ————

Garland E. Allen

RECENT THEOLOGICAL METAPHORS of the Human Genome Project as ·the "Holy Grail" of modern biology and literary references to our "fate being no longer in the stars but in our genes" reveal a pervasive belief, widespread in our high tech society, that much of who we are and what we do as human beings is controlled by the genes we inherit from our parents. In the past fifteen years our understanding of the genetic and molecular basis of many clinically definable physiological traits—cystic fibrosis, the various thalassemias, lipid and carbohydrate storage diseases, chronic granulomatous disease, and more than eight hundred others—has increased exponentially. In that same time period the Human Genome Project has been put in place, amid claims that the new knowledge of our genetic "blueprint" will revolutionize our future and provide solutions to myriads of previously intractable medical and social problems. Techniques involving somatic gene therapy and germ-line gene replacement, or claims that genetic engineering can lead to the design of molecules that substitute for the products of defective genes, all lead to the belief that in genetics lies the answer to many of our society's woes.

Nowhere have genetic claims been more prominent, or received more sensational treatment, than in the area of human mental, personality, and social traits. Whether in the guise of sociobiology twenty years ago, human behavior genetics in the past ten years, or "evolutionary psychology" in the last five, we have all been treated to a continuing barrage of reports on research purporting to show a genetic basis for a wide variety of social behaviors. Headlines on the covers of all our national magazines have driven this point home to even the most casual reader. Everything from general personality to alcoholism, schizophrenia, manic depression, and criminality has been claimed to have a significant genetic basis. We are what we are largely because of our genetics.

Most of these behaviors are presented as pathologies that have led to the observed widespread and significant increase in a variety of social problems, from the alarming rise in crime and drive-by shootings in the last decade to alcoholism, manic depression, and an increase in substance abuse and susceptibility to stress. The implications of these claims are generally twofold:

1. Because behavioral traits are to a significant degree controlled by genes, they are fixed and cannot be altered by environmental change; they can only be managed. Hence, traditional methods of trying to solve social or psychological problems—one-on-one therapy, counseling, reduction in stress—have been shown to be ineffective, and should be replaced by a more rational and medical protocol, employing genetically based, or at least genetically "*informed,*" solutions, including the use of behavior-modifying drugs, which substitute for defective gene products.

2. The second implication, following directly from the first, is that while we may not have full answers yet as to how genes control behavior, and thus to how genetics can inform us about future social decisions, we should nevertheless look to Science (with a "capital S"), particularly Medical Science, rather than to social science, for answers to these large-scale social problems. Biological psychiatry is the medical offshoot of this general spread of what is called scientism, that is, a strong and generally uncritical faith in the power of science.

Thus, genetics has become, in the words of Walter Gilbert, the "Holy Grail" of modern biology and medicine. However, the quest for the Holy Grail of Christian mythology has proved remarkably elusive, and the attempts to call forth genetic explanations for personality and social behavior have not fared much better, as evidenced by a "lack of progress report" published in *Scientific American* in June 1993. Such claims, whatever their scientific merit, or lack thereof, align with endeavors to place the cause of social problems outside the social sphere. The term "genetic (or biological) determinism" has been applied to this "new astrology"—our fate being now, in James D. Watson's words, "in our genes" rather than "in the stars." Despite its scientific clothing, however, there may well be more to worry about with our new biomedical Emperor than meets the eye.

Overview

I do not wish to argue that there is no genetic component to human mental and behavioral traits. I have no doubt that there is, though how significant it is compared to the input from experience over the course of our developmental lifetime is generally difficult, if not impossible, to determine. Nor am I going to argue that technologies such as gene therapy, if they are ever feasible, should be rejected because they bring us too close to "playing God." Genes are real, and we are learning more every day about the conditions they affect and the molecular basis of their functions. Rather, I want to argue that the attempt to promote genetic determinist explanations for social problems is driven more by economic and social contexts than by the availability of new and more reliable scientific data. While all science is to some degree culturally driven, theories of human social behavior are necessarily and overtly more so than most. This need not be a bad thing at all—many culturally derived metaphors or analogies, ways of conceiving of problems or picturing hypotheses, have led to very creative scientific ideas. What does become problematic is when we ignore the fact that science is culturally situated and thereby fail to examine which cultural biases or ideas help and which impede our understanding of the phenomena—in this case, the origins of our social behavior—we are trying to explain.

There are, of course, numerous problems with making strong claims about the genetic determination of complex human traits, especially behavioral ones. These problems reside in both biology and ethics. On the biological side, geneticists years ago moved beyond the view that single genes, or even multi-gene complexes, produce a fixed and invariant phenotype, recognizing that the phenotype for many traits—most principally behavioral ones—is far more plastic than classically portrayed. Rather than invariable outcomes, genes have norms of reaction that in most cases yield a variety of phenotypes under a range of environments. That range of environments includes not only the external environment in which the organism lives, but also the genetic environment—the genetic background, as it is sometimes called—in which every gene functions. Development, the process by which genetic information is ultimately translated into phenotype, has until recently been a little-understood and much-overlooked aspect of genetics. It is just now beginning to come back into its own at the molecular level, where the focus is on how genes are turned on and off and how they interact to produce a particular outcome. That process, as we are beginning to find out, is subject to a wide range of influences, both genetic and environmental.

In addition, defining complex behaviors in any kind of rigorous way (what is an "alcoholic" or a "criminal"?), collecting matched and well-controlled data, and determining the environments to which human beings have been subjected pose staggering methodological problems.

On the ethical side, of course, even to begin to disentangle the respective roles of heredity and environment in the development of behavioral traits requires the sort of rigorous, controlled experiments on human subjects that most scientists are, thankfully, loathe to pursue. So I am not sanguine about the prospects of ever achieving a meaningful answer to questions about any significant genetic components of our behavior.

But it is not the intricate problems involved in the study designs or the statistical analyses of the data about such traits on which I wish to focus here. Rather, in the spirit of George Sarton, one of the first historians of science who recognized science as a cultural product and its very basis as a necessary expression of cultural assumptions, I would like to ask why genetic or biological determinist theories receive the attention that they do *at the time in history* that they do. If the history of science has any heuristic value—and I think that it does—one benefit is surely as a means of understanding the larger picture of how and why certain questions get asked and certain answers get given at any particular time and place. Moreover, once we have answered those questions, I think we can learn from the past to determine how we might respond to similar situations in the present.

Fortunately for our inquiry, history can give us some clues about where genetic theories of social behavior can lead. In the early decades of this century, in many countries, a set of biological determinist claims, similar to those we are encountering today, was promulgated with the scientific authority of the day. Known as eugenics, this organized and influential movement was prominent in most Western countries, especially in the United States, Britain, and Germany. The extensive historical analyses of eugenics now available, by authors such as Daniel J. Kevles, Diane Paul, Mark Adams, Pauline Mazumdar,

Sheila Weiss, Robert Proctor, Paul Weindling, Stefan Kühl, and Nils Roll-Hanson, among others, offer a rich data set on the economic, social, and political context in which that movement developed, as well as the political and social consequences to which it led. The history of eugenics also provides some important parameters for comparison to and understanding of the genetic claims that abound today and suggests how current claims are being or might be used. Nowhere is this history more dramatic and disturbingly relevant than in the case of Nazi Germany, where genetics and its associated eugenic claims became the centerpiece of an economic and a racial ideology that ultimately led to the Holocaust and the deaths of millions of people. It was eugenic principles, both developed in Germany and borrowed from the United States, that gave the Holocaust its scientific legitimacy. We turn now to a brief examination of eugenics as it developed in the early 1900s out of a renewed interest in breeding and heredity in agriculture.

Eugenics and Its Research Program, 1900–1940

"Eugenics" was a term coined in 1883 by Francis Galton, geographer, statistician, and cousin of Charles Darwin. It referred to "the right to be well-born" or, in the words of Galton's foremost American disciple, Charles B. Davenport, the "science of human improvement by better breeding."[1] Eugenics dominated much of the social reform thinking that abounded in the first four decades of this century. Its explanations were couched in terms of the then-new and exciting field of Mendelian genetics. Eugenicists argued that many social problems could be eliminated by discouraging or preventing the reproduction of individuals deemed genetically unfit (negative eugenics), while desirable social traits could be increased by encouraging reproduction among those deemed most genetically fit (positive eugenics). Eugenicists thought of themselves as bringing the latest scientific research to bear on old and previously unsolved social problems.

Many eugenicists, especially those carrying out research work, had a background in biology, but they saw their work as drawing on a wide variety of fields (fig. 1). Many had an interest in, or experience with, agricultural breeding and thought of their work as extending the knowledge of animal husbandry to improving the human species in much the same way as a breeder improves a flock or herd. "The most progressive revolution in history could be achieved," Charles B. Davenport wrote in

FIGURE 1: Eugenics was seen by its advocates as a multidisciplinary enterprise, drawing on fields such as genetics, statistics, psychology (including especially psychometrics, or mental testing), medicine, and anthropology, among others. In the United States and Germany, the genetic, or hereditarian, element in eugenic thinking was particularly strong. The leafy branches of the eugenic "tree" were thought to include a general level of eugenic "education" among the public, social legislation such as voluntary or involuntary sterilization laws, and political reforms such as immigration restriction. This image was the logo for the Third International Congress of Eugenics, held in New York City at the American Museum of Natural History (whose director and president, Henry Fairfield Osborn, was an avid eugenicist), 21–23 August 1932. [From *A Decade of Progress in Eugenics: Scientific Papers of the Third International Congress of Eugenics, held at the American Museum of Natural History, New York* (Baltimore: Williams and Wilkings, 1934), Plate I] A clearer version of this image can be obtained from the Eugenic Image Archive established by the Cold Spring Harbor Laboratory, Cold Spring Harbor, NY, at the following web site: http://vector.cshl.org/eugenics/. Image # 233.

1923 to textile magnate W. P. Draper, "if in some way or other human matings could be placed on the same high plane as … horse breeding." Indeed, as historian of science Barbara Kimmelman has shown, the first organized eugenics group in the United States was founded in 1906 as the Eugenics Committee of the American Breeders' Association, headed by David Starr Jordan, then president of Stanford University.[2] Like the breeder, the eugenicist used pedigree analysis to determine the hereditary makeup of family lines (fig. 2); but unlike the breeder, the eugenicist could not use controlled mating experiments to test conclusions drawn from pedigree analysis. As a result, social transmission and biological transmission were often conflated. Despite this limitation, eugenicists put forth numerous claims for the inheritance of a wide variety of behaviors and conditions, from pauperism to scholastic ability, feeblemindedness, manic depression, pellagra, and thalassophilia (love of the sea). Moreover, they relied on and extended late-nineteenth- and early-twentieth-century lineage studies, such as those of the infamous Juke and Kallikak families, which supposedly documented in a dramatic way the ultimate outcome of hereditary degeneracy (fig. 3).

Much of the research work was carried out by or organized through the Eugenics Record Office (ERO) at Cold Spring Harbor, Long Island. The ERO was the institutional nerve center of North American eugenics. It was directed by Charles B. Davenport and funded by the Harriman family of New York until 1916, after which it was taken over by the Carnegie Institution of Washington and maintained until its final closure in 1940.[3] The ERO was managed by Davenport's enthusiastic minion Harry Hamilton Laughlin, whom he had recruited in 1910 from a teaching position at an agricultural and teacher-training school in northeastern Missouri. Laughlin served eugenics in a number of capacities: superintendent of the ERO (1910–1940), propagandist in state legislatures, "Expert Eugenics Witness" to the House Committee on Immigration and Naturalization in the 1920s, tireless organizer of meetings, author of newsletters and articles on eugenics, and head of a series of summer training sessions for eugenics fieldworkers, held at the ERO and funded by John D. Rockefeller, Jr. In the early years of its existence, the ERO boasted a distinguished board of scientific advisors, including such important figures as W. E. Castle (mammalian geneticist at Harvard), David Starr Jordan (who, before becoming a university president at Indiana, then Stanford, was a well-known ichthyologist), Irving Fisher (economist at Yale), Thomas Hunt Morgan (at the time, just beginning at

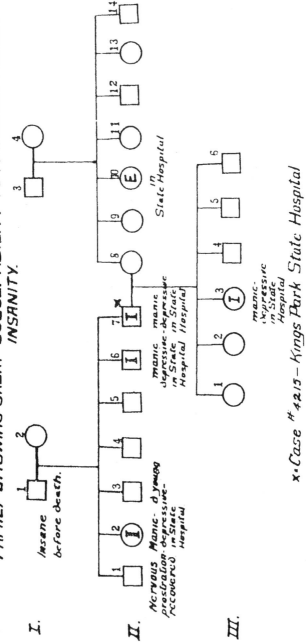

FAMILY SHOWING GREAT SUSCEPTIBILITY TO MANIC DEPRESSIVE INSANITY.

x·Case #4215 – Kings Park State Hospital

FIGURE 2(a)

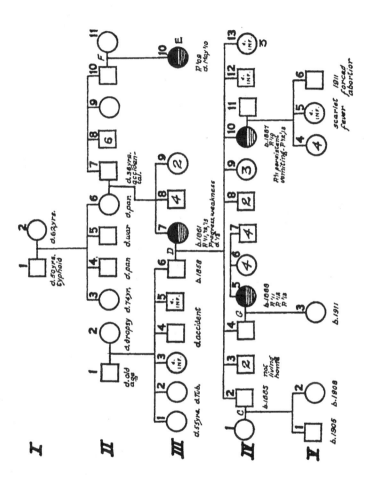

FIGURE 2(b)

FIGURES 2(a) and 2(b): These are two family pedigree charts of the sorts constructed by eugenicists to show that certain traits are genetically determined because "they run in families." The upper pedigree (a) is for the inheritance of manic depression, and the lower (b) is for pellagra (various filled-in and hatched symbols represent individuals with different clinical manifestations of the disease). Manic depression is a complex trait whose cause is unclear even today; pellagra is a documented vitamin B deficiency and as such is dietary in origin. Both conditions may "run in families" because families share cultural, psychological, and dietary, as well as biological, backgrounds. Such pedigrees are usually constructed by starting with a current individual diagnosed as showing a particular trait, and then tracing back his or her ancestry through various public and private records. [(a) in possession of the author; (b) from Charles B. Davenport, "The Hereditary Factor in Pellagra," *Archives of Internal Medicine* 18 (1916): 4–75, fig. 30.]

Columbia the work with the fruit fly *Drosophila* that would later earn him a Nobel Prize), and Alexander Graham Bell. Besides the ERO, many other eugenics organizations existed in the U.S., including state branches of the nationwide American Eugenics Society, the Race Betterment Foundation (funded by the Kellogg cereal family in Battle Creek, Michigan), and the Human Betterment Foundation in Pasadena, California. The ERO, however, served as the major research center and clearing-house for much eugenics work done around the world.

Beyond research, eugenicists were also interested in social action, including education and popularization, and in working to pass laws that would promote eugenic goals. To publicize their views, eugenicists wrote books and magazine articles and promoted exhibits, fitter family contests, eugenic sermon contests, and even eugenic movies (fig. 4). Eugenics became incorporated into most major high school textbooks from the 1920s well into the 1950s.[4] The picture that emerged for even the most casual reader was that eugenics represented the cutting edge of modern science, the application of rational scientific principles to achieve the solution to what had been seen as intractable social problems. Gone were the soft, ineffective hands of charity and social work, well meaning as they might have been. These efforts only perpetuated pauperism, criminality, alcoholism, and other forms of social degeneracy because they did not touch the source of the problem—bad genes. Indeed, charity and public handouts, according to eugenics literature, only increased the problem by allowing the degenerate segments of the population—the "dysgenics," or, as the British labeled them, the "residuum"—to reproduce more. Eugenicists sought to promote their message to as wide an audience as possible.

MARTIN KALLIKAK

He dallied with a feeble-minded tavern girl

He married a worthy Quakeress

She bore a son known as "Old Horror" who had ten children

She bore seven upright worthy children

From "Old Horror's" ten children came hundreds of the lowest types of human beings

From these seven worthy children came hundreds of the highest types of human beings

FIGURE 3: Hereditary studies from the late nineteenth and early twentieth centuries argued that social inadequacy and degeneracy were hereditary. This "cartoon version" of the famous Kallikak study by Henry H. Goddard of the Vineland Training School in Vineland, NJ (1912) shows that from the same father, with different mothers, two very different lines of descendants can emerge. According to eugenicists, heredity was the major factor in the outcome of the two family lines. This image appeared as late as 1961 in an introductory psychology textbook, indicating the persistence of such hereditarian thinking into the later twentieth century. [From Henry E. Garrett and Hubert Bonner, *General Psychology*, 2nd ed. (New York: American Book Co., 1961). Taken directly from Allan Chase, *The Legacy of Malthus* (New York: Alfred A. Knopf, 1977), 155.]

FIGURE 4: Advertisement from the *Chicago Herald* (1 April 1917) for the popular movie *The Black Stork* (1916), about a severely deformed newborn (probably hydrocephalic) in Chicago who was allowed to die on the advice of the family's physician, Dr. Harry Haiselden (who played himself in the movie!). The case was highly controversial, adding to the lure of the movie representation, which took the doctor's side and presented eugenic arguments for the decision. [From Martin Pernick, The Black Stork: *Eugenics and the Death of "Defective" Babies in American Medicine and Motion Pictures since 1915* (New York: Oxford University Press, 1996), fig 6.]

Eugenicists' Political Action Programs

Eugenicists were especially active in the United States in areas of immigration restriction (1921, 1924) and in the enactment of state eugenic sterilization laws. Eugenicists were convinced that the newer immigrants coming to the United States after 1880, mostly from central and southern Europe, the Balkans, Russia, and Poland, were biologically inferior (the "dregs of humanity" as one eugenic pamphlet put it) to the older Anglo-Saxon and Nordic stocks, whose immigration had flourished in the first half of the century.

Laughlin and others carried out studies purporting to show the high rate of pauperism, feeblemindedness, criminality, and other deleterious traits that existed in various ethnic groups, with the clear implication that the traits were genetically determined. Laughlin took his findings to Congress, where he appeared three times, twice (1922, 1924) as the official "Eugenics Expert Witness" to the House Committee on Immigration and Naturalization, whose chairman, Representative Albert Johnson of Washington State, was an enthusiastic eugenicist who had been appointed honorary president of the Eugenics Research Association. Laughlin's data, such as his comparison of intelligence in different national groups (fig. 5), were designed to convince the committee that scientific evidence, not ethnic bias or political expediency, made such immigrant groups a bad risk.

In the immediate post–World War I years, singling out particular national and ethnic groups for restrictive exclusion was obviously a sensitive issue in the arena of international diplomacy, as well as among the country's own considerable immigrant population. Thus, the apparent objectivity of science had considerable political appeal to legislators who wanted to restrict immigration for a variety of economic and social reasons, but could not publicly take such a seemingly crass position. Largely as a result of Laughlin's testimony, the House committee drafted legislation that, by setting immigration quotas on the basis of the 1890, rather than the 1920, census, selectively restricted immigration from the very regions the eugenicists claimed harbored the most degenerate germ plasm. The Johnson Act passed both houses of Congress in 1924, and was signed into law by President Calvin Coolidge, acting on his earlier assertion that the country "cannot have too many inhabitants of the right kind." The Johnson Act had drastic consequences. Among others, ships such as the SS *St. Louis*, bringing refugees from Nazi Germany in the mid- and

INFERIOR INTELLIGENCE

Race, Country of Birth, or Army Rank, and Percent of Men in Each Group, by Army Mental Tests showing Inferior (D), or Very Inferior (D-, E) Intelligence.

- COMMISSIONED OFFICERS
- NON-COMMISSIONED OFFICERS
- ENGLAND
- HOLLAND
- NEGRO OFFICERS
- DENMARK
- SCOTLAND
- PRIVATES
- GERMANY
- SWEDEN
- CANADA
- BELGIUM
- WHITE DRAFT
- NORWAY

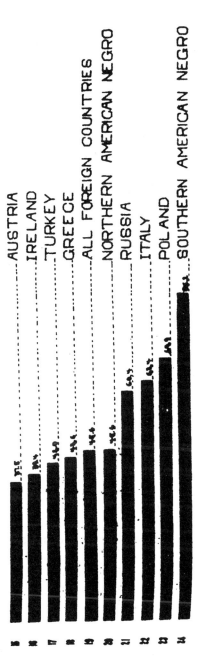

FIGURE 5: One of the many graphs, based on data from the U.S. Army alpha and beta I.Q. tests administered to recruits during World War I, presented by Harry H. Laughlin to the House Committee on Immigration and Naturalization in 1924. The purpose of the graph was to demonstrate that low intelligence ("feeblemindedness," in the parlance of the day) was hereditarily preponderant in populations of "new immigrants"—those from southern and eastern Europe, the Mediterranean, and the Balkans, and among Russian Jews. These sorts of data were important in convincing Congress to pass the Johnson Act in 1924, which restricted immigration most severely from just the areas Laughlin claimed had high rates of feeblemindedness and social degeneracy. [From H. H. Laughlin, *Analysis of America's Modern Melting Pot* (Washington, D.C.: Government Printing Office, 1924).]

late-1930s, were turned back because of the "quota" established by the Johnson Act.

Eugenicists were also instrumental in lobbying for the passage of compulsory sterilization laws. Articles, such as one from *The Daily Oregonian* in 1937, emphasized the cost to the average citizen of maintaining degenerate and inferior people *and their children* at state expense. Laughlin drew up a "Model Sterilization Law" that was sent to all state legislatures. The results were successful: by 1935, thirty states had enacted such laws. These laws allowed inmates of state institutions (prisons, insane asylums, sanitariums, and mental hospitals) to be forcibly sterilized after examination by a "eugenics committee" attached to the institution and consultation with a relative of the inmate. "Habitual criminality," "sexual perversion," "low moral sense," "hereditary feeblemindedness," and epilepsy were all categories that could lead to forced sterilization. By 1935 over twenty-one thousand eugenically motivated sterilizations had been performed, and by the early 1960s an estimated sixty-four thousand people had been sterilized in the U.S. alone.[5] Sweden carried out almost the same number of sterilizations in the same time period, an astonishing total for a much smaller country. In the political arena, eugenics as "Science" was used to promote and/or justify social policies that conformed to common prejudices about racial and ethnic minorities, and the drain they were supposedly exerting on society at large.

Opposition to Eugenics

Eugenicists' claims did not go unchallenged in either the biological or social and political arenas. A number of biologists, including Raymond Pearl and Herbert Spencer Jennings (both of Johns Hopkins), H. J. Muller (then at Texas), T. H. Morgan (Columbia), Abraham Myerson, and a whole committee of the American Neurological Association, to name only a few, wrote and/or lectured about the poor scientific data on which eugenic claims were based. They pointed out the imprecise way in which the behavioral traits were defined, how categories such as "feebleminded" or "manic-depressive" contained a whole hodgepodge of varied behaviors, how anecdotal information was relied upon for diagnosing individual phenotypes and for constructing pedigrees, how small the sample sizes often were, and how groups being compared were not matched for age, sex, or socioeconomic background.

T. H. Morgan, in his 1925 *Evolution and Genetics*, put the opponents' views most eloquently:

> If within each human social group the geneticist finds it impossible to dis-cover, with any reasonable certainty, the genetic basis of behavior, the prob-lems must seem extraordinarily difficult when groups are contrasted with each other where the differences are obviously connected not only with material advantages and disadvantages ... but with traditions, customs, religion, taboos, conventions, and prejudices. A little goodwill might seem more fitting in treating these complicated questions than the attitude adopted by some of the modern race-propagandists.[6]

Many Catholics opposed eugenics on general doctrinal grounds, but in 1930 Pope Pius XI put forward the encyclical *Casti connubi*, specif-ically directed at the eugenics movement and its emphasis on steriliza-tion. In a more secular vein, influential journalist and commentator Walter Lippmann wrote a series of articles for *Atlantic Monthly* and *Century Magazine* attacking, in an amazingly thoroughgoing way, the hereditarian view of intelligence (I.Q.).

But none of this stopped the movement, or even appeared to slow it down to any significant degree. Although scholars differ on the reasons for the failure of criticisms to have much immediate effect, I would argue that the hereditarian claim did not initially rise, nor would it eventually fall, based on the soundness of its scientific findings. It was a movement that grew out of and supported a much larger social agenda. It was the social rather than the scientific content of eugenics that would determine its ultimate course.

Eugenics in Its Social Context

Eugenicists most certainly did not invent the whole raft of social prob-lems at which their genetic solutions were directed. The period during which eugenics thrived was one of great social upheaval and change in the U.S. and, with certain differences in time frame, in most countries of Western Europe as well, especially Germany. These changes grew out of industrialization, with its attendant massive urbanization, and increasingly unstable economic processes, including "depressions" every ten to fifteen years, accompanied by massive unemployment—the period of U.S. history that Sidney Lens has characterized as one of the "Labor Wars."[7] This was also the era of the Bolshevik revolution in

Russia, militant IWW ("Wobblie") agitation in the mining and lumber industries in the Pacific Northwest, the anti-immigrant hysteria of the Sacco-Vanzetti case in Massachusetts (in which two Italian radicals were accused of murder in 1921 and sentenced to death), and the Seattle general strike of 1919.

Eugenicists argued that their approach was the most rational and efficient way to solve such recurrent problems and bring order into the chaotic economic and social arena. The logic of eugenics was compelling. If the increasing number and extent of social problems was largely due to an increasing number of genetically defective people in American society, then the most efficient and effective way to solve the problem was to prevent it at the source, that is, to prevent the reproduction of the defectives themselves. And, of course, those deemed defective were usually the poor and the ethnic and racial minorities, the very people least able to defend themselves. Author Allan Chase put it succinctly when he stated that the eugenicists' policies were "aimed directly at the gonads of the poor."[8] But national efficiency was a major issue in the 1920s and 1930s, not only in the United States but also in Europe; in the U.S., national efficiency and eugenics were incorporated particularly well into the ideology of the progressive era. One headline from a British newspaper found in Laughlin's archive read: "Rationalising Mankind. 'Big Business' Methods in Evolution. Eugenic Reform." Efficiency—"Taylorism" was its industrial name—brought about by the use of technically trained experts was an effective argument in a period when inflation was rampant and, after the Depression, joblessness was high. Historian Diane Paul has pointed out that biologists and others who were opposed to, or at least skeptical about, compulsory sterilization before 1929 were considerably more favorable after the stock market crash of that year.[9] Eugenicists and their supporters played on concerns about livelihood, taxes, safety, and social chaos to build support for supposedly scientific solutions to problems such as immigration restriction and sterilization.

There was also a growing awareness of strong class lines being drawn, especially around labor issues, and eugenicists clearly saw themselves on the side of the privileged and the elite. Like the ruling-class leaders who supported them, eugenicists were largely white, Anglo-Saxon Protestants who viewed the vast cultural, language, and behavioral differences of the new ethnic immigrants as a personal threat as well as a threat to the established social order. Biologically defective racial and ethnic groups were claimed to be the source of society's problems, and by preventing those individuals (and collateral members of their families) from having children, eugenicists were convinced that the problems could be eradicated in a few generations. This view persisted despite the fact that most biologists were aware that even with the most rigorous selection, the elimination of defective genes (especially recessive ones, as the majority were thought to be) from the population would take hundreds of years.

Most importantly, especially to the supporters of eugenics, solving social problems in this way did not require a change in the economic or social status quo. This aspect of eugenic thinking did not escape social critic Harold Ward, who wrote in *The New Republic* in 1935 that the primary focus on eugenics as the cause of social evils bypassed the obvious and most egregious evils of industrial capitalism:

> In a word, eugenics, through its fatal indifference to, or neglect of, the stupendous economic contradictions of modern society, has become a palliative weapon, not a curative—or even preventive—one. It leaves untouched, by any effective criticism, the entire price and profit system out of which, as many of its most loyal advocates fully recognize, issue the very dysgenic (socially undesirable) evils it proposes to attack with secondary biological methods. It tries to save the present system by juggling with the germ plasm....[10]

It is thus not surprising to find that in the United States eugenics was being funded by the wealthiest philanthropic institutions of the day (Carnegie, Rockefeller, Harriman, and Kellogg), all funded by industrialist interests. For instance, the Harriman, Carnegie, and Rockefeller institutes contributed over $1.2 million between 1910 and 1940 to the ERO alone, while other funds supported organizations such as the Race Betterment Foundation, the American Eugenics Society, the Eugenics Research Association, and the Galton Society.[11] The wealthiest class of society had the most to gain by furthering the belief that social problems were due to poor heredity rather than inequity in the economic distribution of wealth and the privileges and problems attendant with it. Eugenicists were not pursuing their program in a vacuum. The very roots of the movement were tied to the recognition of an increasing array of social problems and of the disparity between rich and poor. It stands to reason that the social context, not the genetic data, was the deciding factor in bringing eugenics to prominence in the early decades of the century.

The Nazi Connection

The foregoing suggests that eugenics did not originate with the Nazis. As a movement, eugenics had existed officially in Germany since 1905, when the Gesellschaft für Rassenhygiene (Society for Racial Hygiene) was established in Berlin. By 1907 the society had split into two groups, one in Munich and one in Berlin, and although their emphases diverged over the years, both groups persisted throughout the interwar period.[12] However, during the Weimar years, German eugenicists were not highly successful in passing legislation or putting eugenic principles into effect. It was only with the Nazis' rise to power that eugenics became so central to state policy.

One of the Nazis' most decisive eugenic acts was to pass legislation regulating marriage and authorizing involuntary sterilization of "defectives." The Nazi sterilization law of 14 July 1933, the Law for the Prevention of Progeny of Sufferers from Hereditary Diseases, was based on the 1932 Prussian proposal that had been approved by some of Weimar Germany's most influential eugenicists, including the then-director of the Kaiser Wilhelm Institute for Genetics, Richard Goldschmidt.[13] But as historian Stefan Kühl has shown, the Prussian law was itself an extension of Laughlin's "Model Sterilization Law,"[14] establishing a clear and direct connection between American and Nazi eugenic legislation. So grateful, in fact, were the Nazis for the American experience on which to draw that Laughlin was awarded an honorary M.D. from Heidelberg University in 1936, for being, as the citation read, "a successful pioneer of practical eugenics and the far-seeing representative of racial policy in America."[15]

Like its American counterpart, the German law allowed for the sterilization of those afflicted with feeblemindedness, schizophrenia, manic-depressive disorder, epilepsy, Huntington's chorea, genetic blindness and deafness, as well as those suffering from "serious alcoholism"; however, contrary to popular assumption, the law did not provide for sterilization based explicitly on race.[16] It was the 1933 law that also set up "eugenics courts" to review all cases recommended for involuntary sterilization. Shortly after the establishment of the courts, several North Americans, including Clarence C. Campbell and Charles M. Goethe (both former presidents of the Eugenics Research Association), biologist Marie E. Kopp, and immigration restrictionist Lothrop Stoddard, all visited Germany and reported favorably on the operation of the courts.[17] Stoddard went so far as to claim that Nazi Germany's eugenic program was the most ambitious and far-reaching experiment in eugenics ever attempted by any nation.[18] As is now well known, the Nazis carried their sterilization program far beyond any level reached in other countries, sterilizing over four hundred thousand people by 1940. Of this accomplishment, the American eugenicists were envious. Joseph S. DeJarnette, a member of the Virginia sterilization movement, ruefully commented in 1934: "The Germans are beating us at our own game."[19]

In addition to the sterilization law, the Nazis passed the Nuremberg Laws in 1935, which prohibited marriage and sexual intercourse between "Aryans" and people of more than one-quarter Jewish descent.[20] When criticized for this law, the Nazis responded by pointing again to the United States and several other countries that had had antimiscegenation laws in place for decades, if not centuries. "Wir sind nicht allein" (We are not alone), a phrase appearing on Nazi posters about their sterilization and antimiscegenation laws, indicates the degree to which the Nazis borrowed from already existing programs in other countries and their sensitivity to criticism from the international arena.

The fact that eugenic practices were carried to such extremes in Germany, compared even to the other most eugenically active countries, may be ascribed to the far more severe economic and social constraints under which Germany labored in the interwar period. After Germany's ignominious defeat in World War I, embodied in the Treaty of Versailles, German financial and institutional structures were in shambles. Mass labor demonstrations, the emergence of a well-organized communist front that briefly controlled several large industrial centers, and civil chaos in general all combined to produce a bitter and resentful feeling among large segments of the German middle class. The experiment in democracy that became the Weimar Republic was doomed from the outset by these massive problems. Yet in this chaotic climate, German eugenicists put forward arguments that would bring their concerns directly to the seats of governmental power. Among other factors, eugenicists claimed that Germany's defeat was due to national degeneracy, the influences of racial impurity, declining birthrates among the intelligentsia and economically prosperous, and the antieugenic policies associated with socialist egalitarianism. Postwar eugenicists emphasized more strongly that the government had to step in and strengthen the hereditary health of the nation. Increasingly, economic arguments, such as the costs of caring for the socially inadequate and mentally ill, were employed by those lobbying for government support for eugenics.[21]

Sheila Weiss has stressed the importance of seeing the *logic* of eugenic arguments in Germany as the aspect that resulted in its full co-optation by the Nazis after 1933. That logic gave rise to considerations of "national efficiency" and the elimination of "nonproductive eaters," or "lives not worth living." Given the economic crises besetting the Weimar Republic, especially after the crash of world capitalism in 1929, budget cuts and stringency measures often became the "bottom line" for political decisions. Elimination of those who consumed but did not produce became the byword for efficient management in Germany, more strongly even than in the United States. Eugenics provided the biological justification for drastically cutting all aspects of social welfare, health care, and institutional programs for the old, the indigent, and those thought to be genetically handicapped. Racism and anti-Semitism were only one component, though sometimes a rather vocal one, of pre-Nazi eugenic ideology. Eugenicists in Germany were sometimes divided on their racialist and pro-Nordic stance, but they were seldom divided on the issue of how eugenics could use modern scientific expertise to improve national and industrial efficiency. By the time the Nazis had consolidated their power and established labor and concentration camps, eugenic principles, including racism, had become a mainstay of the Third Reich's political and social policy. The debate over anti-Semitism had ended among most German eugenicists by 1936. By then anti-Semitism was accepted as "scientific fact."

The Decline of Eugenics in the United States

It is clear that by the mid- to late-1930s the older style of eugenics characterized by the claims of Laughlin, Davenport, and others was on the wane. The crude, simplistic genetic claims; the unveiled racial and ethnic biases that eugenicists put forth; the loss of support by wealthy elites, for whom eugenics had by now accomplished its major purpose (to denigrate various sectors of the working class and therefore to divide and conquer the work force); and growing concern about the Nazis' use of racial hygiene and eugenics to justify sterilization and (increasingly) euthanasia all conspired to undermine the movement. It also did not help that Laughlin was himself a victim of late-onset epilepsy, a condition eugenicists sought to eliminate. His near-fatal driving accident in Cold Spring Harbor brought on by an epileptic attack was a matter of considerable embarrassment and concern to the Carnegie Institution of Washington.[22]

Most historians agree that the ideal of eugenics did not die, even after World War II and the full revelation of Nazi atrocities. It carried on in various guises, probably the most influential being the population control movement, which took eugenicists' concerns for the high reproductive rate of the poor at home and projected it onto the growing population of Third World nations abroad. It was no longer just the defective Juke or Kallikak family in the U.S. or Britain that was the problem. These were, in the words of biologist Raymond Pearl, a "drop in the bucket." What biologists had to be concerned about was global population growth, with the least advanced (and supposedly the most biologically defective) countries contributing proportionately the most to future population growth. Such unchecked increase, Pearl predicted in 1926, would be the major cause of all future global problems, from famine and epidemics to pollution and war.[23] While the eugenic ideal of reproductive control did not die, the specific form of it that was so popular in the 1920s gained a tarnished image. After World War II, many biologists and medical personnel shunned the term. Today it is used primarily as a pejorative indictment of any attempts at forced control over reproductive rights.

Conclusion

What, then, can this historical episode inform us about the present? The prevalence of claims today for a genetic basis of social behavior—and therefore for many, if not all, social problems—appears to be equally as extensive, or even more so, than it was during the heyday of the eugenics movement. Indeed, it may be more powerful and persuasive today because it is now integrated into medical science in a way that it was not in the old eugenics movement. At the same time, the data on which modern claims are based, involving the same traits as seventy years ago (alcoholism, manic-depressive disorders, schizophrenia, criminality, I.Q., and "sexual perversion"), which are the focus of modern work, appear little if any more conclusive or free from the same methodological pitfalls as in the movement's previous incarnation. The belief that genetics will be the "Holy Grail" of modern medicine and the salvation of our social and economic future seems as much a myth today as it was a half-century or more ago.

Yet we are now geneticizing and medicalizing behaviors in a far more inclusive way than in the past. Today, medicalization and geneticization go hand in hand. A behavior or personality trait is first given a clinical name. This establishes its supposed scientific legitimacy and also reifies the condition, that is, makes it sound like it is a single entity, arising from a single cause. Medicalization establishes the mental framework for viewing the behavior or trait as a "disorder." The next step is either to treat the condition therapeutically with drugs, or to medicalize it further by claiming a genetic basis. In social and economic terms, the value of geneticization is to locate the cause of the condition unequivocally in the defective biology of the individual and his or her family line. Historically, medical conditions have been thought of as environmentally induced (by diet, infectious agents, accidents, etc.) and therefore amenable to environmental cures. On the contrary, genetically caused diseases have been historically regarded as largely untreatable by any environmental intervention. Genetic causes lie within. Given today's debates about medical care coverage and the desire of insurers to avoid paying for "pre-existing conditions," it is easy to understand why genetic explanations are so attractive, at least to the business and investment community. Discussions are rampant today about whether insurance companies should be allowed to deny coverage for individuals or families with "pre-existing" genetic conditions, such as Huntington's chorea; or whether insurance can be made conditional for selective abortion, and a myriad of related ethical questions. What if this concept could be extended to alcoholism, depression, criminality, risk-taking, homosexuality, and the whole host of behaviors (all viewed as "disorders") that, it is now claimed, have a hereditary basis?

Genetic explanations are also attractive, in certain ways, to the public at large. Genetics absolves individuals of responsibility for their own actions, or for shortcomings or problems experienced by their children. A headline in the *Wall Street Journal* a few years ago read: "Man's Genes Made Him Kill, Lawyers Say" (15 November 1994), while another in the *Los Angeles Times* claimed: "Genes, Not Parenting, the Key to Temperament, Studies Say" (20 February 1994). Although there is nothing inherent in genetic arguments per se that dictates social policy toward individuals with verifiable genetic diseases, we would be well advised to look to history for the *likelihood* of how genetic knowledge might be used. When genetic arguments are extended to all facets of our behavior and personality, as they were during the old eugenics movement and as they are today, we need to take a critical look at both the science being presented and the social environment calling it forth.

Whether such claims have a basis in the findings of modern biology is another issue. My own view, as I pointed out at the beginning of this essay, is one of considerable skepticism. Not only does history not offer much reason to think that present-day claims rest on more solid evidence than in the past, but also advances in biology itself suggest that these claims are based on a naive view of how genes work. In contrast to the 1920s, today's biologists are becoming increasingly aware that the same genotype may produce a wide range of phenotypes, depending on both the genetic (other genes present in the individual's genome) and environmental context. Even in cases such as cystic fibrosis, where the major genetic element has been isolated, individuals carrying that gene run the gamut from showing severe debilitation to no discernible effect at all. This is even more true for behavioral traits, which have evolved in our species over millions of years to provide flexibility in response to changing circumstances.

The question remains: Are we likely to experience a true revival of eugenic thinking or true eugenic practice in the near future? If the argument in this essay—that eugenics is very much a product of deteriorating economic and social conditions—is correct, then much will depend on the overall social context that develops in the United States and around the world in the next decade or two. With the current availability of many genetic screening tests and amniocentesis, we already have in place a kind of "laissez-faire eugenics," to use Philip Kitcher's phrase. Moreover, with the growing pressure from HMOs and other health care providers on families not to have, or to abort, "at risk" offspring, reproductive decisions are already being made with respect to "genetic defects," albeit not under orders from the state. This is what critic Troy Duster has termed "back door eugenics."[24] Is corporate pressure so very different—or less insidious—than state pressure? We may be splitting hairs in trying to answer this question.

But where does all this lead us? We *may* indeed be in danger of slowly evolving a new eugenics, but we do have one advantage that our predecessors lacked—namely, their experience. We know where naive and simplistic genetic thinking can lead in both this country and especially in Germany in the 1930s. The severity of the German outcome compared to our own lies not in abstract differences in "national character" or the tradition of Prussian authoritarianism, but rather in the very concrete differences in the degree of economic and social chaos between the two countries during the interwar period. For Germany, the humiliation of World War I and the forced experiment of a British-style parliamentary system embodied in the weak and divided Weimar government provided a backdrop against which economic deprivation resulting from the Treaty of Versailles—the reparations payments and the loss of overseas colonies—imposed far greater hardships on the average German than the Great Depression did on the average American. If the relationships I have sketched out here are valid, then the difference in both degree and kind between the outcome of German and U.S. eugenics can be understood as a result of the differences in economic and social contexts prevailing in the two countries at the time.

What we can learn from this history is that if we want to avoid a new eugenics, and to avoid the judgment of history falling upon as it has upon the Germans, we must work on several fronts at the present time. Scientists and knowledgeable historians/philosophers of science must challenge simplistic genetic explanations, in both the professional and the popular press. As citizens, we should actively lobby for basic human services, such as national health coverage for all residents and minimum wage for all workers in all jobs, and for limitations in classroom size. Finally, we must demand programs and policies that would alter the economic and social conditions created by our free market economy, which will, if they are allowed to follow their present course, surely create the conditions in which eugenic solutions can, and most likely will, be once again deemed acceptable.

Notes

A preliminary version of this essay was first presented as The George Sarton Award Lecture at the annual meeting of the American Association for the Advancement of Science, 14 February 1998, in Philadelphia. The author wishes to thank both the AAAS and The History of Science Society for their invitation to make this presentation.

1. See Charles Davenport, *Eugenics* (New York: Henry Holt, 1910).
2. Barbara A. Kimmelman, "The American Breeders' Association: Genetics and Eugenics in an Agricultural Context, 1903–1913," *Social Studies of Science* 13 (1983): 163–204.
3. Garland E. Allen, "The Eugenics Record Office at Cold Springs Harbor, 1910–1940: An Essay in Institutional History," *Osiris* (2nd Series) 2 (1986): 225–264.

4. See Steven Selden, *Inheriting Shame: The Story of Eugenics and Racism in America* (New York: Teachers College Press, 1999).

5. Jonas Robitscher, *Eugenic Sterilization* (Springfield, IL: Charles C. Thomas, 1973), 31.

6. Thomas Hunt Morgan, *Evolution and Genetics* (Princeton: Princeton University Press, 1925), 207.

7. Sidney Lens, *The Labor Wars* (New York: Doubleday, 1973).

8. Allan Chase, *The Legacy of Malthus* (New York: Alfred A. Knopf, 1977), 134.

9. Diane Paul, *Controlling Heredity* (Atlantic Highlands, NJ: Humanities Press International, 1995), 134.

10. Harold Ward, "The Dilemma of Eugenics," in *The New Republic* 82 (1935): 304.

11. See Allen, "The Eugenics Record Office."

12. See Robert Proctor, *Racial Hygiene: Medicine Under the Nazis* (Cambridge, MA: Harvard University Press, 1988); and Sheila Weiss, "The Race Hygiene Movement in Germany, 1904–1945," in Mark Adams, ed., *The Wellborn Science: Eugenics in Germany, France, Brazil and Russia* (New York: Oxford University Press, 1990), 8–68.

13. Weiss, "The Race Hygiene Movement in Germany," 43.

14. Stefan Kühl, *The Nazi Connection: Eugenics, American Racism and German National Socialism* (New York: Oxford University Press, 1994), 39.

15. Ibid., 88.

16. Weiss, "The Race Hygiene Movement in Germany," 43.

17. Kühl, *The Nazi Connection*, 54–63.

18. Ibid., 60.

19. Daniel J. Kevles, *In the Name of Eugenics* (New York: Alfred A. Knopf, 1985), 116.

20. Proctor, *Racial Hygiene*, 132–134.

21. Jonathan Harwood, *Styles of Scientific Thought: The German Genetics Community, 1900–1933* (Chicago: University of Chicago Press, 1993), 33–41.

22. Allen, "The Eugenics Record Office," 254.

23. Garland E. Allen, "Old Wine in New Bottles: From Eugenics to Population Control in the World of Raymond Pearl," in Keith R. Benson, Jane Maienschein, and Ronald Rainger, eds., *The Expansion of American Biology* (New Brunswick: Rutgers University Press, 1991), 245–250.

24. See Troy Duster, *Back Door to Eugenics* (New York: Routledge, 1990).

Chapter Two

THE NAZI CAMPAIGN AGAINST TOBACCO
Science in a Totalitarian State

———— ✪ ————

Robert N. Proctor

IN MY RECENT BOOK, *The Nazi War on Cancer*, I explored the curious and heretofore unnoticed fact that the Nazis launched the world's most aggressive anticancer campaign, encompassing bans on carcinogens in food and water, restrictions on the use of asbestos and other carcinogens in the workplace, and novel dietary and chemical therapeutics.[1] I was interested to learn why soybeans were declared "Nazi beans," and how Germany became the first nation to recognize lung cancer and mesothelioma as compensable, asbestos-induced occupational diseases. I looked at the rhetoric of cancer research. It includes the use of reversible metaphors such as "cancer as Jew," "Jew as tumor," "cancer as communist cell," "communist cell as cancer"; the profusion of "ectomies" and "otomies" (lobotomy, chordotomy, laparotomy); and the surprisingly widespread rhetoric of "final solutions." I was interested in why the word "enlightenment" was used more in the Nazi period than at any other time, but also in the political contours of medical memory, the things we tend to forget about life and science—all part of my larger interest in structural apathies, communities of disinterest, and the social production of ignorance (what I call "agnatology").

A particularly important aspect of the Nazi war on cancer was the campaign against tobacco. The approach here is somewhat different from what one normally encounters in studies of Nazi medicine. Medical historians are by and large familiar with efforts by the German medical profession to suppress knowledge of the complicity of physicians in the crimes of the Third Reich—sterilization, "euthanasia," abusive experimentation, and so forth. This essay considers a different kind of forgetfulness, a different kind of taint, having to do, one could say, with the cross-purposes of Germanists, public health activists, and medical historians who make it their business to celebrate "medical firsts."

There are interesting reasons why Germans were able to identify carcinogens very early on, reasons having to do with the insurance economy, industrial paternalism, labor activism, and Germany's famous laboratory traditions. But there are also interesting reasons why the Nazi war on cancer has been overlooked. Anti-tobacco activists cannot really use the issue. One cannot say, "Smoking causes cancer—even the Nazis knew that!" And the people one might be expected to fixate on, including scientists from the Nazi era, have not found a return to the past very rewarding. Nazi tobacco research has had neither prosecutors nor cheering squads, two of the things often needed to focus historical attention.

Stunde Null

Historians have tended to treat the 1950s as the *Stunde Null* ("Zero Hour," or lowest point) of tobacco health research, especially when it comes to the question of when a lung cancer hazard was first recognized. In a recent *New York Times* review of Richard Kluger's *Ashes to Ashes*, for example, Dan Kevles remarked that the danger of smoking to health "rested on little more than anecdotal evidence coupled with moral censure until 1950, when studies appeared in the United States and England [incriminating] cigarettes as a cause of lung cancer."[2] The studies invariably cited are those published by Richard Doll and others in the 1950s, excellent epidemiology that has garnered many laurels. Richard Doll was knighted, for example, and almost won a Nobel Prize.

What I have found, however, is that very similar studies were performed in Germany in the 1930s and 1940s. German tobacco epidemiology was, in fact, for a time the most advanced in the world; indeed, it was in Germany in the early 1940s that we find the world's first broad medical consensus that smoking is the major cause of lung cancer.

That recognition was fostered by a national political climate stressing the virtues of racial hygiene and bodily purity. In the Nazi view of the world, tobacco was a genetic poison; a cause of infertility, cancer, and heart attacks; and a drain on financial resources and public health. The Nazi antismoking campaign was consistent with the regime's policy of doctor-directed *Gesundheitsführung* (leadership in health), which embraced both preventive health and the primacy of the public good over individual liberties. Tobacco was opposed by racial hygienists who feared the corruption of the German germ plasm, by industrial hygienists who feared a reduction of work capacity, and by nurses and midwives who feared harm to the "maternal organism." Tobacco use was attacked as a "plague" and as "dry drunkenness" (older themes), but also as "lung masturbation" and a "relic of the liberal lifestyle." Tobacco was branded "the enemy of world peace," and there was even talk of "tobacco terror" and "tobacco capitalism." The anti-tobacco campaign can be seen as part of a larger climate of "homeopathic paranoia," a fear that small but powerful agents (such as alcohol, asbestos, lead, Jews, Gypsies, and tobacco) were corrupting the German body.

What may be most disturbing about the campaign is the rather uncomfortable light it sheds on the relation between science and politics at this time. The story is not the familiar one of the suppression of science or the unwilling conformity of science to political ideals; the relation between science and politics was more symbiotic. Public health initiatives were launched in the name of National Socialism. Nazi ideals informed the practice and popularization of science, motivating it and reorienting it in subtle and complex ways. It is not enough to speak of the suppression or even survival of science; one also has to see how Nazi ideals worked to inspire and guide the science of the time. As it turns out, some of the most important work on tobacco in this period might never have been done without the direct intervention of Hitler's chancellery in anti-tobacco politics.

Medical Moralism

Anti-tobacco sentiments were, of course, nothing new to the twentieth century. German opposition to tobacco dates from the early seventeenth century, when smoking was introduced into German-speaking territories by Dutch and English soldiers fighting in the Thirty Years' War. Smoking was banned in Berlin in 1723 and in Königsberg in 1742, and penalties for violating such bans could be severe. In Lüneburg in 1691, for example, persons found smoking within the city walls could be put to death. Elsewhere, violation of tobacco laws could lead to beatings, banishment, or the fire-branding of a mark on the offending individual. Many such laws remained on the books until the "professors' revolution" of 1848, a coincidence Nazi-era activists used to associate tobacco with "Jewish liberalism."[3]

Cancer concerns, however, came later. Tobacco had been suggested as a cause of cancer of the lip in the eighteenth century, but smoking remained a relative luxury throughout the nineteenth century, and its contribution to the incidence of cancer must have been minimal. As recently as World War I, lung cancer was still an extreme rarity. In 1912, when Isaac Adler produced the first book-length review of lung cancer, he felt he had to apologize for writing on such a rare and insignificant disease.[4] Medical professors confronted with a case would call in their students to observe, suggesting that they might never see another. Today, of course, it is the world's most common cause of cancer death, claiming more than one hundred fifty thousand victims a year in the United States alone. It is estimated that China will soon have close to a million lung cancer deaths every year.

Smoking became more popular toward the end of the nineteenth century, due to the introduction of mechanized cigarette rolling, tobacco advertising, and state promotion or monopoly of cigarettes to generate revenues. Cigarettes were provided with rations to the soldiers of World War I, and the introduction of milder types of tobacco and flue curing made it easier to inhale, encouraging a shift away from pipes and cigars. Cigarette smoke tended to be drawn deeper into the lungs, delivering a much higher dose of tar, nicotine, and other noxious substances to the bronchial passageways. The cancer consequences were profound, as lung cancer rates grew by leaps and bounds. Smoking was only one of several suspects: the influenza pandemic of 1918–1919 was sometimes blamed, as were automobile exhausts, occupational exposures, chest X-rays, chemical warfare agents from World War I, and even the upsurge of racial mixing.

Some scholars doubted the reality of the increase. In Germany, for example, a 1930 paper argued that lung cancers were simply being diagnosed more often as a result of the increasing use of X-rays,[5] but the more common view by the middle of the Weimar era was that the disease was genuinely on the rise, for as yet unclear reasons. Part of the difficulty in sorting out this question was that many other things were on the rise. Automobile use was growing faster even than lung cancer, which led some to suggest that engine exhausts or road tar might be the decisive factor. Dusts of all sorts were blamed, as people began to realize that the power tools increasingly used in mining, construction, metalwork, and other trades were fouling the lungs of workers to an unprecedented degree. Many of the other theories advanced in the 1920s and early 1930s could be lumped under the broader rubrics of modernization, industrialization, or urbanization, making it difficult to say what was the cause and what was the effect.

Cigarettes began to come under suspicion in the 1920s, especially through the work of Fritz Lickint, a Dresden physician who in 1929 published some of the first statistical evidence linking lung cancer and cigarettes, a "case series" showing that lung cancer patients were particularly likely to be smokers.[6] Lickint went on to become Germany's foremost advocate of the antismoking message, cautioning that tobacco had surpassed alcohol as a public health menace. In his monumental *Tabak und Organismus*, published in 1939, Lickint chronicled an extraordinary range of ills deriving from smoking or chewing tobacco. The 1,200-page volume, surveying eight thousand publications, was advertised as *Das Standardwerk* and is arguably the most comprehensive scholarly indictment of tobacco of the century. The book blames tobacco for cancers all along the *Rauchstrasse* ("smoking street")—lips, tongue, lining of the mouth, jaw, esophagus, windpipe, and lungs. Tobacco was an instigator not just of cancer, but of arteriosclerosis, infant mortality, ulcers, and dozens of other maladies. Lickint also argued that "passive smoking," a term he coined, posed a serious threat to nonsmokers. Lickint calculated that tobacco must play a role in seven thousand male cancer deaths per year in Germany—all preventable.[7]

In 1939 Lickint was praised as the physician "most hated by the tobacco industry," but he was only one of many attacking tobacco at this time. Tobacco was said to hinder the military prowess of the German soldier; smoking was said to cause automobile accidents, prompting criminal penalties for accidents caused by driving "under the influence" of cigarettes. The Nazi Party's Office of Racial Policy pointed out that nicotine had been found in the breast milk of smoking mothers,[8] and Agnes Bluhm, Germany's most prominent female racial hygienist, argued that smoking could cause spontaneous abortions, especially disturbing to Nazi authorities who placed a premium on boosting Germany's birth rate.

All of these dangers were magnified, in the Nazi view of the world, by the fact that tobacco was addictive. Tobacco was said to create an alien allegiance in an era when both mind and body were supposed to belong to the Führer. The impression broadly shared was that while anyone might become addicted, the genetically weak and degenerate were far more vulnerable; hence the charge that smoking was "especially popular among young psychopaths."[9]

It is not yet clear whether tobacco addicts were ever incarcerated for their addiction, but we do know that such a fate befell persons addicted to other substances. In 1941, Reich Health Führer Dr. Leonardo Conti ordered the establishment of an office to register addicts and combat addiction (Reich Bureau for the Struggle against Addictive Drugs); similar registries were established to identify alcoholics, the homeless, and other "asocials."[10] Smokers may have been fearful of such moves, given the widespread conception of tobacco use as a "first stage" in the move toward abusing ever-stronger substances, such as morphine or cocaine.[11]

Franz H. Müller's 1939 Case-Control Study

Documenting the lung cancer hazard of smoking was one of the more remarkable achievements of this period. Angel H. Roffo of Argentina (1882–1947), who published much of his work in German cancer journals, had already shown by 1930 that tars derived from tobacco smoke could induce cancer in laboratory animals. In subsequent experiments he found that certain tobacco tar distillates could produce tumors in as many as 94 percent of all exposed animals.[12] Roffo was also importantly involved in shifting the emphasis from nicotine to tar as the primary tobacco cancer hazard. By 1936, Lickint could state that nicotine was "probably innocent" of carcinogenic potency and that benzopyrene was probably the guilty party.[13] In 1933, Neumann Wender, a Viennese professor, showed that tobacco smoke contained not only nicotine and tar but methyl alcohol and other toxins; he also showed that the tar content of cigarette smoke increased when the woody stems of tobacco leaves were used in the manufacturing process.[14] Enrico Ferrari of Trieste that same year pointed out that since tar was known to have "excellent cancer-causing properties," it was not hard to imagine that the increasing use of these woody parts might be responsible for the upsurge in lung cancer. Ferrari claimed to have been long convinced ("without a doubt") that cigarettes were a major cause of lung cancer; how else could one explain the fact that his native Trieste had both the highest smoking rate in Italy and the highest lung cancer rate in that country?[15]

Lickint had pointed to the preponderance of smokers among lung cancer patients in 1929, and his was the lead most often followed when physicians began to nail down the statistical link. Rudolf Fleckseder of Vienna in 1936, for example, reported a very high proportion of smokers among his fifty-one male lung cancer patients (94 percent were smokers, 69 percent were heavy smokers), and others also noted the disproportion.[16] The stage was thereby set for the era's two most powerful statistical analyses: a 1939 paper by Franz Hermann Müller, a young physician at Cologne's Bürgerhospital, and a 1943 paper by two scholars, Eberhard Schairer and Erich Schöniger, working at Jena's Institute for Tobacco Hazards Research. The papers are of historic interest, given that they provide the most sophisticated proofs up to that time that smoking was the major cause of lung cancer. The 1943 paper is also interesting insofar as it probably would not have been written without the personal intervention of Hitler in the anti-tobacco effort.

Franz H. Müller's 1939 paper, essentially his medical thesis, is apparently the world's first controlled epidemiological study of the relationship between tobacco and lung cancer.[17] The paper, published in Germany's leading cancer research journal, began by noting the dramatic increase in lung cancers in the bodies autopsied at the University of Cologne's pathology institute. Lung cancer had been rare in the nineteenth century, but had recently become the second-largest cause of cancer death in Germany, accounting for 23 percent of all cancer mortality. (Stomach cancer still held first place, with about 59 percent.) Müller mentioned the most commonly cited causes of the increase, such as road dust and macadam tars, automobile exhaust, trauma, tuberculosis, influenza, X-rays, and industrial pollutants, but he argued that "the significance of tobacco smoke has been pushed more and more into the foreground."[18] German tobacco use had grown by a factor of five from 1907 to 1935, exposing lung tissues to unprecedented levels of carcinogenic tar. Roffo and Lickint had shown that smokers of three packs a day would inhale a total of four kilograms of carcinogenic tars over a period of ten years. Müller added that the tar content of cigarettes had risen in recent years, a phenomenon that he blamed, following Wender and Ferrari, on the increasing use of tobacco stems in cigarette manufacture. He was also worried about the economic burden of smoking, trotting out the widely publicized fact that 10 percent of the entire national income was going to cigarettes and alcohol.

Müller's most important contribution, however, was his epidemiologic investigation, prompted by his observation that the lung cancer patients in his care were very often heavy smokers, and that men were far more likely than women to contract the disease. His own Cologne data showed a sex ratio of 6 to 1; a Lickint review of twenty-five publications gave a figure of 5 to 1.[19] Müller's analysis was what we today would call a survey-based retrospective case-control study, meaning that he compared, through questionnaires and medical histories, the smoking behavior of two groups of people: lung cancer patients and a healthy "control group" of comparable age. The survey was sent to the relatives of the deceased (lung cancer kills rather quickly), and included the following questions:

1. Was the deceased, Herr ———— a smoker? If so, how high was his daily consumption of cigars, cigarettes, or pipe tobacco? (Please be numerically precise in your answer!)
2. Did the deceased smoke at an earlier time in his life and then stop? Until when did he smoke? If he did at one time smoke, what was his daily consumption of cigars, cigarettes, pipe tobacco. (Please be precise!)
3. Did the deceased ever smoke more cigarettes than he did at a later time, and then cut down on his smoking? How high was his daily use of tobacco products, before and after he cut back? (Please be precise!)
4. Is there anything you can say about whether the deceased was ever exposed to unclean air for any length of time, either while at work or off the job? Did this unclean air contain smoke, soot, dust, tar, fumes, motor exhaust, coal or metallic dust, chemical substances, cigarette smoke, or similar substances?

Müller does not tell us how many questionnaires were sent out, but we are told that ninety-six "cases" (*Krankheitsfälle*) were eventually obtained, eighty-six males and ten females. All had died of lung cancer, confirmed at autopsy by the University of Cologne's pathology institute or by one of six other pathology institutes at Cologne's regional hospitals. Additional information was gathered from the patients' medical records, and in some cases from the patients' workplace. The eighty-six male "cases" were divided into five classes: "extremely heavy smoker," "very heavy smoker," "heavy smoker," "moderate smoker," or "nonsmoker." The same was done for a group of eighty-six healthy "controls" (*gesunden Männern*) of the same age as the cases.[20]

The results were stunning. The lung cancer victims were more than six times as likely to be "extremely heavy smokers," defined as daily consumers of 10 to 15 cigars, more than 35 cigarettes, or more than 50 grams of pipe tobacco. Furthermore, the healthy group had a much higher proportion of nonsmokers: 16 percent, compared with only 3.5 percent for the lung cancer group. The eighty-six lung cancer patients smoked a total of 2,900 grams of tobacco per day, while the eighty-six healthy men smoked only 1,250 grams. Müller concluded not just that tobacco was "an important cause" of lung cancer but that "the extraordinary rise in tobacco use" was "the single most important cause of the rising incidence of lung cancer" in recent decades.[21]

Müller's article is notable in several other respects. For one thing, there is no obvious Nazi ideology or rhetoric. There is one brief hint that "the genetically vulnerable" should be advised not to smoke, but race is never mentioned and there are no other remarks that would lead one to identify the article as a "Nazi" piece of scholarship. The bibliography (twenty-seven sources) refers the reader to the work of at least three Jewish scientists (Max Askanazy, Walther Berblinger, and Marx Lipschitz), each of whom is also cited approvingly in the text. This is not as unusual as one might imagine: Jewish scientists from the Weimar period were frequently cited in Nazi-era medical literature, despite occasional pressures to put an end to the practice.

Also interesting is the discussion of possible causes of lung cancer other than tobacco. Müller was well aware that tobacco was unlikely to be the sole cause, given that a third of all of his cases were either moderate smokers or nonsmokers. He disagreed with the Englishman W. Blair Bell and other "lead therapy" advocates who claimed that the metal showed promise as a cancer treatment by selectively destroying cancer cells. Müller's inclination was rather to follow Carly Seyfarth's view that workers exposed to the metal—printers, metalworkers, plumbers, and typesetters, for example—faced an increased risk of contracting the disease. In his own sample of eighty-six men with lung cancer, seventeen showed a history of exposure to lead dust, from which he concluded that lead inhalation must be considered a "promoting factor" (*fördernder Einfluss*) in the development of cancer. Other factors were no doubt involved, as was suggested from the work history of his patients, which included a 48-year-old locksmith exposed to soot, smoke, and coal dust; a 26-year-old housewife who for two years had worked in a cigarette factory, inhaling tobacco dust; three women who had worked during World War I in a munitions factory, exposing themselves to nitrates, phosphorous, mercury, chromium, picric acid, and other noxious substances; a 48-year-old dye worker known to have inhaled aniline vapors; and several workers exposed to chromium in one form or another. All were moderate smokers or nonsmokers, leading one to the conclusion that occupational exposures may have played a role in their becoming ill.[22]

Müller's path-breaking article was sometimes cited in the 1950s, when Doll, Wynder, and others reconfirmed the tobacco-lung cancer link.[23] What is not often recognized, however, is that Müller's was not the era's only case-controlled documentation of the tobacco-lung cancer hazard, nor even the most sophisticated. That honor would have to go to a lesser-known paper by Eberhard Schairer and Erich Schöniger that was published in Germany's leading cancer journal in 1943—a paper that extended Müller's analysis and provided the most conclusive evidence up to that time, anywhere in the world, that tobacco was the major cause of lung cancer. We shall turn to that paper in a moment, but first some words on the practical steps taken to combat tobacco in the late 1930s and early 1940s.

Moving into Action

Legal sanctions began to be put into place in 1938. The Luftwaffe banned smoking in its barracks that year, and the post office did likewise. The NSDAP announced a ban on smoking in its offices in 1939, at which time Himmler ordered a smoking ban for all uniformed police and SS officers while on duty.[24] Tobacco rationing coupons were denied to pregnant women and to all women over fifty-five or under twenty-five, and restaurants and cafés were barred from selling cigarettes to female customers. A July 1943 law made it illegal for anyone under eighteen to smoke in public. Advertisements implying that smoking possessed "hygienic values" were barred, as were images depicting smokers as athletes or sports fans. Advertisers were no longer allowed to show smokers behind the wheel of a car, and were barred from ridiculing opponents of smoking, as they were generally fond of doing.[25]

One response was to begin large-scale production of nicotine-free cigarettes. The Reich Institute for Tobacco Research in Forchheim, near Karlsruhe, perfected methods to remove nicotine through novel breeding techniques and chemical treatments. By 1940, fully 5 percent of the entire German harvest, or three million kilos, was "nicotine-free tobacco."[26] There were sixty thousand tobacco farmers in Germany in 1939.

Research was also launched into the psychology and psychopharmacology of smoking. A 1940 medical thesis explored why blind people seldom smoked, and why soldiers found smoking more pleasurable in the daylight hours than at night.[27] Dozens of preparations were available to help people quit smoking, ranging from a silver nitrate mouthwash to a substance known as transpulmin, which was injected into the blood stream to produce an unpleasant sensation. Hypnotism was apparently popular, as were various forms of psychological counseling at dozens of tobacco counseling stations established throughout the Reich.

Karl Astel's Anti-tobacco Institute at Jena

German anti-tobacco activism culminated in 1940 and 1941, encouraged by the success of the early military campaigns and the euphoric effort to find "final solutions" for Germany's problems. The *Endlösung der Brotfrage* ("final solution to the bread question"), for example, required that all bakeries produce whole-grain bread. The most important anti-tobacco research institution, Jena's Institute for Tobacco Hazards Research, was established in April 1941 by a 100,000 RM grant from Hitler's chancellery.

Jena was by this time a center of anti-tobacco activism. Karl Astel, director of the new institute, was also president of Thuringia's Office of Racial Affairs and, since the summer of 1939, president of the University of Jena. A vocal anti-Semite and high-ranking SS officer, Astel was also a militant antismoker and teetotaler who banned smoking at the University of Jena and soon became known for snatching cigarettes from the mouths of students who dared to violate the ban. Tobacco abstinence was a condition of employment at Astel's anti-tobacco institute. Party District Leader (*Gauleiter*) Fritz Sauckel, in his original proposal for the institute, said this was necessary to guarantee the "independence" and "impartiality" of the science produced, and was "as important as Aryan ancestry."[28]

Astel's anti-tobacco institute promoted both medically informed propaganda, including the production of an antismoking film, and politically informed scientific work. The most intriguing work of the institute was the paper by Eberhard Schairer and Erich Schöniger in 1943 on experimental lung cancer epidemiology. It was the most convincing demonstration to date of the role of smoking in the development of lung cancer. The paper is remarkable for its scope and sophistication; it includes a long discussion of potential sources of bias, and an elaborate critique of alternative explanations for rising lung cancer rates. The authors used a more carefully selected group of controls than had ever been used before, standardized not just for age, sex, and (of course) race, but also for health. All of the controls, for example, had some kind of cancer other than lung. The authors showed that people with lung cancer were far more likely to smoke than the control population with other kinds of cancer. The results were declared to be of "the highest statistical significance," and although Schairer and Schöniger did not quantify that significance, one can in fact show that the probability that the results could have come about by chance is less than one in ten million.

Interpretation

How do we interpret the fact that the world's most sophisticated epidemiological study of the link between lung cancer and tobacco was made possible by a grant from Hitler's chancellery? Why has this been ignored, and what are we to make of it? Richard Doll, the Oxford don knighted for similar work in the 1950s, had never seen the paper until he received a copy from me last year. There are only two citations listed in the *Science Citation Index*; it seems to have been erased from medical memory.

It is striking how closely the anti-tobacco campaign was linked to the larger racial ideology of Nazism. Tobacco was perceived to be sapping the strength of the German people, at work, at school, in sports, on the field of battle, in the bedroom and the birthing clinic. But it is also important not to overlook Hitler's personal aversion. Hitler had smoked twenty-five to forty cigarettes per day in his Viennese youth until he realized how much money he was wasting, whereupon he "tossed his cigarettes into the Danube and never reached for them again." He once characterized tobacco as "the wrath of the Red Man against the White Man, vengeance for having been given hard liquor." He also claimed that Germany might never have achieved its present glory if he had continued to smoke: "[P]erhaps it was to this, then [that is, his giving up smoking], that we owe the salvation of the German people."[29] To which one might respond, paraphrasing Freud, that sometimes giving up smoking is just giving up smoking.

This leads us to the larger question of why Germany was able to organize such a powerful anti-tobacco movement, considering that in the 1920s it was the United States that possessed the world's most powerful organized opposition to alcohol and tobacco. A clue is to be found in John Burnham's discussion of American attitudes toward tobacco at this time. Burnham argues that in the U.S., the moralistic certainties that had led to alcohol prohibition and tobacco temperance in the 1920s were under attack by the 1930s. Several of the "diseases" crusaded against at the height of Prohibition turned out to be pseudodiseases, such as masturbation, and it was easy to believe that the same might be true for tobacco. The cultural consequence, one could say, is that the burden of proof shifted from the defenders of tobacco to its accusers. It was rare to find an American physician who criticized tobacco in the 1930s or 1940s, and those who did object were often dismissed as prudes or cranks.[30] Liberals such as John Dewey, for example, were skeptical of claims that tobacco posed a health hazard. Katcher and Pauly have shown that the same thing happened to alcohol. Many of the hazards of alcohol known at the turn of the century were "forgotten" in the postrepeal era, to be rediscovered only in the 1960s and 1970s; these included cirrhosis of the liver, cardiomyopathy, fetal malformities, and esophageal cancer.[31]

Burnham does not discuss the situation in Germany, but what is interesting is how the situation there was inverted. In Germany, the tobacco and alcohol temperance movements of the 1920s were actually strengthened by the rise of National Socialism. Nazi rule was generally welcomed by antialcohol and anti-tobacco forces, even in the United States, where at least one antialcohol journal applauded the election of Hitler.[32] Germans never experienced Prohibition and never suffered the backlash against tobacco moralism felt by American physicians, at least not until the 1950s when one sees the same kinds of skepticism found in America in the 1930s. It was fashionable to attack tobacco in Germany in the 1930s, whereas the opposite was true for the U.S.[33]

Tobacco Collapse

It would be inappropriate to exaggerate the Nazis' success in combating tobacco. Tobacco consumption grew dramatically during the first seven years of Nazi rule, a consequence of the post-1933 economic boom. But this is also evidence that whatever propaganda may have been launched against the habit seems to have had little or no effect on consumption, at least in these early years. The argument has been put forward that smoking itself may have served as a kind of "passive resistance"; people smoked or listened to jazz or went to swing dance parties as a kind of cultural opposition to Nazi machismo and asceticism. We do know that

Nazi officials worried about appearing overly ascetic or puritanical. Nazi tobacco activists were well aware of the American backlash against Prohibition, and used this to caution against a total ban on cigarettes. As one activist put the predicament: "[F]orbidden fruit is tempting."[34]

As the war dragged on, the campaign did in fact lose much of its steam. Wartime urgencies led a military physician in 1944 to write that "only a fanatic" would withhold a drink or a smoke from a soldier trying to calm his nerves after the horrors of battle.[35] Of course, the anti-tobacco campaign never had the priority of, say, the destruction of the Jews. Efforts to link Jews and tobacco in 1940 and 1941 were short-lived and aroused some high-level protests. For instance, the minister of economics, Walter Funk, worried that tobacco workers were going to become victims of state-sponsored violence. Hitler was asked to adjudicate the issue, and although he sided with the anti-tobacco forces,[36] anti-tobacco propaganda was muted after the summer of 1941. That is also about the time that the tobacco industry launched its own medical institute, the Tabacologia medicinalis, to counter anti-tobacco science and propaganda, which foreshadows in many respects the fight between the Tobacco Institute and U.S. health authorities fifteen years later. The major difference, of course, is that in the German case, tobacco lost. The institute was forced to close.

Why was the Nazis' anti-tobacco campaign not more successful? The rapid economic recovery in the first six years of Nazi rule boosted the average German's purchasing power, and tobacco companies took advantage of this to promote their products. There is also the crucial point that tobacco provided an important source of revenue for the national treasury. In 1937, German national income from tobacco taxes and tariffs was in excess of a billion Reichsmarks, a considerable sum. By 1941, as a result of new taxes and the annexation of Austria, the figure had grown to nearly two billion Reichsmarks. Tobacco taxes by this time constituted about a twelfth of the government's entire income.[37] One might compare that with China today, where income from tobacco taxes provides nearly a third of the government's entire revenue. Two hundred thousand Germans were said to owe their livelihood to tobacco, an important argument for the *fluxus quo*.

German tobacco consumption did not begin to decline until the second or third year of the war. Wartime priorities brought rationing, and bombing raids began to cut into supplies. A 1944 survey of one thousand servicemen found that while the proportion of soldiers who smoked had increased since the start of the war, the total consumption of tobacco had actually decreased by about 14 percent.[38] Postwar poverty further cut consumption. Shortages became so severe that American authorities decided to ship tobacco, free of charge, into Germany as part of the Marshall Plan. Ninety-three thousand tons were shipped in 1948 and 1949, and the cost to the U.S. government was on the order of $70 million. The long-term benefit, at least for American tobacco firms, was a gradual shift in German tobacco tastes from the traditionally favored and locally produced black tobacco to the milder, blond-Virginian blend.[39]

Postwar Consequences

I am not going to reproduce here calculations of the impact of the decline in German tobacco consumption, which began about 1941 and continued into the early postwar years. We know that a lung cancer is generated for every two to four million cigarettes consumed in a society, and one can make some interesting calculations of how Germany's declining cigarette consumption found expression in cancer rates, especially among women.

It is important, however, to consider the lasting impact of Nazism on the postwar anti-tobacco movement. After the war, Germany lost its position as home to the world's most aggressive anti-tobacco science and policy. Hitler, of course, was dead, but many of his anti-tobacco subordinates had either lost their jobs or were otherwise silenced. Karl Astel, head of the Institute for Tobacco Hazards Research, committed suicide in his Jena office on the night of 3 April 1945. Astel's death was a major blow to anti-tobacco activism, as was the death of Reich Health Führer Dr. Leonardo Conti, who committed suicide on 6 October 1945 in an Allied prison, while waiting prosecution for his role in the "euthanasia" operation and other crimes. Hans Reiter, the Reich Health Office president who once characterized nicotine as "the greatest enemy of the people's health" and "the number one drag on the German economy," was interned in an American prison camp for two years, after which he worked as a physician in Kassel, never again returning to public service. *Gauleiter* Fritz Sauckel, the guiding light behind Thuringia's antismoking campaign, was executed on 1 October 1946 for crimes against humanity. It is hardly surprising that much of the wind was taken out of the sails of Germany's anti-tobacco movement. Last year, when I gave a talk at Germany's National Cancer Institute, no one there had ever even heard of Astel's institute or the tobacco work it had produced. The same is true of Germany's leading antismoking groups, for whom history begins in 1945.

The Monstrous and the Prosaic

By focusing on the Nazi anti-tobacco campaign, my goal has not been to fabricate banalities (that "good can come from evil," for example) or to salvage the honor of this era. My intention has not been to argue that today's anti-tobacco efforts have fascist roots, or that public health measures are, in principle, totalitarian. It is necessary to make this rather obvious point because some of my work has been used in the popular press to denounce the antismoking movement as fascist; hence the talk about "nico-Nazis," for example.[40] It is important to understand that the Nazification of German science, medicine, and public health was more complex than is commonly imagined. The history of science under National Socialism is a history of both forcible sterilization and herbal medicine, of genocidal "selection" in the camps and bans on public smoking. We will not forget Mengele's crimes, but we should also not forget that Dachau prisoners produced organic honey, that the SS cornered the European market in mineral water, that much of what went on in the name of the *Volk* could today pass for responsible and progressive preventive health care.

There is no inherently totalitarian tendency or "indefatigable self-destructiveness" of enlightenment in modern science, as Horkheimer and Adorno would have us believe.[41] However, it is important to recognize that just as the routine practice of science is not incompatible with the routine exercise of cruelty, so the dictatorial and eliminative aspirations of fascism are not necessarily at odds with the promotion of public health, at least for certain portions of the population. The exclusive focus on the heinous aspects of Nazi medical practice makes it easy for us to relegate the events of this era to the monstrous or otherworldly, but there is more to the story than "medicine gone mad," the title of Art Caplan's 1992 book on Nazi medicine.[42] The Nazi campaign against tobacco and the "whole-grain bread operation" are, in some sense, as fascist as the yellow stars and the death camps. A more differentiated picture may open our eyes to new kinds of continuities binding the past to the present; it may also allow us better to see how fascism triumphed in the first place.

Notes

Parts of this essay appeared earlier in my essay "Why Did the Nazis Have the World's Most Aggressive Anti-Cancer Campaign?" *Endeavour* 23 (1999): 76–79.

1. Robert N. Proctor, *The Nazi War on Cancer* (Princeton: Princeton University Press, 1999).
2. Daniel J. Kevles, "Blowing Smoke," *New York Times Book Review*, 12 May 1996, 13. The book under review was Richard Kluger, *Ashes to Ashes: America's Hundred-Year Cigarette War, the Public Health, and the Unabashed Triumph of Philip Morris* (New York: Alfred A. Knopf, 1996).
3. Edgar Bejach, *Die tabakgegnerische Bewegung in Deutschland mit Berücksichtigung der ausserdeutschen Tabakgegnerbewegung,* Med. Diss. Berlin, 1927, 3–4; Henner Hess, *Rauchen: Geschichte, Geschäfte, Gefahren* (Frankfurt: Campus Verlag, 1987), 20.
4. Isaac Adler, *Primary Malignant Growths of the Lungs and Bronchi* (New York: Longmans, Green, and Co., 1912), 3.
5. Franz Herz, "Hat das Lungenkarzinom an Häufigkeit zugenommen?" *Medizinische Klinik* 26 (1966): 1666–1669.
6. Fritz Lickint, "Tabak und Tabakrauch als ätiologischer Factor des Carcinoms," *Zeitschrift für Krebsforschung* 30 (1929): 349–365.
7. Fritz Lickint, *Tabak und Organismus* (Stuttgart: Hippokrates Verlag, 1939).
8. Werner Hüttig, "Der Einfluss der Genussgifte auf das Erbgut und seine Entwicklung (Alkohol, Nikotin)," *Öffentlicher Gesundheitsdienst* 1 (1935):171.
9. Georg Boehncke, *Die gesetzlichen Grundlagen der Bekämpfung des Tabakmissbrauches in Deutschland* (Berlin: Wacht Verlag, 1937), 4.
10. "Kleine Mitteilungen," *Vertrauensarzt* 9 (1941): 128.
11. Walther Kittel, "Hygiene des Rauchens," in Siegfried Handloser and Wilhelm Hoffmann, eds., *Wehrhygiene* (Berlin: Springer, 1944), 243.
12. Angel H. Roffo, "Der Tabak als Krebserzeugende Agens," *Deutsche medizinische Wochenschrift* 63 (1937): 1267–1271. A good review is his "Krebserzeugende Tabakwirkung," *Monatsschrift für Krebsbekämpfung* 7 (1940): 97. The first efforts to induce cancer using tobacco tars may have been those of the military physician Anton Brosch of Vienna, who painted guinea pigs with "the well-known carcinogens" tar, paraffin, soot, and tobacco juice with unclear results. See his "Theoretische und experimentelle Untersuchungen zur Pathogenesis und Histogenesis der malignen Geschwülste," *Virchows Archiv für pathologische Anatomie* 162 (1900): 32–84.
13. Fritz Lickint, *Tabakgenuss und Gesundheit* (Hannover: Bruno Wilkens Verlag, 1936), 84–85. Fr. Thys of the Fondation Médicale Reine Elisabeth in Brussels was another who claimed that too much attention was being given to nicotine and too little to tar in the genesis of lung cancer. See his "Note sur l'étiologie du carcinome bronchique," *Revue belge des sciences médicales* 7 (1935): 640–644. By 1941, Victor Mertens could claim that nicotine was "seldom blamed" for carcinogenesis. See his "Noch einmal Zigarettenrauch und Lungenkrebs," *Zeitschrift für Krebsforschung* 51 (1941): 183–192.
14. Neumann Wender, "Eine neue Gefahr für den Raucher," *Münchener medizinische Wochenschrift* 80 (1933): 737ff.

15. Enrico Ferrari, "Tabakrauch und Lungenkarzinom," *Münchener medizinische Wochenschrift* 80 (1933): 942. Ferrari endorsed Wender's proposal to ban the use of woody stems in tobacco manufacturing (ibid.).

16. Rudolf Fleckseder, "Über den Bronchialkrebs und einige seiner Entstehungsbedingungen," *Münchener medizinische Wochenschrift* 83 (1936): 1585–1588. Arkin and Wagner in the United States found that 90 percent of their lung cancer patients were heavy smokers; Roffo gave a figure of 95 percent. See Aaron Arkin and David H. Wagner, "Primary Carcinoma of the Lung," *JAMA* 106 (1936): 587–591; Roffo, "Krebserzeugende Tabakwirkung," 97. Franz Strnad at Nonnenbruch's clinic in Prague in 1938 found that the proportion was just under 50 percent and concluded that smoking was important in the onset of the disease; see his article in the *Monatsschrift für Krebsbekämpfung* 5 (1938): 216ff.

17. Franz Hermann Müller, "Tabakmissbrauch und Lungencarcinom," *Zeitschrift für Krebsforschung* 49 (1939): 57–85. A brief abstract of the paper was translated into English and published in the 30 September 1939 issue of *JAMA*, 1372. I have not been able to find out much about Müller's life, not even the dates of his birth and death. According to local archivists, his personnel files at Cologne's city hospital were destroyed by Allied bombing.

18. Müller, "Tabakmissbrauch," 59.

19. Ibid., 57. Walther Reinhard was one of the first to note this sexual asymmetry (there were sixteen male and eleven female lung cancers in his sample); see his 1878 "Der primäre Lungenkrebs," *Archiv der Heilkunde* 19 (1878): 385. Hans Pässler's 1896 review, "Über das primäre Carcinom der Lunge," *Archiv für pathologische Anatomie und Physiologie* 145 (1896): 191–278, included fifty men and eighteen women. Adler's 1912 sample of 374 cases was 72 percent male (*Primary Malignant Growths*, 22). Carly Seyfarth's "Lungenkarzinome in Leipzig," *Deutsche medizinische Wochenschrift* 50 (1924): 1497–1499, reviewed 307 cases autopsied at the University of Leipzig's pathology institute, including 84 percent males. For Seyfarth, the sexual asymmetry was "undoubtedly" due to higher male occupational exposures, an attribution curiously at odds with his recognition that tobacco might play a role in the increase of cancer. For Wilhelm Hueper, interestingly, given his general distrust of the "cigarette theory," the disproportion was most likely due to the fact that men were much heavier smokers. See his *Occupational Tumors and Allied Diseases* (Springfield, IL: Charles C. Thomas, 1942), 426.

20. Müller, "Tabakmissbrauch," 78. Müller does not say much about how the healthy controls were chosen, nor does he say why he ignored the female smokers. All ninety-six individual cases are presented in the published paper, however, including details on occupational exposures, age, type and quantity of tobacco smoked, kind and location of the malignancy, and previous medical history, especially any history of lung disease.

21. Ibid., 78.

22. Ibid., 78–82.

23. See the references cited in note 1; compare also Willem F. Wassink, "Ontstaansvoorwaarden voor Longkanker," *Nederlands Tijdschrift voor Geneeskunde* 4 (1948): 3732–3747.

24. "Rauchverbot für die Polizei auf Strassen und in Diensträumen," *Die Genussgifte* 36 (1940): 59.

25. "Bestimmung des Werberates," *Wirtschaftswerbung*, December 1941, 396–397.

26. Franz K. Reckert, *Tabakwarenkunde: Der Tabak, sein Anbau und seine Verarbeitung* (Berlin: Max Schwalbe, 1942), 31.

27. Wolfgang, Klarner, *Vom Rauchen: Eine Sucht und ihre Bekämpfung* (Nuremberg: Kern, 1940).

28. Fritz Sauckel, "Abschrift," 20 March 1941, R43 II/745b, Bundesarchiv Potsdam (BAP).

29. Henry Picker, *Hitlers Tischgespräche im Führerhauptquartier 1941–42* (Bonn: Athenäum, 1951), 327–328.

30. John C. Burnham, "American Physicians and Tobacco Use: Two Surgeons General, 1929 and 1964," *Bulletin of the History of Medicine* 63 (1989): 10–15.

31. Brian Katcher, "The Post-repeal Eclipse in Knowledge about the Harmful Effects of Alcohol," *Addiction* 88 (1993): 729–744; Philip J. Pauly, "How Did the Effects of Alcohol on Reproduction Become Scientifically Uninteresting?" *Journal of the History of Biology* 29 (1996): 1–28.

32. "Hitler's Attitude Toward Alcohol," *Scientific Temperance Journal*, spring 1933, 18.

33. It is fashionable to challenge the myth of the steady progression of knowledge, but the systematic patterns of forgetfulness remain by and large understudied. Forgetfulness is as much the rule in science as is total recall—it is also sometimes deliberate, or the inadvertent consequence of political struggle. We need to pay more attention to the history of scientific amnesia, the shadow companion to the production of knowledge.

34. Georg Boehncke, *Die Bedeutung der Tabakfrage für das deutsche Volk* (Berlin: Reichsausschuss für Volksgesundheitsdienst, 1939), 10.

35. Walther Kittel, "Alkohol und Wehrmacht," in Siegfried Handloser and Wilhelm Hoffmann, eds., *Wehrhygiene* (Berlin: Springer, 1944), 241.

36. Walther Funk to Partei-Kanzlei, 20 May 1941, R43 II/1226b, BAP; "Form der Propaganda gegen den Tabakmissbrauch," 22 May 1941, R43 II/1226b, BAP; Hans-Heinrich Lammers to Walther Funk, 10 June 1941, R43 II/1226b, BAP.

37. Reckert, *Tabakwarenkunde*, 236; "Erkennung und Bekämpfung der Tabakgefahren," *Deutsches Ärzteblatt* 71 (1941): 184.

38. Kittel, "Hygiene des Rauchens," 245.

39. Friedheim Merz, *Die Stunde Null—Eine Sonderdokumentation* (Bonn: Neuer Vorwärts, 1981), 66.

40. Rosie DiManno, "The New Rednecks: NicoNazis Pushing Bigotry's Borders," *Toronto Star*, 10 March 1997, A7.

41. Max Horkheimer and Theodor W. Adorno, *Dialectic of Enlightenment* (1944) (New York: Herder and Herder, 1972), xi.

42. Arthur L. Caplan, *When Medicine Went Mad: Bioethics and the Holocaust* (Totowa, NJ: Humana Press, 1992).

Chapter Three

PHYSICIANS AS KILLERS IN NAZI GERMANY

Hadamar, Treblinka, and Auschwitz

———— ∞∞∞ ————

Henry Friedlander

IN THIS ESSAY I deal with physicians who personally committed crimes, not with their mentors, those physicians and scientists who furnished the ideological framework and provided the necessary cover for these crimes, and who can be considered *Schreibtischtäter* (bureaucratic, or desk killers). To repeat: I am here concerned with physicians who murdered human beings, thus leaving out those who committed lesser crimes such as, for example, compulsory sterilization, although most graduated from the lesser to the larger crime.

Various myths have been created to explain the role of physicians in Nazi killing operations. Some authors dealing with Nazi medical crimes have ascribed to physicians as a group a unique commitment to serve humanity and have thus viewed their participation in these crimes as a particularly egregious fall from grace.[1] But physicians are professionals no different in their commitment than chemists, engineers, or historians. They wanted to raise their income, advance their careers, and share the world-view of their colleagues. To demystify them and their profession, I use the term "physician," in German, *Arzt*, to describe them, instead of the term "doctor," common in the English-speaking world.

The T4 Killings: The Killing Wards

The killing operations of the Nazi regime commenced as it started World War II in the winter of 1939–1940. The first victims were the disabled in the German Reich: first, disabled children, and, second, institutionalized disabled adults. The killers used the euphemism "euthanasia," but also called it the "destruction of life unworthy of life" (*Vernichtung lebensunwerten Lebens*). The Chancellery of the Führer (*Kanzlei des Führers*, or KDF) directed the killings with the support of the health division of the Reich Ministry of the Interior. For this purpose, the chancellery set up various front organizations, headquartered in Berlin at Tiergarten Street No. 4, and thus known as T4.[2]

Physicians and psychiatrists, mostly professors, hospital directors, and bureaucrats, directed the T4 killings and also served as medical experts (*Gutachter*) to select the victims whom, however, they never saw. The killers came in two groups. The first group killed in hospitals, both in the so-called T4 children's wards and in selected adult wards. In addition to plain starvation, these male and female physicians killed with overdoses of luminal (a sedative) and veronal (sleeping tablets), and also morphine-scopolamine. In this way, children and adults were killed not as a result of the ingestion of alien poisons but through an overdose of a common medicine. Furthermore, overdoses of barbiturates and similar forms of medication did not result in immediate death. Instead, they led to medical complications, especially pneumonia, that eventually—usually in two or three days—resulted in death. The physicians could then report a "death through natural causes."[3] Thus, Hermann Pfannmüller, who after the war denied all evidence that he had starved his patients, also testified to this fiction before the U.S. Military Tribunal at Nuremberg: "I must emphasize this is not a matter of poisoning. The child simply dies of a certain congestion in the lungs, it does not die of poisoning."[4]

Let us look at this particular perpetrator as an example of the T4 physician-killer. Hermann Pfannmüller was born in 1886. He obtained his medical license in 1913 and his specialty certification in psychiatry in 1918. He had joined the Nazi Party in 1922, but, as a civil servant, had to resign and could only rejoin in May 1933. Active in the enforcement of the racial and eugenic laws during the 1930s, Pfannmüller steadily advanced at the large Bavarian state hospital in Eglfing-Haar outside Munich, and, due to his party connections, was appointed director in 1938. For T4 he served as a medical expert for selecting victims, placed his hospital at the disposal of T4 during the phase of "wild euthanasia," and also ran its children's ward.[5] We have unusually graphic testimony about Pfannmüller's treatment of patients at Eglfing-Haar even before the start of the T4 killings. Ludwig Lehner, a Bavarian schoolteacher, who went on an official tour of the hospital, testified in London in 1946:

> After visiting a few other wards, the institution's director himself, as far as I remember he was called Pfannmüller, led us into a children's ward. This hall impressed me as clean and well-kept. About 15 to 25 cribs contained that number of children, aged approximately one to five years. In this ward Pfannmüller explicated his opinions in particular detail. I remember pretty accurately the sense of his speech, because it was, either due to cynicism or clumsiness, surprisingly frank: "For me as a National Socialist, these creatures obviously represent only a burden for our healthy national body. We do not kill with poison, injections, etc., because that would only provide new slanderous campaign material for the foreign press and certain gentlemen in Switzerland. No, our method is, as you can see, much simpler and far more natural." As he spoke these words, Pfannmüller and a nurse from the ward pulled a child from its crib. Displaying the child like a dead rabbit, he pontificated with the air of a connoisseur and a cynical smirk something like this: "With this one, for example, it will still take two to three days." I can still clearly visualize the spectacle of this fat and smirking man with the whimpering skeleton in his fleshy hand, surrounded by other starving children. Furthermore, the murderer then pointed out that they did not suddenly withdraw food, but instead slowly reduced rations.[6]

Most of the physicians who did these killings were much younger. Ernst Illing at Vienna's notorious Am Spiegelgrund children's hospital was certified in psychiatry only in 1937; his predecessor, the Austrian physician Erwin Jekelius, certified only in 1938. Illing had been trained to kill at Hans Heinze's Brandenburg-Görden hospital and research station, and was assigned as a German physician to Vienna for the purpose of implementing children's "euthanasia" "without attracting public notice."[7]

After August 1941, when Adolf Hitler prohibited further gassing of disabled patients because this procedure had become too public, the killings were decentralized. Large numbers of hospitals throughout Germany and Austria thereafter killed disabled adults using medication, as had long been practiced in the children's wards. These killings, known as "wild euthanasia," involved large numbers of physicians. For example, Meseritz-Obrawalde in Pomerania, located on the eastern border of the German Reich in order to hide mass death from the German population, was probably the most notorious killing hospital of "wild euthanasia."[8] Disabled patients arrived at Meseritz-Obrawalde in transports from at least twenty-six German cities, usually in the middle of the night. Physicians and nurses selected for killing those patients who were unable to work, but the process was arbitrary. Those selected included "patients who caused extra work for the nurses; those who were deaf-mute, ill, obstructive, or undisciplined; and anyone else who was simply annoying" as well as patients "who had fled and were recaptured, and those engaging in undesirable sexual liaisons."[9]

At the end, the hospitals of "wild euthanasia" in some ways resembled the concentration camps: patients worked and were underfed, beaten, and tortured. A nineteen-year-old girl, who had been incarcerated at the Eichberg state hospital, was later committed to the concentration camps, and survived Auschwitz and Ravensbrück, wrote after the war: "[A]t the Eichberg I experienced the most painful period of my young life."[10]

The T4 Killings: The Killing Centers

The physicians in the T4 killing centers did not even operate, as did their colleagues in the killing wards, with the deceptive trappings of medicine. These centers, invented in the winter of 1939–1940 for the murder of disabled adults, were simply places designed to murder human beings on the assembly line, involving gas chambers, crematoria, and what the Germans called *Leichenfledderei* (looting the corpses).[11] An American judge would years later describe such centers as a "human abattoir."[12] Three young physicians with relatively recent medical credentials served as physicians-in-charge at killing centers: Irmfried Eberl (certified 1935), Horst Schumann (certified 1932), and Rudolf Lonauer (certified 1931). Not every physician, however, was willing to accept this kind of assignment. Thus, the physician Werner Kirchert, a member of the SS, refused the job but recommended Schumann, a party loyalist but not a member of the SS.[13] Their assistants were even younger and their medical licenses (*Approbation*) more recent. Kurt Borm (licensed September 1938) and Ewald Worthmann (licensed January 1939) were certified shortly before the war. However, Heinrich Bunke, Klaus Endruweit, and Aquilin Ullrich had only just received emergency licenses (*Notapprobation*) in 1939 after the war had started.

In the killing centers these physicians supervised the registration of the arriving victims; wearing a white coat they simply checked the medical files for completeness. They administered the gas and later pronounced the murdered patients as dead. They also participated in looting the corpses. In addition to the extraction of gold teeth for the benefit of the Reich, physicians did autopsies, providing young killing center physicians with training and academic credit toward their specialization, and also recovered organs, especially brains, for scientific study at medical institutes. This had been one of the inducements offered by those recruiting the physicians. They were promised, in addition to the fraudulent title of institutional director, that they would hold seminars, engage in research, and employ pathologists at the killing centers, but these promises never materialized.[14]

Operation 14f13

In the spring of 1941, the T4 killings expanded to include concentration camp prisoners, who were murdered in the T4 killing centers. This new killing enterprise was designated "Special Treatment 14f13."[15] "Special treatment" (*Sonderbehandlung*) was the term prescribed for killing in the language regulations used by the SS and the police.[16] The code "14f13" was the file number used by the Inspectorate of the Concentration Camps for the killing of prisoners in T4 centers. At the Inspectorate, the category 14f included all files involving the death of prisoners. Thus, for example, 14f7 files concerned death through natural causes, 14f8 applied to suicides, and 14f14 involved executions.[17]

The selection of prisoners in the camps represented a close cooperation between T4 and the SS. T4 physicians, in teams or alone, traveled to the camps to validate the preselections made by SS camp physicians. At least twelve T4 physicians participated: Hans-Bodo Gorgaß, Otto Hebold, Werner Heyde, Rudolf Lonauer, Friedrich Mennecke, Robert Müller, Paul Nitsche, Viktor Ratka, Kurt Schmalenbach, Horst Schumann, Theodor Steinmeyer, and Gerhard Wischer. Mennecke has provided us with the most detailed account of such visits. Throughout his professional career, Mennecke wrote innumerable, extremely detailed letters to his wife Eva, whom he addressed as "Mommy," and his letters from various camps remain a revealing and essential primary source. From Ravensbrück he wrote: "The work moves swiftly, because the answers to questions on top have already been typed on the form and I only have to record the diagnosis, chief symptoms, etc." He recounts how the prisoners file past him and the SS physician "supplies information about their behavior in the camp," and thus "everything moves without a hitch." In another letter Mennecke describes the procedure:

"As a second allotment there then followed altogether 1,200 Jews, who did not first have to be 'examined,' but where it is sufficient to extract from the files the reasons for their arrest (often very extensive!) and to record them on the questionnaires."[18]

Let us look at this unusually verbose perpetrator. Friedrich Mennecke was born in 1904 into a working-class family. His father was severely wounded during World War I and died in 1923. An uncle helped support the family but could offer financial help only for the education of Mennecke's older brother. After completing his secondary education in 1923, Mennecke thus worked in the business world for four years while his brother studied law. Only after his brother's graduation did Mennecke begin his study of medicine. Completing his doctorate at Göttingen, he received his medical license in 1935. These early experiences probably had something to do with Mennecke's drive for advancement and status.

As a student, Mennecke joined the Nazi Party at Göttingen in May 1932 and later used his party affiliation to advance his career. Equally important, he had also joined the SS, rising by 1940 to the rank of captain, which also worked to his advantage.

After completing his internship and residency, Mennecke obtained a job at Eichberg early in 1936; the director at the time suspected that Mennecke had been appointed because of his party credentials. Three years later, in January 1939, his career made a spectacular jump forward when he was appointed director at Eichberg.[19] In 1937 he married Eva Wehlan, a medical laboratory assistant and the "Mommy" of his letters.[20]

The Killing Center Treblinka

In late 1941, the T4 technology was exported to the east.[21] There the SS established killing centers, modeled on the T4 centers, for the massive murder campaign against Jews and Gypsies. One of these killing centers was located at Chelmno, and was staffed by police officers who had earlier killed disabled patients in gas vans. The other three were the so-called camps of Operation Reinhard: Belzec, Sobibor, and Treblinka. Although under the command of the SS and the police leader of Lublin, Odilo Globocnik, the camps were staffed and operated by T4 personnel, backed up by Ukrainian volunteer auxiliaries (*Hilfswillige* or *Hiwis*), who trained at the SS camp Trawniki and were also known as

Askaris after the colonial troops used by the Germans in southwest Africa during World War I.[22]

The largest of these killing centers was Treblinka; Irmfried Eberl was its first commandant. Eberl was born in 1910 in Bregenz in the Vorarlberg province of Austria, attended the University of Innsbruck, and received his medical license and his doctorate in 1935. Thereafter, he completed his training in forensic medicine, tuberculosis, and gynecology at various hospitals in Innsbruck and Vienna. Eberl joined the Nazi Party in 1931. In 1936 he moved to Germany, because as a member of the illegal Nazi movement he found it difficult to obtain a hospital appointment. In Germany, he held various hospital and party jobs until he received permanent medical certification in March 1937, and was granted official permission to use the doctor title in May 1937. Thereafter, he was appointed physician with the emergency medical services of the city of Berlin. He did not return to Austria after the Anschluss, the union of Austria with Germany in March 1938, probably because local Austrian Nazis did not want to make room for the illegals that had moved to Germany. He joined T4 early, serving as T4 physician-in-chief first in the Brandenburg and thereafter in the Bernburg killing center.[23]

In June 1938, Eberl married Ruth Rehm. She was born in 1907 in Ulm, Bavaria, and received her schooling in Erfurt and Magdeburg. She studied "scientific graphology" for two years, passed her examination in 1932, and joined the Nazi Party that September. After a year of independent employment as a graphologist, she worked for the Nazi movement in Magdeburg, Erfurt, and Weimar, and, finally, for the German Labor Front in Berlin. She was killed in an air raid in July 1944. She was a strong and determined supporter of the Nazi movement who did not hesitate to denounce fellow Germans to the Gestapo.[24]

In 1942 Eberl went to the east. As he wrote his wife (29 June 1942), private letters were to be mailed to the "SS Special Commando, Treblinka near Malkinia"; packages, however, should be sent to T4 at the following address: "Berlin W 35, Tiergarten Straße 4 (Operation East)."[25]

Only one T4 physician—Irmfried Eberl—was assigned to the camps of Operation Reinhard. He was one of the three senior physicians-in-charge at the "euthanasia" killing centers. Horst Schumann was already assigned to sterilization experiments at Auschwitz. Rudolf Lonauer could not be spared because Hartheim and Niedernhard fulfilled a major responsibility for killings in Austria and at Mauthausen. Eberl's selection was therefore not illogical. For about two months, during July and August 1942, he served as the commandant of Treblinka. Late in August, or early in September, Globocnik relieved him of his command, and he returned to Germany, where he again assumed direction of the Bernburg killing center.[26]

After Eberl's departure, no physician remained in any of the camps of Operation Reinhard. Obviously, the extermination camps of the east functioned well despite the absence of physicians. In the German T4 centers, physicians were employed as a cover for killing centers masquerading as hospitals. They were also needed to check medical records and provide death certificates. And Hitler had ordered that only physicians should turn on the gas. None of these procedures applied in the camps of Operation Reinhard.

The Extermination Camp Auschwitz-Birkenau

Auschwitz (Oswiecim) differed, along with Majdanek, from all other killing centers. It consisted of a killing center located within a regular German concentration camp. This combination created a dual but interlocking system in Auschwitz. SS physicians thus fulfilled both the function of the concentration camp medical officer, a position that had existed since the early 1930s, and also that of the killing center physician, a position that had been created only in early 1940 as part of the T4 operation. The existence—side by side—of concentration camp and killing center did, however, alter the operation of both, thus creating the ultimate form of the German extermination camp.[27]

Auschwitz opened as a concentration camp for Polish political prisoners in April–May 1940 in the annexed area of Upper Silesia. Richard Glücks, the inspector of the concentration camps, appointed SS Captain Rudolf Höss, an old camp hand, as commandant. In March 1941, Himmler ordered the construction of another camp area in nearby Birkenau (Brzezinka). This new camp, in the end much larger than the main camp (*Stammlager*), was mostly built by Soviet POWs. In 1941 the function of Auschwitz started to change.[28]

First, Auschwitz became the arena for the "final solution." The first experimental gassing of Soviet POWs and debilitated Polish prisoners took place in a barrack of the main camp. The innovation was the use of prussic acid in the form of Zyklon B gas, a fumigation agent available in all camps. Thereafter, the old crematorium in the main camp was utilized for gassings. In the spring of 1942, gassings were moved to two converted farmhouses in Birkenau, and in the spring and summer of 1943, four large crematoria buildings (numbered 2 through 5), including gas chambers, opened in Birkenau. Alongside the killing installations, Birkenau had a compound, known in the camp as "Canada," where the belongings of the arriving transports were kept and sorted. In addition, Birkenau grew with numerous separate compounds, each a subcamp with its own electrified barbed wire fence.[29]

Second, Auschwitz became a large slave labor reservoir. Early in 1941, I.G. Farben selected grounds about four and a half miles from Auschwitz for one of its Buna works to produce synthetic rubber. To house the inmates, I.G. Farben built a satellite camp in 1942, known as the Monowitz or Buna camp, which developed into a major labor camp with numerous subsidiary camps.[30]

In November 1943, as Arthur Liebehenschel replaced Höss as commandant, Auschwitz was divided into three parts. The *Stammlager* became Auschwitz I, Birkenau became Auschwitz II, and Monowitz and its subsidiaries became Auschwitz III, each with its own commandant. But the commandant of Auschwitz I served as garrison senior officer, and several departments—including the political department and the SS physicians—continued to serve all three camps.[31]

As part of the administrative structure of the German concentration camps, the office of the SS physician was responsible for the medical care of SS personnel, general sanitation, the prevention of epidemics, and also medical services for the inmates. In Auschwitz, the garrison physician (*Standortarzt*) headed the medical services, directing the work of the SS physicians, dentists, pharmacists, and medics (*Sanitätsdienstgrad*, or SDG). From 1940 to 1945, the following served in Auschwitz (not at same time): forty SS physicians, nineteen SS dentists, three SS pharmacists, and seventy-nine SS medics. From 1942 to 1945, SS Major Dr. Eduard Wirths served as garrison physician. Born 1909 in Würzburg, he had been a general practitioner with a country practice in Baden. A member of the Nazi Party since 1933 and of the SS since 1934, he was drafted into the Waffen-SS and served in Norway and Finland; in April 1934, heart problems led to his transfer to the concentration camps, first to Dachau and Neuengamme, then Auschwitz during the war. We know a great deal about his behavior at Auschwitz from Hermann Langbein, who served as his inmate clerk (*Schreiber*). Through Langbein, Wirths was influenced by the political resistance, and he did attempt to improve the general hygienic and medical conditions in the camp, and to decrease the number of arbitrary killings by injections in the infirmaries. He committed suicide in British custody.[32]

The SS physicians who served in the protective custody camp usually became complicit partners in crime by permitting the continuation of substandard hygienic conditions, poor food, and atrocious working conditions. Moreover, they were responsible for overseeing the inmate infirmary, called *Revier* in most camps and *Krankenbau* in Auschwitz. And there they usually did not ensure that inmates received adequate care. They also participated in inhuman corporal punishment (*Prügelstrafe*), because a physician had to certify that a prisoner was healthy enough to undergo beatings. Of course, not all SS physicians behaved with equal disregard of inmate health. Some did make an effort to improve the lot of prisoners.[33]

In addition to punishments, SS physicians in most camps participated as well in the murder of prisoners. They used medications, usually injections, to kill the sick, the rebellious, or simply those with interesting tattoos.[34] In Auschwitz this method of murder was applied consistently by SS First Lieutenant Dr. Friedrich Entress. Born in Posen in 1914, he had just finished his medical studies when he was assigned to concentration camp duty, in early 1941 at Groß-Rosen and in December 1941 in Auschwitz. As Langbein has noted: "He received his doctorate in mid-1942 without writing a dissertation, a privilege granted to ethnic Germans from the east."[35] In Auschwitz he introduced the use of deadly phenol injections into the heart to kill inmates. He organized it in such a way that the SDG could kill up to one hundred persons a day.[36] Of course, this happened not only in Auschwitz. In Flossenbürg, for example, the camp physician Heinrich Schmitz administered the deadly injections himself—into the vein and not the heart, which took just a little longer. One time he was unable to hit the vein in the arm of a non-German inmate physician, who thereupon told him: "[P]oorly injected, dear colleague, but what you are doing is murder, while as a physician you are supposed to help humanity." Schmitz used the inmate's other arm to give him the deadly injections.[37]

Auschwitz as an extermination camp was also the arena for assembly line murder, and physicians participated in it as well. All medical officers—physicians, dentists, pharmacists—selected those destined for the gas chambers. In rotation, they made selections at the Birkenau siding, the *Rampe*, whenever a transport of Jews arrived. Those selected as unable to work—the very young, the old, the sick, mothers with children—at least 80 percent from each transport, went to the gas chambers. The killing procedure was the same as at Treblinka and the T4 killing centers; only the agent used (Zyklon B) was different. The physicians also supervised the gassing to prevent accidents that could affect the SS.[38]

All SS medical personnel, including the physicians, did this duty at the *Rampe*, some with enthusiasm and some with reluctance. In addition, physicians carried out so-called camp selections, in general and in the infirmary. They all did so. The only difference was that some selected the maximum numbers, while others were less determined.[39]

Let us look at an average medical perpetrator, just one among many physicians. SS Second Lieutenant Dr. Fritz Klein was born on 24 November 1888 at Zeiden near Kronstadt in Romania. He considered himself a "Romanian subject of German nationality." He had "qualified as a doctor in Budapest," and had served in the Romanian army until the summer of 1943. At that point, a treaty with Germany provided that all members of the German minority should continue service in the German army. Klein claimed that he joined the SS "because it was impossible to join the proper German Wehrmacht as one had to have German nationality for that." He was assigned to Auschwitz in December 1943. First he served in the women's compound in Auschwitz, then in the Gypsy camp and in the Theresienstadt family camp in Birkenau, and finally back in the Auschwitz *Stammlager*. He was convicted in the British Belsen trial after the war and executed.[40]

Another physician at Auschwitz was not that average. SS First Lieutenant Dr. Johann Paul Kremer was born in 1883 near Cologne into a farming family. He received his Dr. phil. (Ph.D.) in 1914, his Dr. med. (M.D.) in 1919, and his Dr. habil. (the qualifying degree for university appointment) in 1929. He served as extraordinary professor at the University of Münster from 1936 to 1945. Kremer had joined the Nazi Party in July 1932 and the SS in November 1934. In Auschwitz he served as a replacement (between university semesters) from 30 August to 20 November 1942. The following are some revealing entries in his diary:

2 September 1942
For the first time, at three this morning, present at a Special Operation (*Sonderaktion*). In comparison to this, Dante's Inferno appears to me almost like a comedy. Not without reason is Auschwitz known as the camp for extermination!

5 September 1942
This noon attended a *Sonderaktion* of *Musselmänner* from the FKL: the most horrible of horror. *Hauptsturmführer* (Captain) Thilo—the troop physician—was correct when he told me today that we are located here in the asshole of the world. In the evening around 8 o'clock again attended a *Sonderaktion* from Holland. The men push themselves to participate in these operations, because special provisions are passed out, including a fifth of liquor, 5 cigarettes, 100 grams baloney, and bread. Have duty today and tomorrow (Sunday).

6 September 1942
Today, Sunday, excellent lunch: tomato soup, one-half chicken with potatoes and red cabbage (20 grams fat). Sweets and fantastic vanilla ice cream.... Evening at 8 o'clock outside again for a *Sonderaktion.*[41]

Several months after leaving Auschwitz, the bombing of Münster led Kremer to record in his diary questions of how God could permit such injustice; he meant the bombing. He never made such an entry about the gas chambers. After leaving Auschwitz, Kremer never thought about it, and seemed to have forgotten what he had recorded in his diary. When told by the British that his diary had been found, he was happy because he thought it would prove how badly he had been treated by the Nazis. After the war, he was sentenced to life imprisonment in Poland but released in 1958. In West Germany he received a sentence of ten years, minus the time already served in Poland.[42]

The killing center atmosphere permeated the entire extermination camp. For example, in the SS Hygiene Institute at Auschwitz, the SS physicians, Bruno Weber, Hans Münch, and their colleagues, received beef for growing cultures. They decided that they would eat the meat. To provide a substitute medium for the cultures, they sent an SDG to the crematorium to cut flesh from the corpses of prisoners just killed.[43]

Auschwitz was also the place for unethical human experiments. The best-known outside experimenters were Professor Carl Clauberg and Dr. Horst Schumann.[44] But almost every SS physician at Auschwitz did experiments. Many were young and inexperienced physicians who wanted to learn. They took instruction from renowned inmate physicians, had them write their papers, and did experiments to get degrees or for publications.[45]

The most notorious Auschwitz physician, at least during the postwar years, was SS Captain Josef Mengele.[46] Born in 1911, he received a Dr. phil (Ph.D.) in physical anthropology at Munich under Theodor Mollison in 1935 and a Dr. med. (M.D.) at Frankfurt am Main under

Otmar Freiherr von Verschuer in 1938. He conducted postdoctoral research at the Frankfurt Institute for Hereditary Biology and Race Hygiene as an assistant to Verschuer, who in his 1938 progress report to the Deutsche Forschungsgemeinschaft (DFG—German Research Society) on his sponsored research on the genetic study of twins and families lists the work and publications of his assistant Mengele.[47] Mengele, who was a member of both the Nazi Party and the SS, was drafted into the Waffen-SS, served on the eastern front until he was wounded, and thereafter was posted to the Auschwitz concentration camp in 1943–1944. He served as SS physician in the Birkenau Gypsy camp (BIIe), and during August–December 1944 advanced to senior SS physician in Birkenau.

In Auschwitz Mengele performed the usual duties of a camp SS physician as well as the special Auschwitz assignment of directing selections for the gas chamber. In addition, Auschwitz opened up unlimited opportunities for an ambitious researcher. Research subjects were available in large numbers, and the restraints of medical ethics did not apply. Furthermore, Mengele could compel highly skilled inmate physicians to design and conduct research, perform tests and autopsies, and produce research papers, without the need to share credit with them. It is therefore not surprising that Mengele used Auschwitz as a research laboratory.[48]

Mengele conducted his Auschwitz research under a DFG grant of his old teacher Otmar von Verschuer, by then at the Kaiser Wilhelm Society in Berlin. In his progress report to the DFG, von Verschuer told the foundation about this new research arrangement: "My assistant Dr. Dr. Mengele is another contributor who has joined this research project. He was posted to the Auschwitz concentration camp as an SS captain and camp physician. With approval of the Reich leader SS, he has conducted anthropological research on various racial groups in the camp, and has transmitted blood samples to my laboratory for testing."[49] Mengele mailed the results of his research on Jewish and Gypsy twins to the Kaiser Wilhelm Society. There scientists analyzed the samples of blood obtained before death and the organs obtained after dissection. Mengele's investigation of eye color was only one bizarre example of such criminal experiments. He collected pairs of eyes if one of the pair had a different color, hoping that he could discover ways to change eye color. At one time, Mengele killed an entire Gypsy family to send their eyes for analysis to research assistant Karin Magnussen at the Kaiser Wilhelm Society.[50]

Why Did They Do It?

The motives of the physician perpetrators differed from place to place and person to person. Certainly, these physicians were German nationalists who subscribed to Nazi ideology and to its racist and eugenic components. But it is difficult to assess their commitment to Nazi ideology. One measure is their membership in the Nazi Party, especially the length of their membership. Eberl joined the party in Austria in 1931, and Ruth Rehm, his German wife, also joined prior to 1933. Rehm was considered a "fanatical" Nazi; Eberl's decision to leave Austria for Germany also indicates his strong commitment. The fact that he was chosen to go east to Treblinka is another indication of his ideological motivation. Like the other T4 physicians, Eberl agreed voluntarily to direct a killing center, and even agreed to serve in Treblinka. His motivation appears to have been ideological, although it was also an important job with a future in the thousand-year Reich.

For most of these physician-killers, however, ideology was not the prime motivation, although it served as a rationalization. Good examples are Johann Paul Kremer and Eduard Wirths. Both had joined the Nazi Party early, and both were members of the SS. But this does not tell us enough about them. Obviously, membership in the SS was not absolute proof of criminality; Eberl had never belonged to the black order. Both Kremer and Wirths were situational killers. They found themselves in Auschwitz, the function of which was mass murder on the assembly line. They did not refuse to serve there, but they found these killings sufficiently repulsive to rule out participation for ideological reasons. They did the minimum that their positions required, yet they did collaborate in the destruction process. Their motivation seems to have been their loyalty to the SS, the party formation they had joined years earlier. Although they used ideological arguments to explain or justify their participation, they had sufficiently internalized older ethical codes to prevent their enthusiastic collaboration. They understood that they were crossing a line.

Other physicians were motivated by ambition and greed. Friedrich Mennecke serves as a good example. He used his membership in the party and the SS to further his career, viewing his collaboration with T4 as a path toward advancement. But he also used his involvement for financial gain. Like Hermann Pfannmüller, he collected money for his services as a T4 expert, checking patient questionnaires to decide whether they should be killed. He also enjoyed his excursions to various concentration camps to select the prisoners for killing under Operation 14f13.

A different kind of ambition drove Josef Mengele. Intellectually, he adhered to the eugenic and racial ideology of the Nazi movement. It is not material whether he came to this ideology via the *völkisch* movement or through the professors who taught him. Well educated and from a wealthy family, Mengele combined ideological commitment with academic accomplishment. His ambition was advancement in his scientific profession. Posted to Auschwitz, he exploited the opportunity for medical experiments to aid his professor von Verschuer, to ingratiate himself at the Kaiser Wilhelm Society, and to make a name for himself. Most observers at Auschwitz have described him as arrogant, and this arrogance, together with his eugenic and racial world-view, explains his zealous enforcement of the Auschwitz killing process.

The T4 physicians as well as the SS physicians at Auschwitz were volunteers who could have refused to participate. They became killers because they adhered to the governing ideology and because they were arrogant, ambitious, and greedy.

Notes

1. See, for example, Robert Jay Lifton, *The Nazi Doctors: Medical Killing and the Psychology of Genocide* (New York: Basic Books, 1986).
2. See Henry Friedlander, *The Origins of Nazi Genocide: From Euthanasia to the Final Solution* (Chapel Hill: University of North Carolina Press, 1995). See also Ernst Klee, *"Euthanasie" im NS-Staat: Die "Vernichtung lebensunwerten Lebens"* (Frankfurt am Main: S. Fischer Verlag, 1983).
3. Gerhard Schmidt, *Selektion in der Heilanstalt, 1939–1945*, 2nd ed. (Frankfurt am Main: Edition Suhrkamp, 1983), 115, 132–149; Dokumentationsarchiv des österreichischen Widerstandes (DÖW), file 18282: Landgericht (LG) Wien, interrogation Marianne Türk, 25 January 1946; Staatsanwaltschaft (StA) Hamburg, Anklage Bayer, Catel, 14 Js 265/48, 7 February 1949, 27; StA Hamburg, Anklage Lensch und Struve, 147 Js 58/67, 24 April 1973, 154.
4. United States Military Tribunal, Official Transcript of the Proceedings in Case 1, United States v. Karl Brandt et al., 7392. See also Alice Platen-Hallermund, *Die Tötung Geisteskranker in Deutschland: Aus der deutschen Ärztekommission beim amerikanischen Militärgericht* (Frankfurt am Main: Verlag der Frankfurter Hefte, 1948), 46.
5. On Pfannmüller, see Berlin Document Center (BDC), dossier Hermann Pfannmüller: Reichsärztekammer file card and Nazi Party membership file card;

National Archives and Records Administration (NARA), RG 238: interrogation Hermann Pfannmüller, 5 September 1945; StA München I, Verfahren Hermann Pfannmüller, 1 Ks 10/49 (1b Js 1791/47), Protokoll der öffentlichen Sitzung des Schwurgerichts bei dem LG München I, 19 October 1949, 4–7; StA München I, Anklage Hermann Pfannmüller, 1b Js 1791/47, 16 June 1948; LG München I, Urteil Hermann Pfannmüller, 1 Ks 10/49, 5 November 1949; Adelheid L. Rüter-Ehlermann and C. F. Rüter, eds., *Justiz und NS-Verbrechen: Sammlung deutscher Strafurteile wegen nationalsozialistischer Tötungsverbrechen,* 22 vols. (Amsterdam: University Press Amsterdam, 1968–1981), vol. 8, no. 271: LG München I, Urteil Pfannmüller, 1 Ks 10/49, 15 March 1951 (hereafter cited as *JuNSV*).

6. Nuremberg Doc. NO-863: voluntary testimony, Ludwig Lehner, London, 25 August 1946, repeated (with some stylistic changes) as sworn affidavit for the U.S. Office of Chief of Council for War Crimes, St. Wolfgang, Wasserburg on the Inn, Upper Bavaria, 30 March 1947.

7. DÖW, file E19292: Reich Committee to Ernst Illing, 27 June 1942. On Jekelius, see BDC, dossier Erwin Jekelius: Reichsärztekammer file card and Nazi Party membership file card; DÖW, file E19209, Personalakten Dr. Erwin Jekelius; StA Wien, Anklage Ernst Illing, Marianne Türk und Margarete Hübsch, 15 St 9103/45, 18 June 1946; VG bei dem LG Wien, Urteil Ernst Illing, Marianne Türk und Margarete Hübsch, Vg 1a Vr 2365/45 (Hv 1208/46), 18 July 1946. On Illing, see BDC, dossier Ernst Illing: Reichsärztekammer file card, Nazi Party membership file card, and Personalakten Illing of the Reichsministerium für Wissenschaft, Erziehung und Volksbildung. On the killings in the Vienna hospitals, see Eberhard Gabriel and Wolfgang Neugebauer, eds., *NS-Euthanasie in Wien* (Vienna, Cologne, and Weimar: Böhlau Verlag, 2000).

8. See Generalstaatsanwalt (GStA) Berlin, Anklage Hilde Wernicke und Helene Wieczorek, 11 Js 37/45, 5 February 1946; LG Berlin, Urteil Hilde Wernicke und Helene Wieczorek, 11 Ks 8/46, 25 March 1946; *JuNSV*, vol. 20, no. 587: LG München I, Urteil 112 Ks 2/64, 12 March 1965; StA Hamburg, Anklage Lensch und Struve, 147 Js 58/67, 24 April 1973, 359–388; and StA Hamburg, Verfahren Lensch und Struve, 147 Js 58/67: Gutachten Jozef Radzicki (German translation).

9. StA Hamburg, Anklage Lensch und Struve, 147 Js 58/67, 24 April 1973, 378–379.

10. Hessisches Hauptstaatsarchiv (HHStA), 461/32442/3: letter, "An den Herrn Oberstaatsanwalt bei dem Landgericht Frankfurt a.M.," Frankfurt am Main, 22 November 1946.

11. On the T4 killing centers and their physicians, see Friedlander, *Origins of Nazi Genocide,* chap. 5.

12. *Fedorenko v. United States,* 449 U.S. 490, 493 (1981).

13. GStA Frankfurt/Main, Anklage Schumann, Js 18/67 (GStA), 12 December 1969, 120.

14. GStA Frankfurt/Main, Eberl Akten, II/210/1-3, 1:1–3: Irmfried Eberl to Paul Nitsche, 16 April 1942.

15. GStA Frankfurt/Main, Anklage Werner Heyde, Gerhard Bohne und Hans Hefelmann, Ks 2/63 (GStA), Js 17/59 (GStA), 22 May 1962, 603.

16. Ibid., 604. See also Henry Friedlander, "The Manipulation of Language," in Henry Friedlander and Sybil Milton, eds., *The Holocaust: Ideology, Bureaucracy, and Genocide* (New York: Kraus International Publications, 1980), 110.

17. Zentrale Stelle der Landesjustizverwaltungen, Ludwigsburg (ZStL), Sammlung Arolsen, Bd. 311, S. 01104: Rundschreiben des Inspekteurs der Konzentrationslager, Oranienburg, 21 October 1941.

18. Mennecke letter, Fürstenberg, 20 November 1941, in Peter Chroust, ed., *Friedrich Mennecke, Innenansichten eines medizinischen Täters im Nationalsozialismus: Eine Edition seiner Briefe, 1935–1947*, 2 vols. (Hamburg: Hamburger Institut für Sozialforschung, 1987), 205; Weimar, 25–26 November 1941, ibid., 143–144.

19. BDC, dossier Friedrich Mennecke: Mennecke Reichsärztekammerkarte, Approbationsurkunde, NSDAP master file card, SS-Stammrolle, RuSHA Fragebogen, published in Henry Friedlander and Sybil Milton, eds., *Berlin Document Center*, 2 vols., *Archives of the Holocaust Series*, vol. 11 (New York: Garland Publishing, 1991), docs. 295–299; U.S. Military Tribunal, Transcript of the Proceedings in Case 1, 1866–1868 (testimony Friedrich Mennecke); NARA, RG 238, Microfilm Publication M-1019, roll 46: interrogation Friedrich Mennecke, 11 January 1947, 1–4; HHStA, 461/32442/4: LG Frankfurt, Verfahren Friedrich Mennecke, Walter Schmidt, 4 KLs 15/46 (4a Js 13/46), Protokoll der öffentlichen Sitzung der 4. Strafkammer, 10 December 1946, 1–2 (testimony Wilhelm Hinsen).

20. BDC, dossier Friedrich Mennecke: Friedrich Mennecke to RuSHA, 27 April 1937, published in Friedlander and Milton, *Berlin Document Center*, doc. 300.

21. See Henry Friedlander, "Die Entwicklung der Mordtechnik: Von der 'Euthanasie' zu den Vernichtungslagern der 'Endlösung,'" in Ulrich Herbert, Karin Orth, and Christoph Dieckmann, eds., *Die nationalsozialistischen Konzentrationslager: Entwicklung und Struktur*, 2 vols. (Göttingen: Wallstein Verlag, 1998), 1:493–507.

22. See Adalbert Rückerl, *NS-Vernichtungslager im Spiegel deutscher Strafprozesse: Belzec, Sobibor, Treblinka, Chelmno* (Munich: Deutscher Taschenbuch Verlag, 1977).

23. GStA Frankfurt, Eberl Akten, II/611, 3:1–13: Eberl's handwritten vita, Innsbruck, 4 November 1934, Berlin, 29 August 1937, Berlin, 7 October 1937, and typed vita, Dessau, n.d. See also Eberl's completed Personal- und Fragebogen for the Rassenpolitisches Amt der NSDAP, Bernburg, 18 March 1943 (ibid., II/149, 1:119–121).

24. Eberl to Befehlshaber der Sipo, Paris, 27 March 1943.

25. Ibid., III/683/5, 7:147–148: Irmfried Eberl to Ruth Eberl, 29 June 1942.

26. Friedlander, *Origins of Nazi Genocide*, 299–300.

27. On the history of Auschwitz, see Hermann Langbein, *Menschen in Auschwitz* (Vienna and Munich: Europa Verlag, 1995). See also the reports on the Auschwitz trial in Frankfurt am Main in Bernd Naumann, *Auschwitz: Bericht über die Strafsache gegen Mulka u.a. vor dem Schwurgericht Frankfurt* (Frankfurt am Main: Fischer, 1968); Hermann Langbein, ed., *Der Auschwitz Prozeß: Eine Dokumentation*, 2 vols. (Frankfurt am Main: Büchergilde Gutenberg, 1995).

28. Danuta Czech, "Entstehungsgeschichte des KL Auschwitz," in Franciszek Piper and Teresa Swiebocka, eds., *Auschwitz, nationalsozialistisches Konzentrationslager* (Cracow: Staatliches Museum Auschwitz-Birkenau, 1997), 33; idem, *Kalendarium der Ereignisse im Konzentrationslager Auschwitz-Birkenau, 1939–1945* (Reinbek bei Hamburg: Rowohlt, 1989), 30–31, 34–39; *JuNSV*, vol. 21, no. 595a: LG Frankfurt, Urteil Robert Mulka, 19–20 August 1965, 4 Ks 2/63, 391. See also Rudolf Höss, *Kommandant in Auschwitz: Autobiographische Aufzeichnungen des Rudolf Höss*, ed. Martin Broszat (Munich: Deutscher Taschenbuch Verlag, 1963).

29. See Franciszek Piper, *Vernichtung*, vol. 3 of Waclaw Dlugoborski and Franciszek Piper, eds., *Auschwitz 1940–1945: Studien zur Geschichte des Konzentrations- und Vernichtungslagers Auschwitz*, trans. Jochen August, 4 vols. (Oswiecim: Verlag des Staatlichen Museums Auschwitz-Birkenau, 1999), 137–244; Stanislaw Klodzinski, "Die erste Vergasung von Häftlingen und Kriegsgefangenen im Konzentrationslager Auschwitz," in Hamburger Institut für Sozialforschung, ed., *Die Auschwitz-Hefte: Texte der polnischen Zeitschrift "Przeglad Lekarski" über historische, psychische und medizinische Aspekte des Lebens und Sterbens in Auschwitz*, trans. Jochen August et al., 2 vols. (Weinheim and Basel: Beltz, 1987), 1: 261–275.

30. See Peter Hayes, *Industry and Ideology: IG Farben in the Nazi Era* (Cambridge: Cambridge University Press, 1987), 347–360.

31. Archiwum Panstwowe Muzeum Oswiecim Brzezinka (Archive of the Auschwitz-Birkenau State Museum), hereafter APMO, Standort-Befehl, vol. 2, 219–222, D-AuI-1/49, no. 4579: Standortbefehl 53/43 (sig. Liebehenschel), 22 November 1943.

32. Langbein, *Menschen in Auschwitz*, 537–566.

33. Ibid., 491–536; *JuNSV*, vol. 21, no. 595a: LG Frankfurt, Urteil Robert Mulka, 19–20 August 1965, 4 Ks 2/63, 406.

34. *JuNSV*, vol. 21, no. 595a: LG Frankfurt, Urteil Robert Mulka, 19–20 August 1965, 4 Ks 2/63, 416.

35. Langbein, *Menschen in Auschwitz*, 493.

36. Ibid., 50–58.

37. *JuNSV*, vol. 13, no. 436a: LG Weiden, 29 May 1956, Ks 2/55, 749.

38. See APMO, Kommandanturbefehl, vol. 1, 71, D-AuI-1/90, no. 30685/1: Sonderbefehl sig. Höss, 12 August 1942.

39. *JuNSV*, vol. 21, no. 595a: LG Frankfurt, Urteil Robert Mulka, 19–20 August 1965, 4 Ks 2/63, 416.

40. Raymond Phillips, ed., *Trial of Josef Kramer and Forty-Four Others (The Belsen Trial)*, War Crimes Trials Series, general editor David Maxwell Fyfe, vol. 2 (London, Edinburgh, and Glasgow: William Hodge, 1949), 183–188.

41. *JuNSV*, vol. 17, no. 500: LG Münster, Urteil Johann Paul Kremer, 29 November 1960, 6 Ks 2/60, 8–15.

42. Langbein, *Menschen in Auschwitz*, 509–513.

43. Ibid., 529.

44. See *Medizin ohne Menschlichkeit: Dokumente des Nürnberger Ärzteprozesses* (Frankfurt: Fischer Taschenbuch Verlag, 1960), 240–247.

45. Langbein, *Menschen in Auschwitz*, 491.

46. For biographical data on Mengele, see BDC, dossier Josef Mengele: Reichsärztekammer file card, SS master file card, NSDAP master file card, and RuSHA file.

47. Bundesarchiv, Koblenz (BAK), R73/15342: Otmar von Verschuer to DFG, 30 September 1938.

48. Langbein, *Menschen in Auschwitz*, 496–504.

49. BAK, R73/15342: Verschuer to Reichsforschungsrat, 20 March 1944.

50. ZStL, interrogation Hans Nachtsheim, 19 August 1966. See also Benno Müller-Hill, *Tödliche Wissenschaft: Die Aussonderung von Juden, Zigeunern und Geisteskranken, 1933–1945* (Reinbek bei Hamburg: Rowohlt Taschenbuch Verlag, 1984), 72–74.

PHOTO 1: Carl Clauberg, SS physician who performed sterilization experiments on Jewish and Gypsy women in Auschwitz and Ravensbrück. *Source:* Main Commission for the Prosecution of the Crimes Against the Polish Nation, via the United States Holocaust Memorial Museum.

PHOTO 2: Two doctors in a ward in an unidentified asylum. The existence of the patients is described as "life only as a burden." This photo is from a filmstrip put out by the Reich Propaganda Office showing frightening images of mental patients that were intended to develop public sympathy for the T4 "euthanasia" program. *Source:* United States Holocaust Memorial Museum.

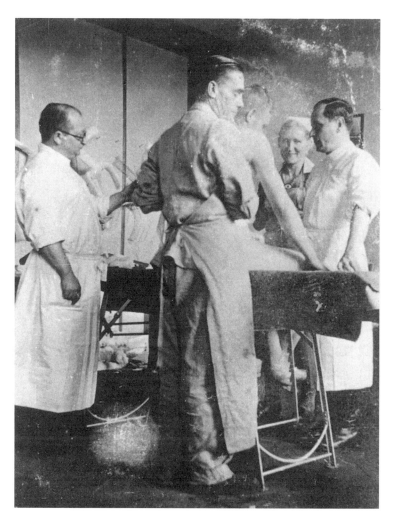

PHOTO 3: Dr. Carl Clauberg (left) with his staff in the operating room in Block 10. Clauberg experimented with nonsurgical methods of sterilization on Jewish female prisoners at Auschwitz I. *Source:* Main Commission for the Prosecution of the Crimes Against the Polish Nation, via the United States Holocaust Memorial Museum.

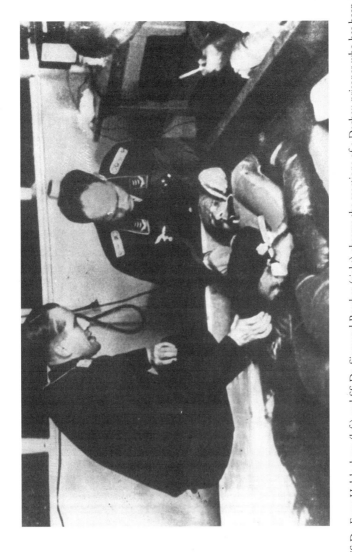

Photo 4: SS Dr. Ernst Holzloehner (left) and SS Dr. Sigmund Rascher (right) observe the reactions of a Dachau prisoner who has been immersed in a tank of ice water in an attempt to simulate the extreme hypothermia suffered by pilots downed over frigid seas. *Source:* Süddeutscher Verlag Bilderdienst, via the United States Holocaust Memorial Museum.

PHOTO 5: SS physicians examine Polish children who have been judged "racially valuable" for adoption by German foster parents. *Source:* Süddeutscher Verlag Bilderdienst, via the United States Holocaust Memorial Museum.

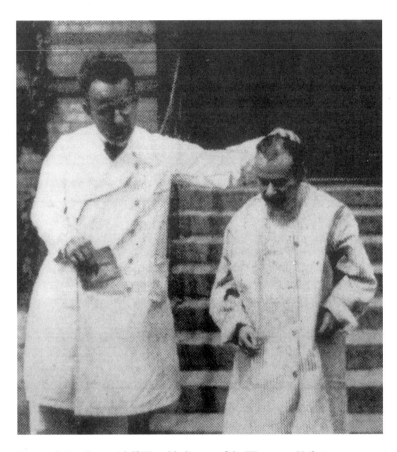

PHOTO 6: Dr. Gustav Adolf Wätzold, director of the Wittenauer Heilstätten, escorts or shows off one of the patients at the mental asylum. *Source:* Archiv Krankenhaus Reinickendorf, örtlicher Bereich Karl-Bonhoeffer-Nervenklinik, via the United States Holocaust Memorial Museum.

PHOTO 7: The Hadamar Institute, near Limburg an der Lahn, was one of six hospitals and nursing facilities in which the Nazi "euthanasia" program was carried out. Hospitalized children and adults who became victims of the program were gassed or killed by lethal injection. Many of them had been sterilized beforehand. Surviving records indicate that ten thousand people were killed at Hadamar before it was liberated by American troops in April 1945. *Source:* United States Holocaust Memorial Museum.

PHOTO 8: View of a corridor called "Death Row" at the Hadamar Institute. Victims in rooms leading off this corridor were marked by Nazi officials for immediate death. *Source:* United States Holocaust Memorial Museum.

Chapter Four

CRIMINAL PHYSICIANS IN THE THIRD REICH
Toward a Group Portrait

———— ∞∞∞ ————

Michael H. Kater

WHAT IS THE MEANING of "criminal"? The *Oxford Universal Dictionary* defines this adjective as "of the nature of or involving a crime, or a grave offense."[1] How can this definition be applied to a professional group such as German physicians between 1933 and 1945? If we accept that the offense be in violation of our currently adopted value system, then we are talking less about crimes in a wider, universal sense, than about those generated specifically and exclusively by physicians as a corporate group.

After targeting physicians in the Third Reich as our group of doctors, and employing profession-specific criteria, we can identify the standards governing two major categories of analysis: first, political association, and, second, professional-ethical conduct. I believe it is possible to find a critical mass of evidence to make the case that physicians in Nazi Germany displayed a proclivity for, first, political and, second, ethical wrongdoing. Whether it is possible to construct from this evidence a group portrait of evil doctors that decisively determined the legacy of German medicine for a large part of this century is perhaps more difficult to assess, but the attempt must nevertheless be made. I shall return to this problem later.

Examining the first category, political association, we find German doctors in the Third Reich to have been culpable to a large degree. These doctors had the choice of belonging, without compulsion, to a number of National Socialist organizations, the four most important of which were the National Socialist Physicians' League (NS-Ärztebund), the Nazi Party proper, the storm troopers (Sturmabteilung or SA), and the SS (Schutzstaffel). Only one of these, the SS, was juridically defined as a criminal organization during the post–World War II Nuremberg trials by the victorious Allies.[2] That judgment was due mainly to ignorance, for by today's standards, all four organizations must be regarded as criminally responsible.

The Nazi Physicians' League was a professional organization formed by the Nazi Party for its doctors in 1929, four years before Hitler's political takeover. Its ideology was closely aligned with that of National Socialism, and its aims were, as were those of similar organizations for other professionals such as lawyers and teachers, to serve as a platform for a special interest group—in this case, doctors. At least nominally, membership in the Nazi Party was a prerequisite for joining the Physicians' League, but this rule was often ignored, as were so many rules in National Socialist practice. High on the agenda of this party group was anti-Semitism. German doctors generally believed that Jewish physicians were overrepresented in the medical profession by a factor of 10 to 1; at the same time, their statistics told them that approximately 10 percent of all non-Jewish doctors were unemployed, in particular, the younger ones. Hence, joining the Nazi Physicians' League even before 1933 was predicated on sincere or opportunistic adherence to Judeophobia. This made Physician League doctors racist, which was then, as now, a moral crime. Yet another unsavory pre-1933 aim was to prevent the spread of the public health care system, a Social Democratic creation and hallmark of the Weimar era, which favored health insurance panels and provided for the sick and the poor at the expense of potentially wealthy, privately billing physicians and financially privileged patients.[3]

On the basis of an extensive computer analysis, I determined several years ago that approximately one-third of all German physicians belonged to the Physicians' League during the Third Reich.[4] Until his death in 1938, Dr. Gerhard Wagner, the former personal physician of Deputy Führer Rudolf Hess, was its leader. Wagner was one of the principal architects of the Nuremberg Racial Laws of 1935, which legalistically discriminated against German Jews, who were defined as Jews if they had at least three Jewish grandparents. The regional and local branches of the Nazi Physicians' League often acted like social clubs. They would collaborate with Nazi cultural organizations such as Alfred Rosenberg's Combat League for German Culture (Kampfbund für Deutsche Kultur), whose specialty was the dissemination of Nazi cultural propaganda, or perhaps attend lectures on Germanic prehistory or concerts of works by Nazi composers performed by Nazi musicians.[5] In October of 1934, for instance, Nazi art historian Juliane Harms spoke to Nazi League doctors in Wiesbaden on the topic of "Old and New Romanticism in Germany," enabling the Physicians' League members to reciprocate a week later, at a similar event attended also by Rosenberg followers, with a lecture on "The General Practitioner and Hereditary Diseases."[6] The Physicians' League was more immediately useful when it spread biographical information about Jewish colleagues who were still practicing medicine at a time early in the regime when many were already being driven out of the profession but some were trying to hold on. It also sought to steer German patients away from the offices of Jewish doctors and those German physicians, perhaps Social Democrats, still known to be hostile to the Nazi regime. Moreover, members were marched off, in mufti or uniform, to significant political events, or merely to drills and flag ceremonies. The league also served as an agency to recruit physicians for weekend service in the Hitler Youth organization (Hitlerjugend) or the Nazi Motor League (NS-Kraftfahrkorps). Of special significance was the so-called Leadership School at Alt-Rehse, situated on a beautiful lake northeast of Berlin. Billed in the Nazi literature as the "character school of the German doctor," it was designed as a Nazi social club as well as a training center for continuing medical education to transmit Nazi biopolitical propaganda, such as the official catechism on eugenics. The regular two-week courses for league members were mandatory; they were antiintellectual, sports saturated, and vitalistic—ultimately, a training ground for martial prowess. Indeed, after the outbreak of World War II, Alt-Rehse was rededicated for purely military purposes, excluding the doctors who were now serving at the front.[7]

By 1939, the Nazi Physicians' League had been eclipsed by the Nazi Party itself. As table 1 shows, nearly 45 percent of all physicians joined the party over the span of the Third Reich; exactly half of all male doctors did so. The 45 percent membership figure for doctors compares with 25 percent for lawyers, 24 percent for teachers, and 22 percent for musicians of all types. The average for the population as a whole never exceeded 9 percent. A majority of those doctors joined around 1937 when it was already apparent that the regime was solving the "Jewish question" to the satisfaction of all of the professions, especially the physicians. In 1937, they tended to be those who had been licensed between 1925 and 1932 and who, before Hitler's rise to power, had

TABLE 1: Professions in Nazi Organizations, 1933–1945

	Physicians	Lawyers	Teachers	Musicians	Total Population
SA (*males only*)	26.0%		11.0%	15.0%	
SS (*males only*)	7.0%		0.4%	3.0%	0.6%
Nazi Party					
Total	45.0%	25.0%	24.0%	22.0%	9.0%
Males	50.0%				
Females	20.0%				
Nazi Physicians' League					
Total	31.0%				
Males	35.0%				
Females	10.0%				

been unemployed. In December 1935, a new, centralizing Reich physicians' code had been promulgated, leading to the creation of a novel Reich Physicians' Chamber (Reichsärztekammer) in April 1936, which did the regime's as well as the doctors' bidding admirably. In fact, the political centralizing tendencies of the Nazi regime over the years coincided with individual centralizing efforts within the medical profession, some of which had been striven for, but never realized, in the years of the pluralistic Weimar Republic. It was a series of centralized sweeps, too, that, in various stages, got rid of the feared Jewish competition by the time of the Crystal Night pogrom on 9–10 November 1938. And such centralization also neutralized the long-hated quacks.[8]

In the Nazi period, 26 percent of all physicians were members of the storm troopers, also known as Brown Shirts, or SA. This compares with 15 percent for musicians and a mere 11 percent for teachers (table 1). The SA was the first paramilitary formation of the Nazi Party, and was headed by former army captain Ernst Röhm. Even for the physicians, membership was significantly low because the SA was a proletarian or lower-middle-class phenomenon, and doctors, of course, belonged to the social elite. Nonetheless, many of the more visceral activities of the SA—perhaps street fights with communist Red Front members before 1933 and roughing up "enemies of the state" after 1933—appealed to certain physically active doctors; besides, they were needed as medics as well. Invariably, doctors instantly attained high rank in the SA, which needed them only after working hours or on weekends, and paid them nothing in money or in kind.[9]

Hitler purged the SA in June 1934 because he suspected it of disloyalty, with the result that Röhm's former subordinate, Heinrich Himmler, who had led a special black-shirted elite unit of the SA called the SS, became preeminent. This meant that many SA physicians now switched over to the SS, which had done a good job attracting doctors even before the so-called "Röhm purge." Eventually, 7 percent of all of the physicians in the Reich became SS comrades. In absolute terms, this figure is low, but it must be remembered that the SS was artificially kept small in order to justify its elite claim. Compared to other professions, however, the doctors were hugely overrepresented there: not even half a percent of teachers were in the SS (just under the Reich average of 0.6 percent), and only 3 percent of all musicians were members (table 1). Only lawyers had a higher representation in the SS.[10]

The reasons for this are significant. Again, Himmler was at that time wooing members of the social and professional elites, and lawyers as well as doctors belonged to both. Always pillars of a more traditional society, lawyers and doctors, who were initially not quite at ease with the political change portended by the Nazis, craved enduring professional and socioeconomic security and desired recognition—even in a "revolutionized" polity such as that which Hitler's new regime claimed to represent. Moreover, the SS was able to impress these professionals with an aura of technical perfection and, at least on the surface, intellectual brilliance.[11]

The SS also held out job-specific prospects. Lawyers were interested in its preoccupation with redefining legal concepts and practice. Legalistic manipulation to justify the concentration camp system or the Nuremberg Racial Laws of September 1935 could appeal to many an ambitious young lawyer; for some of them, it was attractive to rise above the law.[12] For physicians, a different fascination manifested itself, and here we are also touching on the realm of the criminal. As Robert Jay Lifton has observed: "[D]octors regularly function at the border of life and death."[13] Naturally, Nazi doctors were becoming aware of the SS's seemingly limitless control over life and death, a situation resembling their own. Just as for centuries a patient had to place his or her fate into a doctor's hands, any ordinary citizen now was potentially at the mercy of decision-making SS leaders. For a physician in the SS, death took on a different quality than it had in a civilian career or even in the military, whose norms followed accepted codes of behavior of the kind alluded to at the beginning of this essay. The factor of death as such loomed large in the value system of the SS, which brandished a skull as its symbol. For the SS doctor, or his or her patients, death now assumed a more versatile quality in that it might be used in a threatening manner. Traditionally, patients had viewed physicians as professionals whose main aim was to prevent death at all cost; the general public's quintessential respect for doctors was based on this attribute. But in a society whose leaders were in the business not only of saving patients from the process of dying but also of inflicting death at will, doctors could, arguably, command even more respect.

This brings us to the second category, professional-ethical conduct, mentioned at the outset of this essay. The superimposition of new ethical norms observed in the SS over old, accepted ones, including the tenets of the Hippocratic oath, was what facilitated criminal medical practice among Nazi physicians. In fact, many, though not all, of those practices were engaged in by doctors serving in the SS, either after hours or, especially during wartime, as full-time salaried staffers. The ideology of National Socialism was based on crude notions of Darwinism, biopolitics whereby the racial superiority of "Aryans" was axiomatically assumed over that of "non-Aryans," and better "Aryans" were supposed to survive lesser ones. This meant, above all, the physical elimination of racial aliens such as Jews and Gypsies, but also the possibility of their function as human guinea pigs. Furthermore, Hitler's social Darwinism implied the artificial breeding of a pure and an acceptable genotype, which was to result in "internal negative selection"—"internal" because it applied to the German "Aryan" people themselves, "negative selection" because congenitally and other sick persons were targeted for murder in huge "euthanasia" actions.[14]

It is instructive to look at the individual careers of some of the medical murderers involved in these activities. The careers of the most notorious are already known, such as Josef Mengele at Auschwitz, Sigmund Rascher at Dachau, and Werner Heyde, Carl Schneider, and Werner Catel in the "euthanasia" killing centers.[15] But there are lesser-known men, and even a few women, whose death work can now be detailed. Dr. Theodor Steinmeyer, born in 1897, for instance, was a Protestant from Catholic Bavaria who had seen action in World War I before studying medicine in Erlangen. In 1925 he was a general practitioner in Nuremberg. By 1929 he had taken qualifying training as a psychiatrist. He became a tenured civil servant as deputy director of the psychiatric hospital in Wehnen near Oldenburg in northern Germany. In 1934 he changed to a full directorship at the Ellen institution near Bremen. Steinmeyer was an old and proven Nazi hack (in a photo he looks remarkably like Hitler), one who had served in the pre-1933 party hierarchy. Hence, he already believed fully in Nazi social Darwinist tenets by the time of the Führer's takeover in January 1933. He also had been an SA physician, having tended to the wounded after street brawls. Apart from his duties in the Ellen psychiatric wards, Steinmeyer also acted as a judge in one of the regional hereditary health courts, which, after the recommendation of loyal Nazi medical practitioners, routinely determined which patients should be treated in accordance with the newly instituted hereditary laws. Such treatment could mean sterilization, castration, or the forced transfer to a state psychiatric hospital (where the patients would later be killed). Steinmeyer became active in the "euthanasia" killing schemes starting in the fall of 1939, both as a pencil-pushing planner and a hands-on physician who would take people's lives with medications, injections, and the use of poison gas.[16]

Another "euthanasia" physician, hardly known today, was Werner Sengenhoff. This young psychiatrist, married to the daughter of a Lutheran minister and the father of two small children, began his duties as director of killing schemes in one of the administrative regions of Westphalia in western Germany. Sengenhoff, too, wore the badge of an early fighter for the Nazi movement; he had cofounded the National-Socialist Students League (NS-Studentenbund) of Düsseldorf and had become a staff physician in the regional Hitler Youth. He was a huge man with a tendency to overindulge in alcohol and to pick fights. Sengenhoff's documented loyalty to the Nazi movement, his medical degree and specialization, and a large personal ambition enabled him, like Steinmeyer, to become a tenured civil service state physician. After 1939, he became instrumental in "euthanizing" institutionalized babies and toddlers, usually with the help of phenobarbitol or injections of morphine.[17]

All told, the Nazis sterilized upwards of four hundred thousand Germans and "euthanized" more than one hundred thousand.[18] Moving on to the areas of inflicted pain, maimings, and killings, we now focus on victim groups that by Nazi criteria were referred to as "non-Aryans": Gypsies, Slavs, and Jews. The two main categories of activity here are experimentation on humans, often terminal ones, and the individual and mass killings of men, women, and children in German concentration camps and in mass extermination centers in the east. Characteristically, the perpetrators of these crimes again tended to be SS physicians.

Ernst Günther Schenck, who was born in 1904, became a doctor of natural science in 1927 and an M.D. in 1929. He joined the SA in

1933 and the Nazi Physicians' League as well as the Nazi Party in 1937. He was then already an executive physician in a Munich municipal hospital and a lecturer in internal medicine and physiology at that city's university. In 1942 Schenck became an adjunct professor. By that time, he had also become a close adviser to Reich Health Führer (*Reichsgesundheitsführer*) Dr. Leonardo Conti. In April 1940 Schenck had joined the Waffen-SS, the armored wing of the regular black-shirted SS that fought alongside Wehrmacht units at the fronts, reaching by 1944 the rank of lieutenant colonel. Already in 1942 Schenck had become the inspector general of nutrition for the Waffen-SS, and, as such, was responsible to the head of the concentration camp system, SS General Oswald Pohl. Schenck was now charged with improving the diet of the Waffen-SS by finding new and portable natural staples with high protein content. Late in December 1943, Schenck and Pohl conspired to test one of these synthetic products in Dachau, Buchenwald, and Sachsenhausen, using one hundred thousand inmates as guinea pigs. The product was derived from a chemical derivative, cellulose—waste matter that was observed by Himmler to kill fresh water fish. In the end, only one hundred prisoners were fed the "protein sausage," which looked and was artificially perfumed like liverwurst; we do not know what the results were. But in Mauthausen, experiments with this "sausage" were performed on about four hundred inmates in 1943–1944, in the course of which more than half of the subjects died. One of the surviving inmates later said: "Dogs would not touch this sausage."[19]

Dr. Kurt Heissmeyer, born in 1905, was the nephew of a high-ranking SS leader and moved within the circle of SS physicians surrounding Himmler. He was not yet in the SS when he began his research on tuberculosis. Nonetheless, he had been a Nazi Party member since 1937. Licensed as a physician since 1933, he befriended Professor Karl Gebhardt, SS surgeon and director of the SS clinic at Hohenlychen near Berlin, where Heissmeyer took care of tubercular German women after 1938. His ambition was to find a cure for TB and, hence, to become successor to Robert Koch. Having access to the vast human resources in the concentration camps, Heissmeyer conducted experiments on prisoners. His underlying hypothesis, based on the then-current teachings of race hygienists such as Otmar Freiherr von Verschuer, Mengele's teacher, held that TB was not traceable to a specific bacillus, but rather to the congenitally defective constitution of the patient. Hence, Heissmeyer enlisted the aid of Pohl and Himmler himself and began his work in Neuengamme concentration camp near Hamburg in the summer of 1944.

First, Russian and Polish inmates were injected with the TB bacillus, which, under the minimally hygienic conditions, killed many. Twenty Jewish children, all in their early teens, were then brought to Neuengamme from Auschwitz in the fall. They were all infected with the virulent strain of the bacillus, as were actual guinea pigs—which, cynically, bore the same identification numbers as the corresponding children—in a parallel action. Medications as well as adequate nourishment were administered to the patients only to enable them to be of further use for the experiments. As a result, the patients developed a very high fever. Axillary glands were cut out for histological examinations. But by early 1945, Heissmeyer was running out of time; the Red Army was fast approaching the Elbe River. Hence, on 20 April 1945, Hitler's last birthday, all of the children were sedated with morphine and then hanged. The French inmate physicians who had been compelled to assist Heissmeyer were also precipitously killed.[20]

Johann Paul Kremer was a professor of medicine at the University of Münster when he arrived in Auschwitz in August 1942 to serve for three months as a camp physician. His SS membership dated from 1934. At Auschwitz, Kremer participated in selections of inmates for the gas chamber. In addition, he sampled "live-fresh material from the human liver, spleen, and pancreas," according to one of the reports on his research on hunger. These organs were cut out of the bodies of specially chosen prisoners after they had been killed for this very purpose. Back in Münster, Kremer wanted to use his "Auschwitz material" to force his colleagues into greater recognition of his status as a scientist after he had authored a book that was to be titled "Histological Regression." To this day, the manuscript remains unpublished.[21]

Dr. Herta Oberheuser worked at Ravensbrück, the only concentration camp solely for women. This pediatric dermatologist, born in 1911, had joined the Nazi Party in 1937 as a 26-year-old intern. By 1942 she was assisting Professor Karl Gebhardt, that one-time student of Ferdinand Sauerbruch and Munich schoolmate of Himmler, in gas gangrene experiments at Ravensbrück. Several women inmates had to suffer deep cuts in their legs and arms; bacteria and sulfonamide were simultaneously injected. The pharmaceutical giant I.G. Farben, as well as the Wehrmacht, had an active stake in these trials, which caused the death of at least three women. Oberheuser also participated in Gebhardt's infamous bone transplants, in which women were operated upon to become cripples. The aim was to observe how these cripples would move, if they survived at all. Before dying, these patients suffered much pain.[22]

One inmate who heard the screams of these dying patients in the summer of 1942 was the (in Nazi terms) quarter-Jewish Inga Madlung, the 18-year-old daughter of a prominent half-Jewish Hamburg lawyer, who had already been removed from his post. Inga, whom I interviewed in her London apartment in the late 1980s, had been sent to Ravensbrück with her older sister Jutta because both had been notorious members of the Hamburg swing scene. They loved to listen and dance to illicit recordings of Benny Goodman's jazz and to imitate the American singers the Andrews Sisters, usually in the villas of their wealthy parents. With their unconventional lifestyle, including an uninhibited sexuality that had made the Madlung sisters extremely popular with the boys, the "Swings" were regarded as degenerates by the Nazi regime. Upon arrival at Ravensbrück, Inga was slapped in the face as a jazz and BBC broadcast lover and burned with a heated coin. Later, sick with hunger and diagnosed with scarlet fever, she was placed on a chair outside the barracks and forced by an SS physician, with a German shepherd as his aide, to look straight into the sun. If she tried to move her head just an inch in order to avoid the rays, the dog's nose would be right in her face. This continued for two weeks, under the watchful eye of the sadistic and ever-present SS doctor, whose name history has not recorded. At the end of this torture, Inga Madlung was virtually blind. She would not regain her eyesight until the 1970s, when a London opthalmologist was able to operate on her successfully.[23]

SS physicians conducted the selections for the gas chambers on the ramp at Auschwitz, where more Jews were liquidated than at any other single Nazi killing center. The most notorious of the physician-killers was Josef Mengele, a former medical student of Frankfurt race hygienist Otmar Freiherr von Verschuer. Mengele conducted lethal medical experiments on the side for his former teacher, newly ensconced at the Kaiser Wilhelm Society in Berlin.[24] During the selections, according to social Darwinist teachings, what counted was the inmates' usefulness for work. The Berlin nightclub guitarist Coco Schumann, delivered to Auschwitz from Theresienstadt on 4 September 1944, remembers. He was nineteen years old at the time, with blue eyes, looking young and strong. "Where are you from," barked Mengele. "Berlin, Herr Obersturmbannführer!" shouted Schumann in his best High German. "What do you do?" "Plumber, Herr Obersturmbannführer!" Schumann was a musician, not a plumber, but he knew that a practical occupation might save his life. Indeed, Mengele was quick to acknowledge Schumann's straightforward manner, the Berlin origins, and an honest trade that might be useful in the concentration camp where the inmates worked, apart from the killing center in Birkenau. Mengele told Schumann to step to the left, which was to save his life. From then on, he never worked as a plumber, but played in one of the numerous inmate bands for the SS, on a guitar left over from the recent Hungarian Gypsy transport.[25]

Apart from such a typical selection on the ramp at Auschwitz-Birkenau, selections could go on virtually anywhere else in the camp—in the medical blocks, during roll calls, and at work *Kommandos* (work details). The groups that were selected varied in size from tens to hundreds of people at any one time. From a survivor, Lifton has recorded details of a typical procedure:

> The camp doctor, accompanied by some SS, went from block to block. He received from the office the number of Jews in each single block. The Jews were taken from the blocks ... and their numbers were checked at roll call. Then they had to strip completely, whether it was summer or winter. And now the doctor went along the rows of naked people, and all who appeared weak or frail, who had bandages, showed boils, or even scars or scabies, were ... sent along with those to be killed.[26]

* * * *

BY WAY OF A CONCLUSION, I should attempt to answer two important questions. The first is the one posed by the title of this essay and already alluded to at the beginning: Can one construct a group profile of Nazi medical criminals? At this point, the question must remain open, at least until further research has been accomplished. It would be mandatory, initially, to gather as much evidence on commonalities as possible: What common factors drove these men and some women? What characterized them? Some answers are already available. A large number of these professionals were seeking to improve their job standing, using lobby connections, conventional politics such as Nazi Party membership, and the time-honored mechanics of economic advancement. Some of the assignments in the "euthanasia" apparatus represented a promotion with higher pay, a more prestigious title, and higher standing in the civil service or professional pecking order. Such postings distinguished the careers of the aforementioned Drs. Steinmeyer and Sengenhoff. In the camps, ample opportunities for what passed as scientific research existed, which could be used for academic purposes, such as acquiring the *Habilitation*, or second scholarly book, enabling one to teach in a medical faculty or even become a professor. This drove Heissmeyer at Neuengamme, Mengele at Auschwitz, and Sigmund Rascher, who conducted high-pressure experiments with terminal results, at Dachau. Sadism—the experience of pleasure derived from inflicting pain on others—may have been a motive; it probably moved Inga Madlung's tormentor. This particular motivation often overlapped with others, as it did in the case of Mengele, who was both sadistic and highly ambitious. Were sadism and professional ambition aided and abetted by the incompetence of many SS camp physicians? For example, a certain SS physician in Bergen-Belsen was incapable of sewing up the wound of an inmate patient after a hernia operation.[27] Gender bias was a factor in the sad efforts by Dr. Herta Oberheuser to measure up to her male colleagues at Hohenlychen and Ravensbrück. Female Nazi physicians in the Third Reich, who had a documented record of feeling displaced, tried to organize themselves to prove their worth as the equals of their Nazi male colleagues. Their attempts were effectively quashed by Wagner and Conti in 1938–1939.[28] And the racist call for the physical elimination of allegedly biologically inferior "non-Aryans" turned into a mandate actually believed in by a plurality of Nazi doctors, to the extent that they took Nazi ideology at all seriously.[29] This must have been a significant factor in the high percentage of physicians in the Nazi Physicians' League, the Nazi Party, the SA, and the SS, although we still do not really know why their membership in these organizations overshadowed that of most other professions. One important methodological task, then, is to determine precisely the size of that plurality and render it measurable and comparable, expressed as a ratio vis-à-vis other Nazi or German doctors, or all Nazis, or the German population as a whole.

My catalog is incomplete, for these are just some of the research tasks awaiting present-day historians, sociologists, ethicists, demographers, and medical scientists. The final question concerning us today is one to be asked against the larger canvas of the medical culture, both then and now. At the top looms the concern of how much of what today we can recognize as perversions entered the curricula of the Third Reich's medical schools, which, after all, produced a fresh generation of physicians officiating in the 1950s and 1960s. The effect of the medical canon on Third Reich students who would practice in the Federal Republic or East Germany must not be underestimated. Although basic elements of the Hippocratic oath had been violated for years, post-1945 German medical faculties did not find it necessary to inaugurate medical history courses detailing the abuses of the Third Reich as a mandatory part of the curriculum. In fact, as has been observed, they did not even institute any medical history courses with an emphasis on universal ethics or bioethics.[30] When asked, many post-1945 physicians found nothing wrong with the way they were taught, even though a younger generation that started to practice in the 1960s and 1970s became much more reflective and, presumably, better doctors. Today, the awareness that much was wrong with the medical culture in Germany between 1914 and 1945 is particularly strong among younger physicians. This was evident at the October 1996 Nuremberg conference of the International Physicians for Peace and against Nuclear War, which attracted hundreds of young doctors and medical students.[31] In Germany, there is now an ever-growing, documented, and credible literature on the abuses of the past, while on the other hand, the teaching of the subject still leaves much to be desired.

In North America, moreover, awareness of the potential for medical crimes as demonstrated by the bad examples of history certainly is not as deep and as broad as it should be. The subject of Nazi medical theory and practice tends to be missing from the curricula of U.S. and Canadian medical faculties as well; research institutes totally disregard this history. Risky medical experiments might still be performed under ethically questionable circumstances, in venues such as prisons or psychiatric wards. In April 2000 the Canadian press reported that a victim of Dr. Ewen Cameron's infamous "mind-patterning" experiments in Montreal, which occurred some thirty years ago, was denied compensation for her suffering by a Canadian court. Less than a year later, almost half of the University of Toronto's medical students were reported to have felt pressure from their teachers "to act unethically, including being asked to perform pelvic examinations on women under general anesthesia who had not given their consent." Several alleged to have been asked to do "unnecessary procedures on unwary patients, including those who were comatose or unconscious."[32] In some medical quarters, the viability of data gathered from Nazi medical experiments, captured by the Allies after 1945, is still earnestly being discussed.[33] At Columbia University in New York, Howard Israel, an oral surgeon, was shocked in 1994 to find that a popular anatomical textbook originating in Austria but routinely translated into English and used in medical courses on this continent featured illustrations of what could well be the cadavers of Jews murdered by Nazis during the 1940s. Since then, Israel, along with William E. Seidelman of Toronto, has pursued the matter with the University of Vienna, which only in 1997 saw fit to authorize an examination of the case.[34] The issue of involuntary sterilization has still not been set aside once and for all. All this means that the negative paradigm of Nazi medicine must be circumscribed and the facts sought with greater accuracy than in the past, so that on both sides of the Atlantic, and wherever else medicine is being taught and practiced, further salutary lessons may be learned.

Notes

1. C. T. Onion, ed., *The Oxford Universal Dictionary on Historical Principles*, 3rd ed. (Oxford: Oxford University Press, 1955), 423.

2. *Der Prozess gegen die Hauptkriegsverbrecher vor dem Internationalen Militärgerichtshof: Nürnberg, 14. November 1945–1. Oktober 1947* (Nuremberg, 1947; reprinted Munich: Delphin Verlag, 1984), 1:307–309.

3. Michael H. Kater, *Doctors Under Hitler* (Chapel Hill, N.C. and London: University of North Carolina Press, 1989), 63–65.

4. Kater, *Doctors Under Hitler*, 63.

5. Alan E. Steinweis, "Weimar Culture and the Rise of National Socialism: The *Kampfbund für deutsche Kultur*," *Central European History* 24 (1991): 402–423.

6. Althen to members of Wiesbaden chapter, NS-Ärztebund, Wiesbaden, 1 October 1934, Hessisches Hauptstaatsarchiv Wiesbaden, 483/3159; entry for May 1935, in *Deutschland-Berichte der Sopade*, 7 vols. (1934–1940), 5th ed. (Frankfurt am Main: Petra Nettelbeck Zweitausendeins, 1980), 2:538.

7. Kater, *Doctors Under Hitler*, 65–68.

8. Ibid., 19–25, 54–62.

9. Ibid., 68–69.

10. Ibid., 295, n. 57.

11. Heinz Höhne, *Der Orden unter dem Totenkopf: Die Geschichte der SS* (Gütersloh: Sigbert Mohn, 1967), 53–74.

12. This has not yet been fully dealt with. Thus far, see Gunnar C. Boehnert, "The Jurists in the SS-Führerkorps, 1925–1939," in Gerhard Hirschfeld and Lothar Kettenacker, eds., *Der "Führerstaat": Mythos und Realität: Studien zur Struktur und Politik des Dritten Reiches* (Stuttgart: Klett-Cotta, 1981), 361–374; Ulrich Herbert, *Best: Biographische Studien über Radikalismus, Weltanschauung und Vernunft, 1903–1989*, 3rd ed. (Bonn: J.H.W. Dietz Nachfolger, 1996), 88–322; Bernhard Diestelkamp, *Drei Professoren der Rechtswissenschaft in bewegter Zeit* (Mainz: Akademie der Wissenschaften und der Literatur, 2000).

13. Robert Jay Lifton, "Medicalized Killing in Auschwitz," *Psychiatry* 45 (1982): 286.

14. For ideological and pseudoscientific background, see the relevant sections in Paul Weindling, *Health, Race and German Politics between National Unification and Nazism, 1870–1945* (Cambridge: Cambridge University Press, 1989), and Robert N. Proctor, *Racial Hygiene: Medicine Under the Nazis* (Cambridge, MA, and London: Harvard University Press, 1988).

15. Robert Jay Lifton, *The Nazi Doctors: Medical Killing and the Psychology of Genocide* (New York: Basic Books, 1986), 337–383; Michael H. Kater, *Das "Ahnenerbe" der SS, 1935–1945: Ein Beitrag zur Kulturpolitik des Dritten Reiches*, 2nd ed. (Munich: R. Oldenbourg, 1997), 231–245; Henry Friedlander, *The Origins of Nazi Genocide: From Euthanasia to the Final Solution* (Chapel Hill, NC: University of North Carolina Press, 1995); Michael Burleigh, *Death and Deliverance: "Euthanasia" in Germany, c. 1900–1945* (Cambridge: Cambridge University Press, 1994).

16. Franz-Werner Kersting, *Anstaltsärzte zwischen Kaiserreich und Bundesrepublik: Das Beispiel Westfalen* (Paderborn: F. Schöningh, 1996), 284–300; Bernd Walter, *Psychiatrie und Gesellschaft in der Moderne: Geisteskrankenfürsorge in der Provinz Westfalen zwischen Kaiserreich und NS-Regime* (Paderborn: F. Schöningh, 1996), 684–687, 715–718.

17. Kersting, *Anstaltsärzte zwischen Kaiserreich und Bundesrepublik*, 300–305.

18. Burleigh, *Death and Deliverance*; Friedlander, *The Origins of Nazi Genocide*.

19. Kater, *Doctors Under Hitler*, 123–124; Ernst Klee, *Auschwitz, die NS-Medizin und ihre Opfer* (Frankfurt am Main: Fischer Verlag, 1997), 179–189 (inmate's quote, 183).

20. Günther Schwarberg, *Der SS-Arzt und die Kinder: Bericht über den Mord vom Bullenhuser Damm* (Hamburg: Gruner und Jahr, 1979).

21. Kater, *Doctors Under Hitler*, 125.

22. Angelika Ebbinghaus, "Dokumentation: Die Ärztin Herta Oberheuser und die kriegschirurgischen Experimente im Frauen-Konzentrationslager Ravensbrück," in idem, ed., *Opfer und Täterinnen: Frauenbiographien des Nationalsozialismus* (Frankfurt am Main: Fischer Taschenbuch Verlag, 1996), 313–343.

23. Michael H. Kater, *Different Drummers: Jazz in the Culture of Nazi Germany* (New York: Oxford University Press, 1992), 190–191.

24. Benno Müller-Hill, *Murderous Science: Elimination by Scientific Selection of Jews, Gypsies, and Others, Germany, 1933–1945* (Oxford: Oxford University Press, 1988).

25. Ibid., 179–180; William E. Seidelman, "Mengele Medicus: Medicine's Nazi Heritage," *Milbank Quarterly* 66 (1988): 221–239.

26. Lifton, *The Nazi Doctors*, 181.

27. Thomas Rahe, "Zeugen Jehovas im Konzentrationslager Bergen-Belsen," in Hans Hesse, ed., *"Am mutigsten waren immer wieder die Zeugen Jehovas": Verfolgung und Widerstand der Zeugen Jehovas im Nationalsozialismus* (Bremen: Edition Temmen, 1998), 123. On physicians' cruelty, particularly in Auschwitz, Ravensbrück, and Bergen-Belsen, see Miklos Nyiszli, *Auschwitz: A Doctor's Eye Witness Account of Mengele's Infamous Death Camp* (New York: Arcade, 1993); Lifton, *The Nazi Doctors*; and Raymond Phillips, ed., *Trial of Josef Kramer and Forty-four Others (The Belsen Trial)* (London: William Hodge, 1949).

28. On the latter phenomenon, see Kater, *Doctors Under Hitler*, 92–98.

29. See Proctor, *Racial Hygiene*; and idem, *The Nazi War on Cancer* (Princeton: Princeton University Press, 1999).

30. Ulrich Tröhler, "Graduate Education in the History of Medicine: Federal Republic of Germany," *Bulletin of the History of Medicine,* 63:1989, 435–443; William E. Seidelman, "Current Problems of Medical Ethics and Practice," critical comment delivered at the conference, "Medicine in 19th- and 20th-Century Germany: Ethics, Politics, and Law," German Historical Institute, Washington, D.C., 1–4 December 1993.

31. Stephan Kolb and Horst Seithe, eds., *Medizin und Gewissen: 50 Jahre nach dem Nürnberger Ärzteprozess—Kongressdokumentation* (Frankfurt am Main: Mabuse Verlag, 1998).

32. *Globe and Mail,* Toronto, 23 March 2001.

33. See the contributions by Robert S. Pozos, Robert L. Berger, Jay Katz, Benjamin Freedman, and Velvl W. Green in Arthur L. Caplan, ed., *When Medicine Went Mad: Bioethics and the Holocaust* (Totowa, NJ: Humana Press, 1992), 95–170.

34. Werner Platzer, ed., *Pernkopf Anatomy: Atlas of Topographic and Applied Human Anatomy,* 3rd ed. (Baltimore and Munich: Urban & Schwarzenberg, 1989), 1:fig. 325, 2:figs. 334, 335, 336; Nicholas Wade, "Doctors Question Use of Nazi's [*sic*] Medical Atlas," *New York Times,* 26 November 1996; Howard Israel and William E. Seidelman, "Nazi Origins of an Anatomy Text: The Pernkopf Atlas," *Journal of the American Medical Association* 276 (1996): 1633; Peter Malina, "Eduard Pernkopfs Anatomie oder: Die Fiktion einer 'reinen' Wissenschaft," *Wiener Klinische Wochenschrift* 109 (1997): 935–943; Gustav Spann, "Untersuchungen zur anatomischen Wissenschaft in Wien, 1938–1945: Senatsprojekt der Universität Wien: Eine Zusammenfassung," *Dokumentationsarchiv des Österreichischen Widerstandes Jahrbuch 1999,* 43–52.

Chapter Five

PATHOLOGY OF MEMORY

German Medical Science and the
Crimes of the Third Reich

———— ∞∞∞ ————

William E. Seidelman

A MAJOR DEVELOPMENT in medicine in the last century was the clinical and pathological elucidation of neuropsychiatric disorders affecting memory and behavior. The singular condition associated with impaired memory is known by the eponym for the German psychiatrist who first described the clinical and pathological entity, Dr. Alois Alzheimer.[1] Alzheimer's description and definition of dementia occurred within the context of a dynamic intellectual environment comprising the psychiatrists, neurologists, pathologists, universities, hospitals, clinics, and research institutes of Germany. Alzheimer, his specific discovery, the general study of brain disorders and dementia, and the establishment of new psychiatric diagnoses were part of this remarkable confluence of people and ideas. This intellectual cauldron gave birth to modern psychiatry as we know it today.

Alzheimer's discovery occurred within the context of the specialized discipline of academic psychiatry dedicated to teaching and research. In the early part of the last century, German academic psychiatry had achieved world dominance. By 1911, the year that Alzheimer published his second case of dementia, almost fourteen hundred German physicians were specializing in psychiatry. German psychiatry was to flourish further under the leadership of Alzheimer's professor and mentor, Emil Kraepelin, who is considered the founder of modern psychiatry. The focus of academic psychiatry was the investigation into the organic causes of psychiatric disorder.[2]

Academic psychiatry in Germany (and Austria) flourished in a scholastic, clinical, and research community that fostered the development of modern medical science, clinical medicine, and university-based medical education. The hospitals, clinics, and laboratories of Germany and Austria in the late nineteenth and early twentieth centuries were responsible for some of the greatest advances in the history of modern medicine and medical science.

German psychiatry, as epitomized by Kraepelin, embodied the synergy of psychology, neurology, and pathology, both macroscopic and microscopic. Alois Alzheimer and the neurohistologist Franz Nissl were part of Kraepelin's team of structural researchers who worked with Kraepelin in Heidelberg and subsequently in Munich. According to the historian Edward Shorter: "What Nissl and Alzheimer could find under their microscopes they declared 'neurology.' What they couldn't find was psychiatry."[3]

In 1917 Kraepelin established the German Institute for Psychiatric Research in Munich. A major benefactor of the Munich institute was the American-born Jewish philanthropist, and at one time a patient of Kraepelin's, James Loeb.[4] The Munich psychiatric institute, which in 1924 joined with the Kaiser Wilhelm Society, became the first and foremost psychiatric research institute in the world. The building of the new institute, which opened in 1928, was the first major construction project of the Kaiser Wilhelm Society to be financed by a grant from the medical division of the Rockefeller Foundation.[5]

Tragically, the same academic and research institutions that gave birth to modern medicine and medical science and medical education also fostered what was to become the greatest program of human destruction in the history of humankind. While some of those institutions were to become pioneers in the study of memory disorders, the memory of their own role in the terror and tragedies of the Third Reich is itself disordered. Most of those institutions have yet to demonstrate any memory, any accountability, any conscience for their role. The institutions include the Department of Psychiatry of the University of Heidelberg and the Kaiser Wilhelm/Max Planck Institute of Psychiatry, both once headed by Kraepelin.

German and Austrian medical science "scientifically" defined individuals who were considered inferior and therefore expendable by the state. Hundreds of thousands of German and Austrian citizens were sterilized because of the medical diagnosis of a condition (e.g., "feeble-mindedness," schizophrenia, manic-depressive disorder) considered both undesirable and hereditary. Medical science selected mentally and physically handicapped children and adults for extermination in killing operations designated by the euphemism "euthanasia." The definition of a "desirable" Aryan or an "undesirable" non-Aryan under the Nuremberg Racial Laws arose from medicine and was based on a medical history and examination.[6] The extermination process of the "final solution" evolved from eugenic sterilization and medical "euthanasia."[7] The concentration and extermination camps of the Third Reich were viewed by some German and Austrian medical scientists as a research opportunity in which the hundreds of thousands of hapless victims were perceived to be potential subjects for inhuman experimentation. The infamous selection process on the ramp at Auschwitz was a medical selection made by physicians responsible for determining who was fit for slave labor and who would die in the gas chamber.[8] The infamous gas chamber arose from the T4 "euthanasia" medical killing program.[9] The turning on of the gas in the "euthanasia" program was deemed to be a medical act assigned to a physician.[10] Medical scientists associated with some of the most prestigious universities and research institutes in the world exploited the killing programs of the Nazi regime to acquire anatomical and pathological specimens from the victims. Such specimens are still to be found to this very day.[11] Three institutions that acquired specimens were the Department of Psychiatry of the University of Heidelberg, the Kaiser Wilhelm/Max Planck Institute of Psychiatry and the Kaiser Wilhelm/Max Planck Institute for Brain Research. Each of these institutions played an important role in the development of modern psychiatry and neurology and in the study of the pathology of behavior and memory.[12]

A piteous irony of the Shoah is the fact that while eminent academic institutions may have forgotten, survivors of the Holocaust, many suffering from dementia of the Alzheimer's type, have not. Examples of this can be found at the Baycrest Centre for Geriatric Care in Toronto where 50 percent of the one thousand residents are survivors of the Shoah, many with Alzheimer's. Some have forgotten the names and faces of their children and grandchildren but still remember the names and faces of those who tormented and murdered their loved ones and irrevocably destroyed their families and communities during the Shoah. Some Baycrest residents fear taking showers. One resident, who was the subject of vivisection, refuses surgery.[13] Robert Proctor described a case reported to him by a German physician friend. Proctor's friend cared for a Holocaust survivor who had had a heart attack. After her heart attack, the woman began to dream that she was back in Auschwitz. "That was her very last dream on this earth; she died shortly after telling my friend this story, and asking 'why won't these memories disappear?'"[14]

While these memories won't disappear from the minds of the tormented survivors, they appear to have no presence in the institutions that gave birth to the evil and the destruction. In the universities and research institutes that fostered and exploited evil, there is no memory. Neither the history of medicine in the Third Reich nor medical ethics are part of the formal curriculum of German and Austrian medical schools today. Indeed, physicians graduating in medicine in Germany and Austria today are probably ignorant of the Nuremberg code on human experimentation and its origins in the medical crimes of German and Austrian physicians.[15]

Psychiatry, Eugenics, and Sterilization

One of the researchers who joined Kraepelin in Heidelberg was the Swiss-born psychiatrist/geneticist Ernst Rüdin. Like Alzheimer and Nissl, Rüdin accompanied Kraepelin when he moved from Heidelberg to Munich. In 1909 Rüdin succeeded Alzheimer as senior physician at the Munich psychiatric hospital. In Munich, Rüdin led the genealogical/demographic research department of the Kaiser Wilhelm Society. The focus of Rüdin's research was on the inheritance of psychiatric disorders, and his 1916 paper on that subject is considered a classic that continues to be cited in the literature on the genetics of schizophrenia.[16] After a brief period as professor at the University Hospital of Neurology and Psychiatry in Basel, Rüdin returned to the newly constructed Munich psychiatry institute where, in November 1928, he became director of a "greatly expanded" genealogical department. In 1931 he ascended to the leadership of the world's preeminent psychiatric research institute.[17] Rüdin built on Kraepelin's relationship with two major benefactors, the Rockefeller Foundation and James Loeb. His research was well endowed with funding from Rockefeller and the Loeb estate. Loeb, who died in 1933, had been a generous supporter of the institute from its inception. As his final gift, Loeb bequeathed $1 million to the Munich institute.[18]

After Hitler's rise to power, Rüdin became an active supporter of the eugenic and racial hygiene policies of Hitler's regime. He was an intellectual leader of the Nazi program of enforced eugenic sterilization entrenched under the 1933 sterilization law. He was honored twice by Hitler for his contribution to German eugenics.[19]

The 1933 sterilization law established diagnostic categories for enforced sterilization. Two of the categories were for psychiatric conditions first described by Kraepelin and investigated by Rüdin, namely, schizophrenia and manic-depressive disorder.[20] An estimated four hundred thousand German citizens qualified for sterilization under the law. This goal was achieved.[21]

The Munich psychiatry institute became a major academic eugenic center during the Hitler period. In 1935 the Rockefeller Foundation withheld funding for genealogical and demographic research. In 1940 the executor of the Loeb estate ceased payment to the institute. Desperate for support for his institute and his research, Rüdin turned to the SS terror organization for salvation. In 1939 the SS incorporated the world's first and foremost psychiatric research institute as part of its own research organization, the notorious Ahnenerbe.[22]

Neuropathology: The Brains of the Dead

Parallel to the Heidelberg/Munich-based work of Kraepelin, Alzheimer, Nissl, and Rüdin was the Berlin initiative in brain research by the husband-and-wife team of Oskar and Cecile Vogt. Oskar was a psychiatrist/neurologist; French-born Cecile was a neuropathologist. With financial support from the German government, the Rockefeller Foundation, and the Krupp family, the Vogts were able to establish a large institute for brain research as part of the Kaiser Wilhelm Society. It was constructed in the Berlin suburb of Buch and opened in 1931.[23]

Like many psychiatrists of the day, Oskar Vogt combined the practice of psychiatry with that of neurology. Psychiatrists/neurologists often performed autopsies on their deceased patients. Such was the case of Vladimir Lenin, whom Vogt was called to examine after Lenin had suffered a stroke. After the death of Lenin, Vogt was given possession of Lenin's brain for study.[24] Lenin's brain became the prize specimen in the collection of a new institute for the study of genius established in Moscow by Vogt. With the arrival of Hitler's regime, Vogt's well-known links with the Soviet state were not viewed with favor, and in 1937 he was forced or encouraged to leave the directorship of the institute that he and his wife had founded.[25]

The Vogts were succeeded by their associates, Hugo Spatz and Julius Hallervorden. Hugo Spatz had been a student of Alzheimer's colleague Nissl,[26] working with Nissl and Walther Spielmeyer at Kraepelin's psychiatric research institute where he and Hallervorden first met. Hallervorden was in Munich at the invitation of Spielmeyer. The two neuroscientists went on to achieve fame through the eponymous designation of a congenital neurological disorder first identified by them, Hallervorden-Spatz disease.[27]

Neuropathology depends on the acquisition of brain specimens for analysis. During the Third Reich, the acquisition of brains was greatly enhanced by the killing programs of Hitler's state, the first being the murder of neurologically handicapped children.

Under the eugenic sterilization program promoted by Rüdin, all newborn handicapped children were registered with the state. The sterilization law mandated an expert subcommittee that was responsible for planning a program for the intentional killing of the registered children. This was done in special *Kinderfachabteilungen* (pediatric departments) established in psychiatric hospitals throughout the Reich. Children transferred to these pediatric departments were killed by intentional starvation in "hunger houses" and by the administration of high doses of medication, in particular phenobarbital.[28] Two of the pediatric killing centers, Görden near Brandenburg and Eglfing-Haar near Munich, were designated as clinical teaching units for instruction in the killing of patients.[29]

A psychiatrist who played a key role in this program of killing and scientific study was Professor Carl Schneider of the University of Heidelberg. Schneider assumed the chair previously held by Kraepelin. In addition to being a leader in the "euthanasia" actions, Schneider exploited the killings for his own research. Schneider and his colleagues performed psychological studies on children doomed to die. The brains of the murdered children were collected and studied in order to correlate neuroanatomical findings with the results of the psychological tests.[30]

Professor Hallervorden exploited the T4 adult "euthanasia" killing program to acquire brains for the neuropathological collection at the Kaiser Wilhelm Institute for Brain Research. The main collection site for Hallervorden was the T4 "euthanasia" killing center in the town of Brandenburg. Hallervorden was present at the time of killings and removed brains from the murdered victims. Hallervorden also sent containers with preservative to the other killing centers in the hope of acquiring additional specimens for his institute.[31]

Some of the Brandenburg victims were killed at the Görden hospital, and their brains were removed at the research institute on the hospital grounds. Hallervorden and his associates worked at this laboratory. Peiffer has documented that from 1939 to 1944 a total of 1,651 brains was examined in the Görden laboratory. Sixty-eight brains were sent from the Görden institute to the Kaiser Wilhelm Society in Berlin for examination.[32] Many of the brains collected by Hallervorden were preserved as part of the largest neuropathological collection in the world at the Kaiser Wilhelm Institute for Brain Research. With the Soviet occupation of Berlin, the institute and its collection of brain specimens was moved to West Germany and subsequently to a location near the University of Frankfurt. After the war, the Kaiser Wilhelm Society and the member institutes were renamed after the noted German physicist and Nobel Laureate, Max Planck. Despite the change in name, the organization remained the same.

The collection of brain specimens remained at the Frankfurt institute until 1990. In the late 1980s, the origins of some of the neuropathological collection were reported by a German investigator. After initially denying the existence of the specimens, the Max Planck Society acknowledged the origins of the collection. In addition to the specimens from the Frankfurt institute, the Max Planck Society affirmed the existence of suspect specimens from murdered children in the collection of the Munich psychiatric institute. The collection of specimens, mainly glass slides, was buried in the Forest Cemetery in Munich. The collection was so large that two adjoining gravesites had to be used. In May 1990 the Max Planck Society held a ceremony at the Munich cemetery.[33] Despite the Max Planck Society's reputation as a leading research organization, there was never a proper scientific investigation of the neuropathological collections prior to the burial. Instead, it was decided to remove all specimens from the Hitler period and bury them. There was no documentation in the public domain.[34]

Hallervorden himself was able to continue to work on the neuropathological collection. After the war, he was appointed head of the renamed Max Planck Institute for Brain Research, which had been temporarily relocated to Giessen. In 1982 the medical faculty of Giessen, on the occasion of its 375th anniversary celebration, honored Hallervorden's contribution as "the grand old man of German and international neuropathology."[35] Hallervorden's biography can be found in an English-language anthology of founders of pediatric neurology.[36] While Hallervorden is remembered, the victims whose brains he collected have been forgotten. The memory is buried at the Forest Cemetery in Munich.

Hallervorden's coworker, Professor Berthold Ostertag, was involved in the exploitation of child murder in Berlin. Ostertag was a pathologist at the Rudolf Virchow Hospital in Berlin, a major teaching hospital affiliated with the former University of Berlin. Ostertag examined the brains of 106 children murdered at the children's ward of the Berlin mental hospital Wittenau. After the war, Ostertag continued his academic career as the head of neuropathology at the University of Tübingen.[37]

Despite their forced retirement from the Kaiser Wilhelm Society, Oscar and Cecile Vogt were able to continue to pursue their joint careers in neuropathology. With the support of the Krupp family, the Vogts established a brain research institute in the town of Neustadt in the Black Forest.[38] Eventually, the Vogt institute was moved to Düsseldorf, where it continues to function at the University of Düsseldorf. In 1985 a paper on the pathology of basal ganglia and the limbic system in people with schizophrenia was published in the *Archives of General Psychiatry*.[39] The authors were, at that time, with the Cecile and Oskar Vogt Institute for Brain Research of the University of Düsseldorf. The thirteen brains of schizophrenic patients that formed the basis of the study were from the collection of the Vogt institute. Subsequent to the publication of that paper, two scientists at the National Institutes of Health, Dr. Elliott Gershon and Dr. Margaret Hoehe, raised questions about two of the specimens reported on in the article. Those two specimens were from twin brothers who died in a psychiatric institution in Berlin named Heilstaetten. One of the brothers died in December 1941, the other in April 1942. An inquiry revealed that the brothers probably died as a result of intentional starvation. Whereas most patients who died at the Heilstaetten institution were autopsied at that hospital, in the case of the brothers, their cadavers were autopsied at the Kaiser Wilhelm Institute for Brain Research. The ultimate destination of their brains was the shelves of the Vogt institute in Düsseldorf.[40] As far as is known, there is no record of the Vogt institute having ever undertaken a proper examination of its collection with a report in the public domain.

The three institutes established by the Vogts continue up to this day. They are the Max Planck Institute for Brain Research in Frankfurt, the Cecile and Oskar Vogt Institute for Brain Research at the University of Düsseldorf, and the Institute for the Study of Genius in Moscow. Lenin's brain still resides at the Moscow institute.

Murder and Deception in Vienna: The Case of Dr. Heinrich Gross

The pathology and perversity of memory is illustrated by the child-killing program at the Vienna Psychiatric Hospital and the outrageous case of Dr. Heinrich Gross. The killing of children as part of the child "euthanasia" action took place in the children's section of the Vienna hospital. The children's section was established in 1940 as the Wiener Städtische Jugendfürsorgeanstalt am Spiegelgrund (City of Vienna Young People's Welfare Institution am Spiegelgrund), commonly referred to as "Spiegelgrund." At its inception, Spiegelgrund had 640 beds. In 1942, Spiegelgrund was expanded and divided into the Wiener Städtische Erziehungsheim am Spiegelgrund (City of Vienna Educational Establishment am Spiegelgrund), with 680 beds, and the Heilpädagogische Klinik am Spiegelgrund (Hospital for Curative Paedogogics [Child Psychiatry] am Spiegelgrund), with a designated 220 beds. The latter was subsequently renamed the Wiener Städtische Nervenklinik für Kinder (City of Vienna Psychiatric-Neurological Hospital for Children). Responsibility as a designated *Kinderfachabteilung* for the killing of children rested first with the Wiener Städtische Jugendfürsorgeanstalt, then with the Heilpädagogische Klinik, and continued under the renamed Nervenklinik für Kinder. The founding director of the Nervenklinik für Kinder, Dr. Erwin Jekelius, and his successor, Dr. Ernst Illing, had previously trained and worked at the "euthanasia" killing center at Görden.[41]

During the tenure of Jekelius and Illing, 772 children at Spiegelgrund were killed; 336 of the murdered children were from the infants' ward, which was headed by Dr. Heinrich Gross from 1941 to 1943. During the years 1942 and 1943, Gross shared the directorship with Dr. Marianne Türk. In 1941 and 1942 Gross attended instruction courses at the "euthanasia" clinical teaching unit at Görden. In 1943 Gross was drafted into the Wehrmacht, but during a leave from the army in 1944 he worked at Nervenklinik für Kinder in place of Dr. Türk, who had taken ill. Gross, like so many physicians, saw the availability of the children as a research opportunity ready for exploitation. Despite his lack of academic connections, Gross undertook studies without any potential benefit to the subjects. His research on the children included subjecting them to an excruciatingly painful procedure known as a pneumoencephalogram, in which cerebrospinal fluid is removed via a lumbar puncture and air is injected into the spine and the brain. This procedure was a radiological diagnostic tool in which the injected air enhanced the visualization of the structure of the brain on X-ray. Some of the children died as a result of this procedure. A number of studies carried out on children by physicians at Spiegelgrund were done in collaboration with members of the faculty of medicine of the University of Vienna. Gross's first "scientific case," presented in 1942 to the Vienna Medical Society and published in 1944 and 1952, was done with the guidance of Dozent Wirtinger of the Institute of Anatomy of the University of Vienna.

At the end of the war, Illing, Türk, and others were charged with and convicted of murder in the killing of children at Spiegelgrund. Illing was hanged, while Türk and others were imprisoned for their crimes. In 1948 Gross, who had been captured and incarcerated by the Soviet army in 1945, was apprehended by the authorities in Vienna and charged with murder in the killing of children at Spiegelgrund. Gross was prosecuted under the German penal code, which held (until 1997) that the definition of murder did not apply in the case of mentally handicapped persons, as such persons were not considered capable of reasoning. Gross was found guilty, not of the murder of the handicapped children, but of manslaughter. The case was appealed to the Supreme Court, which suspended the verdict and referred the case back to the original court. The prosecutor, for as yet unknown reasons, withdrew the indictment against Gross, and in May 1951 the case was closed.

A free man, Gross resumed his professional career without impediment. His professional trajectory was facilitated by membership in the Socialist Party and the Union of Socialist Scholars, which he joined in 1953. After further training, Gross returned to the same institution that included the pavilions where he had previously carried out the activities that formed the basis of his 1948 murder/manslaughter indictment. In 1957 he was appointed head of what is now known as the Second Psychiatric Department and the Neurohistology Laboratory. He was also appointed as a paid psychiatric consultant to the law courts. In his capacity as a forensic expert, Gross provided an expert opinion on more than twelve thousand cases, including one involving a former inmate of Spiegelgrund who had known Gross between 1941 and 1943.

Gross's return to the former Spiegelgrund gave him access to the pathological specimens derived from the murdered children. It is believed that this collection originally comprised one thousand specimens of which over four hundred still exist. Gross continued his research using these specimens. In the 1960s he was successful in obtaining funding for his research from the Ludwig Boltzmann Society and the City of Vienna. In 1968, the Boltzmann Society established the Ludwig Boltzmann Institute for Research on Malformations of the Nervous System, which was to be headed by Gross and to be situated as a functional unit of the Neurohistology Laboratory of the Vienna Psychiatric Hospital, also headed by Gross. Thus, Gross's professional path was facilitated by access to and research on specimens derived from children murdered at an institution that he had once directed and in whose death he had been implicated.

Gross published thirty-five papers based on observations made on the brains of the "euthanasia" victims, some in conjunction with colleagues from the University of Vienna. In addition, brain preparations from the "euthanasia" victims were stored in the Institute of Neurology of the University of Vienna until 1998, at which time they were returned to the Vienna Psychiatric Hospital. Gross's career as head of the Second Psychiatric Department came to an end in 1981 following a lawsuit initiated by Gross against accusations made by a Viennese physician, Dr. Werner Vogt. Vogt accused Gross of complicity in the murder of children at Spiegelgrund. The first verdict in the lawsuit was in Gross's favor. Gross lost on appeal by Vogt. The judge's decision in the appeal included detailed allegations of homicide against Gross. But despite the verdict of the High Court and the detailed allegations against him, Gross had the audacity to continue (and the institution the audacity to sustain his appointment) in his position as head of the merged Ludwig Boltzmann Institute for Research on Malformations of the Nervous System as well as the Neurohistology Laboratory of the Vienna Psychiatric Hospital. Thus, he continued to have unfettered access to the brains of the murdered children. A further outrage is that Gross was permitted to continue as an expert forensic witness to the courts, a position he held until 1996.[42]

In 1999 Gross was again indicted for the murder of children at Spiegelgrund. This indictment is based on evidence derived from the records of the Secret Service of the former East Germany, the Stasi.[43] In March 2000, the criminal proceedings against Gross were suspended because of the finding of psychiatrists that he was unable to understand the proceedings against him due to Alzheimer's dementia. Under Austrian criminal procedure, Gross's mental status and capacity to stand trial will be reviewed by the court every few months. In all likelihood, this process will continue for the remainder of Gross's natural life. The burial of the remaining collection of brains from the murdered children awaits the completion of the criminal proceedings against Gross, an event that may not occur until the natural end of his life. Thus, the final interment of the remains of the murdered children must be delayed until the end of the natural life of their alleged killer.

While Gross may be suffering from a disorder of memory that has incapacitated his intellect, so, too, have the systems—professional, scientific, academic, political, and legal—that have employed and protected him for almost six decades. Because of this intellectual, professional, and moral negligence, there may never be a proper judicial accounting for what happened to those children. The question to be asked now is whether the memory of the children and what happened to them will be buried with the interment of their brains.

Institutional Disorder

Paradoxically, the pathology of institutional memory is also exemplified by the very organization responsible for the momentous advances in the pathology of memory and behavior, namely, the Kaiser Wilhelm/Max Planck Society. The Kaiser Wilhelm Society, which was established in 1911, spawned some of the most prestigious and influential scientific and academic institutes in the world. In addition to the aforementioned institutes of psychiatry and brain research, Kaiser Wilhelm institutes encompassed such scientific and academic disciplines as physics, chemistry, biology, cell biology, metallurgy, and law. Many of the Nobel Laureates of the past century were associated with Kaiser Wilhelm institutes. Between its founding in 1911 and 1948, when it was renamed after the physicist Max Planck, the Kaiser Wilhelm Society supported thirty-five institutes in Germany and other countries.[44] The international esteem of the Kaiser Wilhelm institutes is reflected in the support of the Rockefeller Foundation. In addition to its major contribution to the construction of the institutes of brain research and psychiatry, the Rockefeller Foundation provided financial support to other institutes adversely affected by World War I and the ensuing Depression.[45] The Rockefeller Foundation was influenced in this effort by the American educator Abraham Flexner, whose major interest was in the reform of medical education.[46] Flexner's model for the reform of medical education in the United States and Canada was Germany. James Loeb influenced the decision by the Rockefeller Foundation to provide a substantial grant to the Munich psychiatry institute through Flexner, who was a powerful official in the Rockefeller organization.[47]

As the preeminent scientific and research organization in Germany, the Kaiser Wilhelm Society, through its scientists and institutes, was, not surprisingly, involved in the eugenic and racial programs of the Third Reich. What is perplexing is the difficulty that the present-day Max Planck Society has had in confronting its own history. Despite the evidence linking Kaiser Wilhelm/Max Planck (KW/MP) scientists and researchers with the crimes of the Third Reich, it has taken the KW/MP Society over half a century to begin an examination of its own history. In spite of the documented involvement of KW/MP scientists and researchers in a number of nefarious scientific activities during Hitler's regime, the organization has yet to formally apologize for the suffering and death inflicted by its scientists and researchers on untold numbers of innocent human beings. Hiding under the veneer of academic and scientific objectivity, officials suggest that an apology would be premature and should await the completion of the much-belated investigation that would document exactly what the Max Planck Society should apologize for.[48] It is expected that this investigation will be completed in 2004.

Evidence of the complicity of KW/MP scientists has been in existence for over a decade. The activities included the scientific legitimization and advancement of eugenics and racial hygiene by the Kaiser Wilhelm Institute of Psychiatry (Rüdin) and the Kaiser Wilhelm Institute of Anthropology (Eugen Fischer, Fritz Lenz, Otmar Freiherr von Verschuer); the exploitation of the "euthanasia" killings to acquire brain specimens of the murdered victims by the Kaiser Wilhelm Institute for Brain Research (Hallervorden); and genetic research on Jews and Gypsies in Auschwitz by the Kaiser Wilhelm Institute of Anthropology (von Verschuer/Mengele). The Max Planck Society has publicly acknowledged its moral responsibility (in the absence of any preceding investigation) for the exploitation of the "euthanasia" murders to acquire the brains of the victims.[49] The connection between von Verschuer and Josef Mengele has been well known since it was first reported by Professor Benno Müller-Hill in 1984.[50] In the words of a German social scientist published over a decade ago: "In fact, through Verschuer the institute [Kaiser Wilhelm Institute of Anthropology] was to become directly connected with the murderous 'experiments on humans' at Auschwitz. Even though this connection was never substantiated in a court of law, evidence accumulated over the years leaves little doubt."[51]

Despite the evidence, the Max Planck Society appears to be demon-strating signs and symptoms of disordered memory and conscience. This disorder of memory is exemplified by the society's own 1998 descriptive history of the Berlin institutes of the Kaiser Wilhelm/Max Planck Society. The monograph disputes the wording of a commemo-rative plaque on the building that formerly housed the anthropology institute. According to the 1998 document: "The text of the plaque, which was revised many times, however, falsely suggests that the con-centration camp doctor Josef Mengele was a member of the Kaiser Wil-helm Society. He did, however, send blood and organ samples for testing. The statement that the staff of the institute made an 'active contribution to selection and murder' by virtue of issuing professional opinions seems exaggerated, however."[52]

The formal examination of the history of the Max Planck Society was undertaken one year after the publication of the aforementioned dissembling statement. In 1999, the Max Planck Society established an "autonomous" Presidential Commission ("History of the Kaiser Wilhelm Society in the National Socialist Era").[53] With two cochairs and nine members (one from the United States and one from the United Kingdom), and a staff of resident and visiting researchers, the commission has embarked on a major research program encompassing the following:

- The organization, policy, and administration of the Kaiser Wil-helm Society
- Racial hygiene, genetic, medical, and psychiatric research in Kaiser Wilhelm institutes
- Military research: war-related and applied sciences in Kaiser Wil-helm institutes under the supervision of the Four-Year Plan and the war economy
- *Ostforschung* (research on the east) and *Lebensraumforschung* (re-search on living space) at Kaiser Wilhelm institutes in the context of expansionistic and occupation politics

One commission researcher, Volker Roelcke of the University of Lübeck, has documented that Ernst Rüdin provided intellectual and financial support for murderous experiments on children performed by the Heidelberg psychiatrist Julius Deussen.[54] Another commission researcher, Robert Proctor, has been given access to the archives on Adolf Butenandt, which show that Butenandt "was aware of and sup-ported a research project involving blood samples from Auschwitz in an unsuccessful effort to find disease-fighting proteins specific to race."[55] The report of the commission is expected in 2004.

There is no question that the Presidential Commission will add greatly to the body of knowledge concerning the history of science and medicine during the Third Reich. However, the issuance of an explicit apology on the basis of what is already known should in no way prejudice the research into what is not yet known. The half-century delay in documenting the society's own history is of itself deserving of a public apology. The moral imperative is emphasized by the fact that the Max Planck Society today encompasses institutes embracing such areas as human development, criminal law, and foreign and international private, public, and social law. The Max Planck Society is now more than an organization for basic or applied scientific research; it is also an organization with an explicit moral mandate to study the human condition. In so doing, it also has a moral responsibility for its own actions and for those of its members, both past and present.

What the Max Planck Society appears to continue to ignore, or to avoid facing, is the fate of the victims—those who perished and those who survived. Given the fact that fifty-nine years will have elapsed between the end of the Third Reich and the end of the mandate of the Presidential Commission, few of the survivors will still be living. If a formal apology should be forthcoming, few, if any, will be alive or capable of receiving it. By the time the Max Planck Society has recovered its own institutional memory, there will be few survivors who remember. And the pathology of memory will endure.

Afterword

On 7 June 2001 in Berlin, Professor Hubert Markl, the president of the Max Planck Society, addressed a symposium on the subject "Biomedical Sciences and Human Experimentation at Kaiser Wilhelm Institutes— The Auschwitz Connection." In his speech, Markl acknowledged the moral continuity and responsibility of the Max Planck Society with the Kaiser Wilhelm Society and institutes during the Hitler period. He admitted to the culpability of Kaiser Wilhelm institutes and scientists in the development of the eugenic and racial hygiene policies and programs of the Third Reich as well as to the criminal conduct of Kaiser Wilhelm scientists. While eschewing any formal link between the Kaiser Wilhelm Society and Dr. Josef Mengele, Markl does acknowledge the

relationship between Mengele and his mentor Otmar Freiherr von Verschuer during von Verschuer's term as director of the Kaiser Wilhelm
Institute for Anthropology. He admits: "[I]t is safe to say that Verschuer
knew that crimes were being committed at Auschwitz, that he and his
employees used the victims for scientific purposes, and that he probably
had an active influence on how these crimes were carried out." Markl's
speech, which was given at a symposium organized by the Presidential
Commission of the Max Planck Society, is included in the appendix of
this volume. It is a remarkable and profound document that was presented before an audience that included surviving victims of the Men-
gele/von Verschuer Auschwitz twin experiments. Markl's dissertation is
an important symptom of a possible recovery of the institutional memory of German science. Much, however, still remains to be done.

Notes

1. German E. Berrios, "Alzheimer's Disease: A Conceptual History," *International Journal of Geriatric Psychiatry* 5 (1990): 355–365.
2. Edward Shorter, *A History of Psychiatry: From the Era of the Asylum to the Age of Prozac* (New York: Wiley, 1997).
3. Ibid., 109.
4. Ron Chernow, *The Warburgs: The Twentieth-Century Odyssey of a Remarkable Jewish Family* (New York: Random House, 1993).
5. Kristie Macrakis, "The Rockefeller Foundation and German Physics under National Socialism," *Minerva* 27 (1989): 33–57.
6. "Federal Commission for the Protection of German Blood," *Journal of the American Medical Association* 106 (1936): 1214–1215.
7. Michael Burleigh, *Death and Deliverance: "Euthanasia" in Germany, c. 1900–1945* (Cambridge: Cambridge University Press, 1994); and Henry Friedlander, *The Origins of Nazi Genocide: From Euthanasia to the Final Solution* (Chapel Hill: University of North Carolina Press, 1995).
8. William E. Seidelman, "Medical Selection: Auschwitz Antecedents and Effluent," *Holocaust and Genocide Studies* 4 (1989): 435–448.
9. Friedlander, *The Origins of Nazi Genocide*, 215, 286.
10. Ernst Klee, "'Turning on the Gas Was No Big Deal'—The Gassing Doctors during the Nazi Period and Afterwards," *Dachau Review* 2 (1990): 46–66.
11. William Seidelman, "Medicine and Murder in the Third Reich," *Dimensions* 13 (1999): 9–13; idem, "The Legacy of Academic Medicine and Human Exploitation in the Third Reich," *Perspectives in Biology and Medicine* 43 (2000): 325–334; idem, "Medicine and the Holocaust: Physician Involvement in Genocide," in

Israel W. Charney, ed., *Encyclopedia of Genocide* (Santa Barbara: ABC-CLIO, 2000), 412–415.

12. William Seidelman, "Erinnerung, Medizin und Moral: Die Bedeutung der Ausbeutung des menschlichen Körpers im Dritten Reich," in Eberhard Gabriel and Wolfgang Neugebauer, eds., *NS-Euthanasie in Wien* (Vienna: Böhlau Verlag, 2000), 27–46.

13. Paula David and Jodeme Goldhar, "Caring for Aging Survivors of Early Life Trauma Due to War; Survivors of the Holocaust: Case in Point Training Manual," in *"If Not Now…": An Internet Journal for Individuals and Agencies Working with Survivors of the Holocaust and Their Families.* vol. 1 (2000) http://www.baycrest.org /ifnotnow.html; and Michael Gordon, "History Taking in Patients Who Are Survivors," in *"If Not Now…": An Internet Journal.*

14. Robert Proctor, e-mail message to William Seidelman, dated 29 September 1999 (author's files).

15. George J. Annas and Michael A. Grodin, *The Nazi Doctors and the Nuremberg Code: Human Rights in Human Experimentation* (New York: Oxford, 1992).

16. Ernst Rüdin, *Zur Vererbung und Neuentstehung der Dementia praecox,* vol. 1 of *Studien über Vererbung und Entstehung geistiger Störungen* (Berlin: Springer, 1916). For a contemporary discussion of the Rüdin legacy in psychiatric genetics, see Irving Gottesman and Aksel Bertelsen, "Legacy of German Psychiatric Genetics: Hindsight Is Always 20/20," *American Journal of Medical Genetics (Neuropsychiatric Genetics)* 67 (1996): 317–322; Edith Zerbin-Rudin and Kenneth S. Kendler, "Ernst Rüdin (1874–1952) and His Genealogic-Demographic Department in Munich (1917–1986): An Introduction to Their Family Studies of Schizophrenia," *American Journal of Medical Genetics (Neuropsychiatric Genetics)* 67 (1996): 332–337; Kenneth S. Kendler and Edith Zerbin-Rudin, "Abstract and Review of *Studien Über Vererbung und Entstehung Geistiger Störungen. I. Zur Vererbung und Neuentstehung der Dementia praecox* (Studies on the Inheritance and Origin of Mental Illness: I. To the Problem of the Inheritance and Primary Origin of Dementia Praecox), *American Journal of Medical Genetics (Neuropsychiatric Genetics)* 67 (1996): 338–342; Kenneth S. Kendler and Edith Zerbin-Rudin, "Abstract and Review of *Zur Erbpathologie der Schizophrenia*" (Contribution to the Genetics of Schizophrenia), *American Journal of Medical Genetics (Neuropsychiatric Genetics)* 67 (1996): 343–346; Mathias Weber, "Ernst Rüdin, 1874–1952: A German Psychiatrist and Geneticist," *American Journal of Medical Genetics (Neuropsychiatric Genetics)* 67 (1996): 323–331; Pablo V. Gejman, "Ernst Rüdin and Nazi Euthanasia: Another Stain on His Career," *American Journal of Medical Genetics (Neuropsychiatric Genetics)* 74 (1997): 455–456; Elliot S. Gershon, "Ernst Rüdin, a Nazi Psychiatrist and Geneticist," *American Journal of Medical Genetics (Neuropsychiatric Genetics)* 74 (1997): 457–458; Bernard Lerer and Ronnen H. Segman, "Correspondence Regarding German Psychiatric Genetics and Ernst Rüdin," *American Journal of Medical Genetics (Neuropsychiatric Genetics)* 74 (1997): 459–460; Kenneth S. Kendler, "Reply to Gejman, Gershon and Lerer and Segman," *American Journal of Medical Genetics (Neuropsychiatric Genetics)* 74 (1997): 461–463.

17. Weber, *Ernst Rüdin, 1874–1952.*

18. "The German Eugenic Society," *Journal of the American Medical Association* 12 (1933): 101, 943.

19. Paul Weindling, *Health, Race and German Politics Between National Unification and Nazism 1870–1945* (Cambridge: Cambridge University Press, 1989); Robert S. Wistrich, *Who's Who in Nazi Germany* (London: Weidenfeld & Nicholson, 1982); Weber, *Ernst Rüdin, 1874–1952.*

20. The Law for the Prevention of Progeny of Sufferers from Hereditary Diseases (*Gesetz zur Verhütung erbkranken Nachwuchses*) enacted 14 July 1933 (Berlin: Reichsausschuß für Volksgesundheitsdienst Berlin) (Paris: Archives du Centre de Documentation Juive Contemporaine, Document #B15076).

21. Robert Proctor, *Racial Hygiene: Medicine under the Nazis* (Cambridge, MA: Harvard University Press, 1988), 108.

22. Weindling, *Health, Race and German Politics,* 537–539.

23. Webb Haymaker, "Cecile and Oskar Vogt: On the Occasion of Her 75th and His 80th Birthday," *Neurology* 1 (1951): 179–204; Webb Haymaker, "Cecile Mugnier Vogt (1875–1962) Oskar Vogt (1870–1959)," in Webb Haymaker and Francis Schiller, eds., *The Founders of Neurology* (Springfield, IL: Charles C. Thomas, 1970); and Walter Bruetsch, "In Memoriam: Oskar Vogt, M.D., 1870–1959," *American Journal of Psychiatry* 116 (1960): 958–960.

24. Haymaker, "Cecile and Oskar Vogt"; Ute Deichmann, *Biologists Under Hitler* (Cambridge, MA: Harvard University Press, 1996).

25. Haymaker, "Cecile and Oskar Vogt."

26. Ibid.

27. Ludo van Boagaert, "Hugo Spatz (1888–1969)" in Haymaker and Schiller, *The Founders of Neurology;* Edward Richardson, "Julius Hallervorden," in Steven Ashwal, ed., *The Founders of Child Neurology* (San Anselmo, CA: Norman Publishing, 1990).

28. Burleigh, *Death and Deliverance,* 102; Friedlander, *The Origins of Nazi Genocide,* 53–54.

29. Burleigh, *Death and Deliverance,* 43, 109.

30. Ibid., 263–265; Friedlander, *The Origins of Nazi Genocide,* 130–131.

31. Leo Alexander, "Neuropathology and Neurophysiology, Including Electroencephalography, in Wartime Germany," Combined Intelligence Objectives Sub-Committee G-2 Division SHAEF (Rear) APO 413, (Washington D.C.: National Archives, Document No. L-170 cont'd. 20 July 1945); Benno Müller-Hill, *Murderous Science: Elimination by Scientific Selection of Jews, Gypsies, and Others, Germany, 1933–1945* (New York: Oxford University Press, 1988); Jürgen Peiffer, "Neuropathology in the Third Reich: Memorial to those Victims of National-Socialist Atrocities in Germany Who Were Used by Medical Science," *Brain Pathology* 1 (1991): 125–131; Jürgen Peiffer, "Assessing Neuropathological Research Carried Out on Victims of the 'Euthanasia' Programme," *Medical History Journal (Urban & Fischer)* 34 (1999): 339–356; Michael Shevell, "Racial Hygiene, Active Euthanasia, and Julius Hallervorden," *Neurology* 42 (1992): 2214–2219.

32. Peiffer, "Assessing Neuropathological Research."

33. Georg Kreutzberg, "Verwicklung, Aufdeckung und Bestattung: Über den Umgang mit einem Erbe," in Franz-Werner Kerstig, Karl Teppe, and Bernd Walter, eds., *Nach Hadamar: Zum Verhältnis von Psychiatrie und Gesellschaft im 20. Jahrhundert* (Paderborn: Ferdinand Schöningh, 1993); Seidelman, "Erinnerung, Medizin und Moral."

34. Seidelman, "Erinnerung, Medizin und Moral."

35. Wolfgang Neugebauer and Georg Stacher, "Nazi Child 'Euthanasia' in Vienna and the Scientific Exploitation of Its Victims before and after 1945," *Digestive Diseases* 17 (1999): 279–285.
36. Richardson, "Julius Hallervorden."
37. Peiffer, "Neuropathology in the Third Reich," and "Assessing Neuropathological Research."
38. Haymaker, "Cecile and Oskar Vogt"; idem, "Cecile Mugnier Vogt"; Bruetsch, "In Memoriam."
39. Bernhardt Bogerts, Elizabeth Meertz, and Regina Schonfeldt-Bausch, "Basal Ganglia and Limbic System Pathology in Schizophrenia: A Morphometric Study of Brain Volume and Shrinkage," *Archives of General Psychiatry* 42 (1985): 784–791.
40. Ibid.; Bernd Becker and Martina Kruger, Elliot Gershon and Margaret Hoehe, "Brains of the Vogt Collection," *Archives of General Psychiatry* (Letter to the Editor) 45 (1988): 774–776.
41. The principal source on Heinrich Gross, and the most detailed English-language documentation on the subject is the paper by Neugebauer and Stacher, "Nazi Child 'Euthanasia' in Vienna."
42. Ibid.; Jonathan Silvers and Tom Hagler, "In the Name of the Führer," *The Sunday Times Magazine* (London), 14 September 1997, 32–41
43. Silvers and Hagler, "In the Name of the Führer."
44. Bernd Wirsing, "Opening the Archives (letter)," *Haaretz Magazine,* 4 August 2000, 2.
45. Macrakis, "The Rockefeller Foundation and German Physics."
46. Steven C. Wheatley, *The Politics of Philanthropy: Abraham Flexner and Medical Education* (Madison: University of Wisconsin Press, 1988).
47. Weindling, *Health, Race and German Politics*, 432; and Wheatley, *The Politics of Philanthropy.*
48. Hubert Markl, "Anmaßung in Demut: Erst forschen, dann handeln. Eine Erwiderung auf Ernst Klee," *Die Zeit* 7 (February 2000); Robert Koenig, "Reopening the Darkest Chapter in German Science," *Science* 288 (2000): 1576–1577; and Alison Abbott, "German Science Begins to Cure Its Historical Amnesia," *Nature* 403 (2000): 474–475.
49. Wirsing, "Opening the Archives"; MPG Pressinformation, "Den Opfern zum Gedenken—den Lebenden zur Mahnung," 25 May 1990.
50. Benno Müller-Hill, *Tödliche Wissenschaft* (Reinbeck: Rowoholt, 1984).
51. Peter Weingart, "German Eugenics between Science and Politics," *Osiris* (2nd series) 5 (1989): 260–282.
52. Eckart Henning and Marion Kazemi, *Dahlem-Domain of Science: A Walking Tour of the Berlin Institutes of the Kaiser-Wilhelm/Max Planck Society in the "German Oxford"* (Munich: Max Planck Society, 1998), 42.
53. Wirsing, "Opening the Archives."
54. Abbot, "German Science Begins."
55. Koenig, "Reopening the Darkest Chapter."

Chapter Six

THE LEGACY OF NAZI MEDICINE
IN CONTEXT

Michael Burleigh

THERE IS NO IDEAL CONCLUSION in a collection such as this, but there are plenty of dilemmas associated with writing one. Should one merely summarize what has been so cogently expressed before by many of the leading scholars in their respective subdisciplines? But that is surely the proper function of an introduction, and Professors Nicosia and Huener have provided a splendid introduction already. Or should one expand on themes that have been alluded to in passing, or for which no room was found at the time of the book's conception, but which may well seem necessary at its completion? Which elements of the complex of themes often all too facilely described under the rubric "Nazi medicine" is one supposed to emphasize?

As Robert Proctor suggests, there is the serious risk of missing the *simultaneity* of heinous criminality, whether murdering sick people or carrying out vile "medical" experiments on the living, with research that may have been pioneering in such fields as oncology. One suspects that the leading British cancer expert, Sir Richard Doll of the University of Oxford, can live with the shocking news that an otherwise obscure German scientist, Fritz Lickint, may have reached some of his conclusions about the relation between cigarette smoking and certain cancers a couple of decades earlier. Neither Lickint nor Franz Müller was the first to make such a connection, for in the eighteenth and nineteenth centuries, some doctors in Britain, France, and Germany had linked pipe smoking with certain cancers of the lips, mouth, and nose. Sir Richard studied in Frankfurt for a fortnight in the 1930s. He was naturally more startled by a German lecturer who employed a slide in which the cancer cells "were Jews" and the X-rays bombarding them "were Nazi Stormtroopers," than by the quality of what he calls the Germans' "bad epidemiology."[1]

But regardless of whether or not Proctor has overplayed the significance of methodologically indifferent work by some German scientists, which is certainly how such major scientific figures as Doll view things, how does one reconcile his conclusions with Henry Friedlander's revelations regarding the cupidity and cruelty of Nazi physicians involved in the "euthanasia" programs, or those eminent scientists, such as Julius Hallervorden or Otmar Freiherr von Verschuer, who benefited from research materials derived respectively from the "euthanasia" programs or the activities of the latter's protégé, Mengele of Auschwitz? For as William Seidelman demonstrates, the odor of these examples of medicalized criminality extends from the concentration camps and the six asylums directly implicated in the "euthanasia" program up to and beyond the portals of such august institutions as the Kaiser Wilhelm/Max Planck Society. He further demonstrates in his finely gauged study how the modern German scientific establishment has dealt with this past; an institutional equivalent of Alzheimer's disease seems to have afflicted the collective memory of many of the lineal successors of these grand establishments until very recent times.

Maybe, faced with these almost irreconcilable perspectives, an ideal concluding essay should strive unofficiously, in the Hippocratic sense, simply to acknowledge what is valuable in the book we have before us, while indicating things that have inadvertently been left unsaid or underscored. Certainly, any introduction or conclusion on this complex of subjects should first pay generous tribute to the pioneers in this field, such as Alice Platen-Hallermund, whose important book on "euthanasia" was studiously ignored when it first appeared in 1948, to the German documentary filmmaker and freelance researcher Ernst Klee, whose monumental studies of the Nazi "euthanasia" program still represent an unrivaled quarry of original materials, or to Daniel Kevles, whose book on eugenics still eclipses many in the field, and which reminds us that this story does not just involve Germany. The fact that the first two scholars are Germans is certainly worthy of attention.[2]

Appropriately enough, this important volume's point of departure is Garland E. Allen's wide-ranging discussion of eugenics in the United States and Germany between 1900 and 1945, in which he observes that eugenics did not begin with the Nazis. Without wishing to diminish in any way the content of what Professor Allen has written, it is his illustrations that may surprise and shock English-speaking readers, for here ideas that are increasingly exclusively associated with Germans and Nazis, at least in the mass media, are visualized in the English language in American contexts. The illustration showing the "good" and "bad" lineages of the Kallikak family is a case in point, for the Kallikaks were taken over—lock, stock, and barrel—in German eugenicist publications and propaganda. Although on a significantly smaller scale than in Germany, we know that tens of thousands of U.S. citizens were involuntarily sterilized with state approval, including, as has recently been revealed in the case of Virginia, adolescent boys who went on to become much decorated soldiers during World War II.

Professor Allen's study suggests that eugenics flourished in a wide variety of cultural, historical, and political settings. Indeed, the past tense is depressingly inappropriate if one thinks of contemporary Singapore or the People's Republic of China, both of which practice more or less "hard" or "soft" eugenic strategies in the present day. Oddly enough, while many studies of Nazi eugenics make warning noises about potentially dangerous developments in the genetic present, few of them even take note of very worrying current eugenic practices in other parts of the world. Do we need, perhaps, fewer attempts to strain connections between eugenics and contemporary genetics, which scientists increasingly dismiss, and not without reason, as a form of historical Ludditism, and a greater willingness to look at other cultures in which the old ideas are worryingly evident in the present? Why so much concern with what *might* happen, when there are abundant causes for concern with what *is* happening, say in contemporary China? Could this reticence be due to a residual *gauchiste tiers mondisme*, a sort of self-inhibition on the part of Western intellectuals and scholars when it comes to criticizing unpleasant developments in the "Third World"?[3]

But before venturing into the contemporary world, let us explore the historical record more closely. Eugenics movements existed in both predominantly agrarian and industrial societies, including Great Britain, Germany, Denmark, Sweden, and the United States. Clusters of precursors coalesced into activist lobby groups, which in turn forged international connections. Relatively backward countries, or regions within them, turned to those with a more developed grid of scientific inquiry, whether in the case of Argentina vis-à-vis Italy or the U.S. Southern states, which genuflected toward the prestigious and progressive universities in the northeast of the nation.[4]

In very broad terms, these movements represented a confidently sci-entistic response on the part of the anxious middle class to a variety of what one might describe as urgent social challenges. Some of these were real enough; others were mythologized into what were tantamount to moral panics, on the order of those that subsequently accompanied the appearance of the Beatles and Elvis Presley. With the exception of the Frenchman Sicard de Plauzoles, aristocrats were conspicuously under-represented in eugenic circles, being more relaxed about Bluebeards and Draculas lurking in the family background. Middle-class eugenic anxieties included the deleterious effects of industrialization, urbaniza-tion, welfare, and warfare, as well as the acquisition, or loss, of popula-tion through migration of what were regarded, to use the eugenic argot of the times, as either low- or high-value people. These anxieties were an offshoot of middle-class encounters with the urban poor, encounters that had begun with Engels, Dickens, Disraeli, and Jack London in the case of Britain, and that both there and elsewhere appeared to receive alarming confirmation through such exercises as large-scale military conscription. Eugenicists in predominantly rural societies tended to concentrate on the alleged dysgenic effects of what Marx uncharmingly called "the idiocy of rural life," such as deaf-mutism through consan-guinity. As the example of the United States shows, concern for poor "white trash" was intimately connected with latent racial anxieties about an African-American population, which itself was controlled through disciplinary measures other than eugenics.[5]

So we are dealing with middle-class professionals who were, in the main, members of the techno-bureaucratic intelligentsia, although there were many intellectual and artistic luminaries, such as Nietzsche and Shaw, among eugenic enthusiasts. As Henry Friedlander remarks in the context of his fair-minded and informed discussion, Nazi physi-cians were "professionals no different in their commitment than chemists, engineers, or historians." One might elaborate this realist approach in the case of turn-of-the-century eugenicists. We can enhance their collective social profile beyond their predominantly mid-dle-class social origins by alluding to the fact that many of them were engaged in the caring professions; many were women; and, in each national context, liberals and socialists were generously represented. In these circles, loathing of the poor tended to be commingled with guilt, although the effects of guilt, evident in Weimar Germany in the 1920s and in Scandinavia as recently as the 1970s, were no less harmful to those who were the objects of such eugenic "concern." One might even speculate in a not altogether counterfactual fashion that a Social Democrat-dominated Germany might have introduced the sort of negative eugenic policies that came to characterize the welfare states of Social Democratic Scandinavia.

The reasons why such people were enthusiastic about eugenics are not especially difficult to fathom. Eugenics promised to raise the status of an intermediary class of professional experts, regardless of their motives. As they saw it, they would, in their extended reveries, become biocratic sentinels guarding the national gene pool, a project with tremendous appeal to those whose unromanticized role in life was dispensing aspirins and suppositories, dealing with the delinquent or difficult, or, in the case of psychiatrists, warehousing the chronically mentally ill and retarded.[6] Michael Kater implies at various points in his study of Nazi doctors that eugenics would restore a measure of control to careers that had been blighted by such factors as inflation, Jewish immigration, or the tangible loss of professional control that was a consequence of the growth of patient rights' groups or socialized medical systems. Of course, this last explanation may suit interwar Germany, but it sits ill with some North American examples in which eugenicists who thrived in public health contexts, such as the psychiatrist Alfred Blumer, had to tone down their enthusiasm for sterilizing patients when employed in a private context: the rich relatives of people in asylums in Rhode Island did not take kindly to loose talk about eugenic sterilization. A heavily deterministic discipline proved ironically amenable to environmental influence.[7]

But there was quite possibly something else at work, which may require slightly more explicit comment than has been given in this book. Just as we might be in danger of overmedicalizing Nazi criminality, so too might we be in danger of taking the scientific pretensions of eugenics at their face value. After all, eugenics was a gigantic leap of faith, which, by its very ambition, raised its devotees way above ordinary mortals. Its effects not being visible until the distant future, it was work that literally spanned the generations. In view of the criticism that eugenics received from a wide range of commentators, pundits, and scientists in Britain alone, encompassing the anti-Semitic Roman Catholic moralist G. K. Chesterton and the Marxist biologist J. B. S. Haldane, insistence upon this form of scientist "fix" to complex social problems represented nothing less than an act of faith on the part of eugenic enthusiasts. It was part of a broader displacement of religious authority by the secular creed of science, which does not mean that many Christians were not drawn to such ideologies, as the cases of the Germans Hans Harmsen of the Protestant Inner Mission and the former Jesuit Hermann Muckermann suggest. Perhaps in the last few decades historians have been overliteral in treating eugenics as simply science, or, at any rate, in seeking to expose the nonscientific character of the "science" that was used to arrive at such dubious conclusions. For just as there was rather more to Nazism than "applied biology," in the sense that it drew upon bastardized, redemptive religiosity as well as bastardized science, so the interest in eugenics may have been an example of *fides quaerens intellectum*, that is, faith seeking understanding. In their introduction, Nicosia and Huener suggest that eugenics enthusiasts believed that "[s]cience, not religion or philosophy, would direct humanity toward a biological, social, and moral utopia"; the Nazis were not alone in conceiving of science in a quasi-religious, redemptive fashion.[8]

Of course, just as when we look at virtually any great painting, the blank spaces around the figures or objects have as much importance to the composition as the things themselves, so too should we be more conscious of contexts in which eugenics was unsuccessful, leading literally to a dead end. As Professor Allen shows, not everyone found the claims of eugenics compelling. The British case, briefly touched on above, illustrates something to which these essays briefly allude, namely, the reasons why eugenics was more successful in some political contexts—including, most obviously, Nazi Germany—than in others. Allen tells us much about the formation of national eugenic societies; the elaboration of their international contacts and organizations; their funding by wealthy philanthropists, such as the Carnegies, Harrimans, Kelloggs, Loebs, and Rockefellers; and so on, down to the proven connections, researched earlier by Stefan Kühl, between North American and German eugenicists such as Harry Laughlin.[9]

But no matter how well organized and vociferous eugenicists might have been, they still had to negotiate what might, for convenience sake, be called the local political culture. In the British case, the usual suspects, whose social profile was outlined above, tried to put eugenic sterilization on the statute books. The left-wing Fabians and the founders of the "progressive" London School of Economics and Political Science, Sidney and Beatrice Webb, were zealous in their belief that one must "interfere, interfere, interfere." In 1931, for instance, Webb's protégé, Major Church of the National Union of Scientific Workers, introduced a bill proposing voluntary sterilization of the mentally deficient. But try as the medico-technocratic lobby within the Labour Party might, these goals were never achieved. There were popular folk memories of people being "cut up" by crazed bodysnatching scientists, notoriously Burke and Hare in gothic Edinburgh.[10] There was an elite that valued gentleman amateurs, preferably trained in classics, over expert scientific professionals, in a country where the adjective "clever" is rarely a social compliment. These entirely healthy philistine prejudices were also exploited by a vociferous Catholic lobby, whether hailing from working-class, and Labour-voting, Glasgow or Liverpool, or by Chesterton, who traduced eugenics as the handiwork of "tenth-rate Prussian professors"—a remarkable act of legerdemain since Francis Galton, who coined the term "eugenics," was in fact an Englishman. Although British eugenicists, who were not so easily thwarted, subsequently tried to pack a parliamentary committee investigating these issues, the bureaucratic Sir Humphreys of Whitehall quietly killed their proposals by claiming that they were receiving "the active attention of Ministers," the local code for "nothing doing." There seems, then, to be value in giving more attention than we customarily do to national cases in which the local culture actively frustrated the *progressive* visions of the biocratic utopians.[11]

Of course, if the interesting cases (the Netherlands, France, and southern Europe would be others) of countries that did not go down the eugenic route, at least in terms of government policy, is one theme only marginal to this book, so too is the prehistory of eugenics in Germany, excepting developments that led directly to the medicalized crimes of National Socialism. Some of the most compelling recent research on Germany, notably by Michael Schwarz, has not been on such avatars of Nazi racial hygiene as Lenz or Ploetz, but rather on the ways in which a lower-profile eugenics adapted to the democratic political circumstances of the Weimar Republic. There the political running was not made by National Socialism, which was politically marginal until 1930 in any case, but by the Roman Catholic Center Party, various kinds of liberal parties, and, last but not least, the Social Democratic Party. For if the ostensible point of current interest in "Nazi" medicine is not to rummage around in the box of horrors for its own sake, but instead to find serviceable lessons for today, then there is surely some point in studying the responses of democratic German institutions to an insistent eugenics lobby, which was virtually indistinguishable, except in name, from its confreres elsewhere. Perhaps we need to know more about why eugenics appealed so much to the Social

Democratic Party as well as the National Socialist German Workers Party to find idioms appropriate to discussions in contemporary North America or Europe regarding the new genetics. How were these ideas pushed within the parties of humanity, and who opposed them—both within these parties and beyond them?[12]

Surprising as it may be, even Adolf Eichmann, during his trial in Jerusalem, was quite capable of placing himself in the context of Kant's categorical imperative, informing Judge Raveh: "I mean by my remark about Kant that the principle of my will must always be such that it can become the principle of general laws." While Kant would have been horrified to have this particular "disciple," it is instructive that Eichmann was cognizant of the terms in which ethical issues are discussed. And in fact, as numerous speeches by Himmler show, even at the very epicenters of Nazi criminality, hard by the death camps and shooting pits in the east, a form of moral discourse was perpetually in evidence, as these killers sought to rationalize their own depredations in quasi-moral terms by alluding to their own enduring decency and incorruptibility. One cannot simply ignore this discourse, with its direct or distorted echoes of the language of Kant or Nietzsche.

Various parts of this book also allude to the subject of medical ethics, although the book contains no sustained discussion of this theme. Ironically, the absence of such a discussion replicates the marginalization of a discipline that is almost universally regarded as one of the principal safeguards against the recurrence of physicians becoming involved in mass murder. We insist on enhancing the medical awareness of physicians by telling them about Nazi criminality, yet we tell them nothing about the ethical context that accompanied the criminality. Thanks to the research of the German historians Andreas Frewer and Clemens Eickhoff, we are beginning to know something about the shifting content of major journals of medical ethics, although not enough about the ethical components of medical training. This is a serious omission, for Nazism was, if nothing else, related to Bolshevism and fascism in being a dystopian attempt to fabricate "new" men and women by erasing or transforming their "inherited" ethical values in favor of others derived from a modernized and scientized version of pre-Judeo-Christian conduct. In other words, it was a case of ancient or primitive civilizations put through the refracting mirrors of Darwin and Nietzsche. Again, we may be overstating Nazism as an aberrant branch of the scientific imagination, thereby overlooking the extent to which even the scientists were informed by what might be described as historical fantasizing. This is something we are quite prepared to accept in the case of Croat or Serb aggression in contemporary Albania or Bosnia, but not, apparently, in the more "cultivated" context of twentieth-century Germany. Given the twentieth century's casual attitudes toward the sanctity of human life, this can hardly be said to be a peripheral issue. Interestingly, while studies of Nazi medicine and science are commonplace, the field of ethics in Nazi Germany is barely explored, nor is the fact that Nazi publications were saturated with references to the mores of prehistoric or barbaric societies deemed worthy of special mention. This is unfortunate for discussions of eugenics and euthanasia, since both the Nazis and their moral progenitors were adamant in their desire to re-create what they imagined to be the simpler habits of earlier (more primitive) societies, explicitly rejecting what they regarded as the liberal-sentimental "humanitarianism" of the Pyrrhic "welfarist" nineteenth and twentieth centuries.

In 1870, Ernst Haeckel wrote: "[I]f someone would dare to make the suggestion, according to the example of the ancient Spartans and Redskins, to immediately kill after birth the miserable and infirm children, to whom can be prophesied with assurance a sickly life, instead of preserving them to their own harm and the detriment of the whole community, our whole so-called 'humane civilization' would erupt in a cry of indignation." In the aftermath, a number of authors, including Adolf Jost and Alexander Tille, turned to the theme of euthanasia, often arguing that the rights of the collective had primacy over those of the sick or suffering individual. This theme was most systematically explored in the notorious 1920 tract by Karl Binding and Alfred Hoche, *Permission for the Destruction of Life Unworthy of Life*, wherein Hoche claimed that just as present-day societies were condemnatory of the "barbaric" past, so future societies would shake their heads over the "overexaggerated notions of humanity and overestimation of the value of existence" in the present. This provided the ethical-historical rationale for "euthanasia" programs during the Nazi period. This background—of collectivist social Darwinism, extreme economism run riot, racism, and imaginings regarding ancient history—may caution us against making forced analogies between Nazi crimes committed under the camouflage of "euthanasia" and attempts to legalize voluntary euthanasia for terminally ill individuals in the present. Moreover, the example is instructive in a further sense: as no one would seriously indict the discipline of classics because eugenicists admired the Spartans, so we should be careful indeed in indicting contemporary genetics on the basis of the eugenic horror of the earlier decades of the last century.

Professors Friedlander and Kater are correct in emphasizing the baleful role of physicians in eugenic sterilization programs and the successive stages of the "euthanasia" programs, and as both selectors and "researchers" within the concentration camps. However, we should neglect neither the part played by health administrators, who, after all, through their decisions shaped the environments in which the physicians labored, nor that of the nursing and ancillary staffs, who worked on the instructions of the doctors. Friedlander almost matches the morally outraged tone of the pioneer German researcher Ernst Klee by highlighting the depressingly base motives that were all too evidently at work in the case of many physicians in Nazi Germany. How else could any decent-minded person respond when confronted by the grossness of a Mennecke or Pfannmüller, whose crimes have been frequently reported in the literature on Nazi "euthanasia"?

Historical accounts that eschew moral perspectives are surely of limited use, for human beings are, if nothing else, moral actors, equipped with such senses as guilt and shame, good and evil, right and wrong, which seem to me to be of the essence of any account of human behavior. But while one applauds the deliberate demystification of any profession, especially one that has been the subject of so much elegant psycho-historical speculation, in this case there were many prior and ambient economic, ideological, scientific, and professional *structural* circumstances that may have contributed to the ease with which certain physicians became participants in mass murder. We need to learn more about the nuts and bolts of the fiscal climate in which asylums and the like operated, for by concentrating on doctors alone, one may unwittingly confirm their own self-image as "Gods in White Coats," thereby buying into their own professional propaganda. Likewise, it would be interesting to know what role such innovations as occupational therapy or the various forms of shock therapy might have played in separating curable acute patients from those chronic cases who were abandoned to the back wards, increasingly beyond the orbit of moral concern. For although one would not seriously contest Friedlander's view that some Nazi doctors were "arrogant, ambitious and greedy," this does not apply to all of those involved, and may fall short of explaining the full spectrum of culpability. When the Erlangen psychiatrist Valentin Faltlhauser was tried for "euthanasia" killings, a Protestant pastor remarked: "[H]e seemed to me to be a typical example of what happens when a man abandons one principle, and then is unable to stop." The crucial point here is not the slippery slope itself, but the fact that Faltlhauser, an intelligent man who had once coauthored the standard work on care in the community and who ran a progressive regime at Erlangen, had principles that needed incrementally to be abandoned. While on the subject of the physicians Friedlander discusses, it would also be interesting to establish what effect their membership in the SS, which inevitably involved exposure to a series of ideological norms, had on their prior education as physicians.[13]

Of course, physicians were hardly the sole group of people responsible for medical criminality, as recent publications reveal. Apart from my own work on such regional health bureaucrats as Fritz Bernotat and Walter "Bubi" Schultze, and on ancillary staff and nurses, we now have the nuanced, if rather costively written, study of nurses in the Third Reich by Bronwyn Rebekah McFarland-Icke, although we should not overlook the pioneering research of the German Hildegard Steppe. One of the merits of McFarland-Icke's work is to establish the widest institutional and professional contexts in which nurses had to function, before tracing the moral conduct of nurses in some of the asylums involved in the "euthanasia" programs. Readers of McFarland-Icke get a vivid sense of people gradually coming to terms with insidious practices, as it dawned on them that the dosages of medicines they were being ordered to give were lethal, or that the fate of patients they took to certain parts of their institution was predetermined. Short snatches of recorded conversation are inserted in her analysis, giving a genuine flavor of the sorts of dilemmas people experienced. For example, after three patients had died following her administering above-average doses of Luminal or scopolamine, nurse Margarete Goebel asked a Dr. Mootz: "Must we really burden ourselves so?" to which his reply was: "We have a duty." Other nurses claimed not to feel personally responsible for killing people, insofar as they had only moved patients into so-called killing "spaces," which, after all, were multifunctional. They had merely put a headboard up and puffed up pillows so that another nurse could pour a sedative fluid down a patient's throat, or had only mixed certain drugs together or filled syringes, which were then used by others. Somewhere or other, they often told themselves, somebody within the institution must be responsible, and, notwithstanding the constant emphasis upon secrecy, surely these things (they meant crimes) could not be done without legal sanction. That normal in-house disciplinary codes were maintained throughout these events (that is, people were disciplined or dismissed for having parties or sex) must have led to further layers of moral confusion. Among the ancillary staff who had to deal with the grim realities of mass murder, attitudes toward work as such were relatively easy to carry over to the horrid business of disposing of large numbers of corpses. In other words, perhaps we need to pay much more close attention to the simultaneity of the abnormal and the normal if we are to grasp the subtle realities of the contexts in which this killing took place.[14]

There remains a gap between the authors of these essays who excoriate Nazi physicians and today's medical and scientific establishments in Austria and Germany that have evaded the issue of Nazi medicalized criminality. The gap exists despite the efforts of the Allied authorities, and of the German institutions that gradually took over for them, to bring to account people responsible for massive crimes. Virtually all of the documentation that researchers, German and non-German alike, have on Nazi medical criminality represents the painstaking efforts of the West German federal prosecution service, which, now acting for a united Germany, has been based for some time in Ludwigsburg. We would know virtually nothing about these subjects without the files and files of interrogations of the accused or depositions from witnesses. Anyone who has worked with this documentation will know its sheer scale. Moreover, although the subject has been systematically ignored by most mainstream historians in Germany, with the conspicuous exception of East German researchers connected with Achim Thom, virtually every asylum and institution in Germany has been studied by people often with a local or professional interest in their recent past. There are exceptionally fine studies of eugenics and "euthanasia" in Badenese or Bavarian asylums by Heinz Faulstich and Bernhard Richarz, to mention only the most outstanding works in that genre, as well as very fine monographic studies of such constituencies as the blind or deaf during the Nazi period. It would be quite misleading to convey the impression to American readers that German or Austrian scholars have been negligent in studying their own recent history. Unfortunately, not much of this outstanding research work finds its way into the apparently insatiable Anglo-Saxon market for books on National Socialism.[15]

At several points in this book, the editors and authors allude to the lessons for the future that this dreadful history will hopefully convey. Of course, it is by no means self-evident or obvious that any lessons can be easily drawn by comparing events in Germany in the 1930s and early 1940s to the very altered democratic conditions of the genetic revolution in the present, although there are some startling continuities between the eugenics of the past and the eugenics of the present in, for example, the People's Republic of China. Most leading contemporary scientists are fully prepared to acknowledge the crimes of the Nazi past, which they rightly associate with both a certain progressive and snobbish fear of disorder and disorderly people on the part of the aristocrats of the intellectual Left, as well as with the collectivist eugenic engineering that so tantalized at least one of the totalitarian dictatorships of the past. But that is not really what is at issue in the genetic present.

There is a world of difference, which deserves more notice than it seems to receive, between the state deciding to "tidy up" individuals of whom the eugenic experts disapprove and society's current preoccupation with the awful dilemmas that chronically ill people or parents of severely handicapped children have to face. This is a discourse, as far as I can see, that deals solely with compassion for the suffering of individuals. Perhaps the key differences between the dictatorial Nazi past and the democratic genetic present and future are that present-day geneticists presumably do not operate with a blueprint for what the ideal person should be, lack any sense of collective social Darwinist notions of "racial" defense and offense, and are focused on the choices made freely by individuals or the suffering of individual patients. Such a concern was anathema to the collectivist-oriented physicians of Nazi Germany, who above all else were concerned with the health of a racially specific gene pool. Indeed, concern for individual patients accounts for those rare instances in which physicians refused to take part in the murder of their patients in the service of abstract objectives. Likewise, we should be skeptical of efforts to use the Nazi past to frustrate such developments as the legalization of voluntary euthanasia in the present. There are certainly many legitimate objections that one might make, on social or religious grounds, to the legalization of voluntary euthanasia, but constant invocation of the peculiar circumstances of Nazi Germany over half a century ago is not necessarily among them. If we take a far less familiar case, such as that of the Netherlands, the relevance of history is by no means self-evident.

Like Britain, the Netherlands is an example of a country that rejected the demands of its domestic eugenics lobby, chiefly on the grounds that the state had no role to play in individual reproduction. Dutch physicians—who played a noble role in resistance to Nazi wartime occupation, including being assimilated into German medical structures, which would have meant pressure to adopt the same heinous measures—actually knew virtually nothing about Nazi "euthanasia" policies. In fact, they only began to discuss the issue of euthanasia after a particularly controversial case in the early 1970s. In 1973, a doctor responded to the repeated requests of her chronically ill mother to give her a large dose of morphine. A trial and public debate ensued, in which the Dutch public, who are democratic, individualistic, and resistant to the paternalism of both the medical profession and the state, responded sympathetically to the accused physician. From 1974 onward, both the medical profession and the Dutch Ministry of Justice worked out criteria whereby although physician-assisted suicide is illegal, it is not pursued through the courts in practice. By 1998, these arrangements seem to have been endorsed by 90 percent of the Dutch public.

After a series of milestone test cases in the Netherlands Supreme Court, assisted suicide was effectively decriminalized by the Social Democrat-Liberal coalition government in August 1999. Doctors have to report cases in which they have helped patients to die, according to stringent conditions, which automatically triggers an investigation by regional euthanasia committees, appointed by the health and justice state secretaries. Special care has been taken to establish the prior consent of people who have lost the power of independent judgment, such as patients with Alzheimer's disease, while efforts to bring twelve- to sixteen-year-old minors within the scope of these measures—in the sense that if seriously ill, they can decide to end their lives regardless of parental objections—have yet to be determined. These discussions take place without any reference to events in Germany half a century earlier. It may be time to generalize the Dutch approach, which in terms of the tenor and tone of the debate seems eminently reasonable, insofar as the Dutch seem capable of discussing a series of important medical and social issues without the need to constantly invoke the horrors of Nazi medicine. Unfortunately, this is often not the case in the more charged atmosphere of North America, where individuals have been called "Nazis" when, like the parents of poor Nancy Cruzan, they have had to make agonizing private decisions about their unfortunate children. Nancy's parents were not and never will be "Nazis," so it is grotesque to even contemplate applying such loaded terminology to them.[16]

This concluding essay has involved highlighting the major themes in the book, while indicating areas that have not been included, notably eugenics in the contemporary world, or that have not been more fully developed, such as medical ethics or the wider philosophical setting. Without quite wishing to play the devil's advocate, I have also tentatively questioned the assumption that medical science in the Nazi period is, in any direct sense, relevant to what humankind is doing in the present, or may entertain in the future, for why should this dreadful, extreme case be of any greater (or lesser) "relevance" than the examples of past and present democratic societies such as Great Britain, France, or the Netherlands? Scientists are beginning to mutiny at the constant stream of "warnings from the Nazi past," to adapt the rather trite title of a recent British television series. There are things to be learned from the Nazi experience, but what those things are should be as demonstrable as any other scientific proof, rather than somehow assumed, as they often are in much historical discourse. This book is an excellent place to begin thinking about all of these issues.

Notes

1. Adrian Weale, *Science and the Swastika* (London: Channel 4 Books, 2001), 56–62.
2. Alice Platen-Hallermund, *Die Tötung Geisteskranker in Deutschland* (Bonn: Psychiatrie Verlag, 1998); Daniel J. Kevles, *In the Name of Eugenics: Genetics and the Uses of Human Heredity* (Cambridge, MA: Harvard University Press, 1985); Ernst Klee, *"Euthanasie" im NS-Staat: Die "Vernichtung lebensunwerten Lebens"* (Frankfurt am Main: S. Fischer Verlag, 1983).
3. Frank Dikoetter, *Imperfect Conceptions: Medical Knowledge, Birth Defects, and Eugenics in China* (New York: Columbia University Press, 1998).
4. See the excellent book by Edward J. Larson, *Sex, Race, and Science: Eugenics in the Deep South* (Baltimore: Johns Hopkins University Press, 1995), as well as Nancy L. Stepan, *"The Hour of Eugenics": Race, Gender, and Nation in Latin America* (Ithaca: Cornell University Press, 1991).
5. See Nicole Hahn Rafter, ed., *White Trash: The Eugenic Family Studies, 1877–1919* (Boston: Northeastern University Press, 1988).
6. Michael Burleigh "Eugenic Utopias and the Genetic Present," *Totalitarian Movements and Political Religions* 1 (2000): 56ff.
7. On Blumer, see Ian Robert Dowbiggin, *Keeping America Sane: Psychiatry and Eugenics in the United States and Canada 1880–1949* (Ithaca: Cornell University Press, 1997), 70ff.
8. I have explored these relationships at greater length in *The Third Reich: A New History* (New York: Hill and Wang, 2000).
9. Stefan Kühl, *The Nazi Connection: Eugenics, American Racism, and German National Socialism* (Oxford: Oxford University Press, 1994).

10. See the fascinating study by Jon Turney, *Frankenstein's Footsteps: Science, Genetics and Popular Culture* (New Haven: Yale University Press, 1998), 26–42.

11. G. K. Chesterton, *Eugenics and Other Evils* (London: Cassell, 1922), 294.

12. Michael Schwartz, *Sozialistische Eugenik: Eugenische Sozialtechnologien in Debatten und Politik der deutschen Sozialdemokratie 1890–1933* (Bonn: J.H.W. Dietz, 1995).

13. See the pioneering work of Hans Ludwig Siemen, *Menschen blieben auf der Strecke…: Psychiatrie zwischen Reform und Nationalsozialismus* (Gütersloh: J. van Haddis, 1987).

14. Hildegard Steppe, ed., *Krankenpflege im Nationalsozialismus* (Frankfurt am Main: Mabuse Verlag, 1989); Bronwyn Rebekah McFarland-Icke, *Nurses in Nazi Germany: Moral Choice in History* (Princeton: Princeton University Press, 1999).

15. Achim Thom and Genadij Ivanovic Caregorodcev, eds., *Medizin unterm Hakenkreuz* (Berlin: Verlag Volk und Geschichte, 1989); Heinz Faulstich, *Von der Irrenfürsorge zur "Euthanasie": Geschichte der badischen Psychiatrie bis 1945* (Freiburg im Breisgau: Lambertus, 1993); Bernhard Richarz, *Heilen-Pflegen-Töten: Zur Alltagsgeschichte einer Heil- und Pflegeanstalt bis zum Ende des Nationalsozialismus* (Göttingen: Vandenhoeck & Ruprecht, 1987).

16. See Gerrit K. Kimsma and Evert van Leeuwen, "Euthansie in den Niederlanden," in Andreas Frewer and Clemens Eickhoff, eds., *"Euthanasie" und die aktuelle Sterbehilfe-Debatte: Die historischen Hintergründe medizinischer Ethik* (Frankfurt am Main: Campus Verlag, 2000), 276ff. See also Gerald Dworkin, R. G. Frey, and Sissela Bok, eds., *Euthanasia and Physician-Assisted Suicide: For and Against* (Cambridge: Cambridge University Press, 1998), 122–127. I have discussed some of these issues in my "The Nazi Analogy and Contemporary Debates on Euthanasia," in *Ethics and Extermination: Reflections on Nazi Genocide* (Cambridge: Cambridge University Press, 1997), 142–152. The Netherlands Senate recently voted to approve a bill enabling physicians to end the lives of terminally ill patients in certain circumstances. Apparently, 90 percent of the Dutch population support this measure. See *The Guardian*, 11 April 2001.

APPENDIX

Speech given by the President of the
Max Planck Society for the Advancement of Science

Hubert Markl

on the occasion of the opening of the symposium entitled
"Biomedical Sciences and Human Experimentation at
Kaiser Wilhelm Institutes–The Auschwitz Connection"

Berlin, 7 June 2001

(Date of release: Thursday, 7 June 2001, 1:00 P.M.)

The role played by science during the Nazi dictatorship is one of the
many chapters of Germany's past that remains insufficiently unveiled
up to the present day. This also holds for the Kaiser Wilhelm Society as
predecessor of the Max Planck Society. The symposium entitled "Biomedical Sciences and Human Experimentation at Kaiser Wilhelm Institutes—The Auschwitz Connection" taking place this afternoon and
tomorrow is part of a research program based on selected instances and
scientifically examining the actions of the Kaiser Wilhelm Society and
its scientists during the period of National Socialism. This symposium
is therefore part of the Max Planck Society's efforts through the tool of
historical research to unreservedly reveal all the facts about its history,
thereby shedding light on the dark chapters of its own past. We must
be prepared as well—no matter how painful it may be, and even precisely because it hurts—to accept the truth and face up to our responsibility to learn for the present and the future from insight into the past.
We owe that above all to the victims of National Socialist ideology. We
owe it to the many who perished as much as we do to the few survivors.

Source: The Max Planck Society, http://www.mpg.de. This document is reprinted with
the permission of the Max Planck Society.

The existence of mere suspicions instead of established facts can easily give rise to distorted historical accounts, allow stubborn denial and glossing over to persist, and all too easily turn an admission of responsibility into pure lip service, whereas the unadulterated, historically documented knowledge of the crimes committed back then cannot be avoided. This is with certainty one area where the Max Planck Society and so many post—World War II organizations, companies, and institutions in Germany have failed. For way too long, many questions were not asked; for way too long, many connections remained uninvestigated or only dealt with by outsiders; and for way too long, many documents lay in the archives, either inaccessible because they remained classified or because people were all too glad to disregard them. For too long, colleagues supported each other by remaining silent and not asking questions instead of opening the door to honest investigation that was needed. Too many had collaboration with the Nazi dictatorship, either actively or passively, to the point where they were happy to hide their own joint responsibility or even complicity so that, undisturbed and unburdened, they could be a part of the new, democratic, post-war society.

Today's greater willingness to face up to the facts of the past is therefore not an expression of a hypocritically repetitive fault-finding attitude or even moralizing arrogance of the *Spätgeborene* (those too young at the time to possibly bear any guilt for the events of the day). Instead, it is the fulfillment of a duty which those who were directly involved and affected did not see themselves capable of performing for a long time or which they, having been directly associated with the events, shunned while those not involved exercised what they misperceived as consideration for others. Yet, we owe it to ourselves as well as the generations to come to no longer attempt to avoid the necessary investigation into the truth.

As an organization at the leading edge of German research, the Max Planck Society has a tremendous responsibility to do its part to uncover the past, particularly its own. On the one hand, it is true that the Max Planck Society was founded in 1948 at the behest and with the support of the American and British occupying forces quite intentionally as a new institution, a democratic organization for research in a new and democratic Germany. On the other hand, however, the Max Planck Society stood at the same time in many scientific aspects in the tradition of the Kaiser Wilhelm Society, for it felt obligated towards the best of scientific heritages that had been passed down to it and which it has

Appendix

sought to preserve to this very day. As far as personnel at the two organizations is concerned, there were also close ties due to the fact that many of the newly founded Max Planck Society's leading scientists had previously worked at Kaiser Wilhelm Institutes.

So, although today's Max Planck Society is not identical to the Kaiser Wilhelm Society, due to a significant number of connections between the two, it has without a doubt taken possession of its predecessor's inheritance in many aspects. Even the simple fact that the Society was named after Max Planck—one of the most outstanding physicists of the 20th century, a man of impeccable character, Nobel Prize laureate in 1918, President of the Kaiser Wilhelm Society from 1930 to 1937 and in 1945/46—was a deliberate expression of ideal continuity, but at the same time also one signifying a new moral beginning. Taking possession of an inheritance, however, means accepting responsibility for everything, both the positive—in particular the great scientific tradition of individuals named Adolf von Harnack, Albert Einstein, Lise Meitner, Max von Laue, or Max Planck—and the negative, which means, if need be, admitting guilt.

Over the past few decades, the Max Planck Society has launched a series of initiatives aimed at actively coming to grips with its past. For example, as early as the 1950s, we signed long-term cooperation agreements with Israel's Weizmann Institute, long before the Federal Republic of Germany was able to establish diplomatic relations with the nation of Israel. In 1973, we set up our own archive with the task of securing, examining, and making the files of the Kaiser Wilhelm and Max Planck Societies accessible to the public and, in particular, researchers, provided they meet certain legal requirements. In 1983, President Reimar Lüst gave inspiration to a *festschrift* [*sic*] in celebration of the Kaiser Wilhelm Society's 75th anniversary. It was edited by Rudolf Vierhaus and Bernhard vom Brocke, who used it to lay the foundation for further investigation. When it became known that tissue samples from victims of Nazi crimes were still in the possession of some Max Planck Institutes, the Max Planck Society, then under the leadership of Heinz Staab, did everything conceivable to establish the facts and to pay due respect to the victims. In 1990, their remains were ceremoniously laid to rest in a Munich cemetery, and a memorial was set up in their remembrance. On October 14 of last year, together with the Hermann von Helmholtz Association and the Deutsche Forschungsgemeinschaft, a memorial to the victims of "euthanasia" murder, and with that of blinded science, was unveiled in the Berlin suburb of Buch.

Following preparations by my predecessor, Hans Zacher, in 1997 I received permission from the Senate of the Max Planck Society to set up a research commission whose task would be to delve scientifically into the history of the Kaiser Wilhelm Society during the Nazi era and draw the most precise picture possible of the events of those days and their consequences. The commission's co-chairmen are Professors Reinhard Rürup of the Technical University of Berlin and Wolfgang Schieder of the University of Cologne. Both of these men are internationally respected historians, and neither of them—and this was of particular importance to us—is a member of the Max Planck Society. The remaining members of the commission are Professors Doris Kaufmann (of the University of Bremen), Hartmut Lehmann (MPI for History in Göttingen), Jürgen Renn (MPI for the History of Science in Berlin), Hans-Jörg Rheinberger (MPI for the History of Science in Berlin), Michael Stolleis (MPI for European Legal History, Frankfurt), Paul Weindling (Oxford Brookes University, Oxford), and Fritz Stern (Columbia University, New York). Jochen Frowein (MPI for International Law, Heidelberg, and Vice President of the Humanities Section of the Max Planck Society) is also a member of the commission. He takes the place of Franz Emanuel Weinert (MPI for Psychological Research, Munich, and former Vice President of the Max Planck Society), who passed away much too soon in March of this year. Without any outside influence from the administration of the Max Planck Society and having to answer only to the commission, guest scientists and doctoral candidates from Germany and abroad work together on the research program. Historian Dr. Carola Sachse is in charge of project management.

The commission and its workers have free access to all the files the Max Planck Society possesses. The commission puts out its own series of publications and holds public lectures, symposiums, and workshops in order to generate discussion of the results of its work among not just the scientific community but the general public as well. Its members are aware that the task of scientifically clearing up the Kaiser Wilhelm Society's role in the Third Reich can never be accomplished on its own. It reviews and evaluates the status of research on specific fields of related topics, it compiles its own reports, it brings initiatives for further research work and sees to it that they are carried out or that the work is performed by a separate body. No matter how costly and ambitious a research program may be, it could hardly evaluate all the sources and illuminate all the aspects on its own with limited time and limited resources. Confronting the history of Nazism is primarily a permanent task for the science of history and the whole of German society, a task with which they see themselves faced over and over again.

Bit by bit, the commission's fact-finding mission will, however, be able to bring confirmation to the areas where previously there was often no more than suspicion. It can lay a strong foundation based on fact, one that will enable assessments to go beyond the general expression of dismay at the crimes committed during the Nazi era. It can contribute to uncovering the names of victims and perpetrators. Most of all, it can attempt to expose their motives and the reasons for their moral failure. It will be able to provide concrete documentation of guilt, thereby fulfilling the prerequisite for an honest confrontation with the past. However, it should also make it clear to see those areas where moral character and scientific ethos caused people to resist the temptation of research opportunities that we describe in German as *entgrenzt,* an adjective literally meaning "with its borders removed" but indicating something morally unrestricted, in particular the research and experiments conducted by the Nazis.

The Kaiser Wilhelm Society and its administration were a part of the times back then. Therefore, the diverse facets of political and social reality in those days were also reflected in the reality of the Kaiser Wilhelm Society. Yet, one cannot judge or condemn the people of Germany as a whole any more than one can view the Kaiser Wilhelm Society without making any distinctions, for that would not do it or its key players real justice. It was deeply imbedded in the National Socialist thinking and prejudices of its time—even those which it claimed to be studying and justifying through science—just as they were widespread in other countries. It is for that very reason we are left with the task of explaining why, of all places, it was in Germany—in those days at the peak of scientific civilization—that opinions turned into incendiary slogans, preconceived notions into condemnation, more or less abstruse theories into actions, and chauvinistic literature into bloody crimes.

Dealing with historical responsibility requires from us Germans a high degree of sensitivity. Even though most of us today cannot be held personally responsible since we were born later, it remains the task of today's and all future generations to look the historical truth in the eye. When doing so, we must insure that guilt and responsibility do not degenerate into empty words of politically correct rhetoric by either demanding or giving confessions in an abstract manner, so lacking in specific reference to deeds and perpetrators that, to make up for it, they are given even stronger moral impetus. That is why I have always placed great importance on investigating and examining past events with all due diligence of historical science first before carrying out an evaluation on the scientifically secure foundation of historical fact.

The research program, set up to be carried out over a period of five years, was opened in March 1999 with a four-day conference taking place to review current research and give interpretive perspectives on the history of science under National Socialism. Numerous internationally renowned historians from Germany and abroad carried out a survey based on the level of research up to that point of what had been discovered and documented about the role played by the Kaiser Wilhelm Society and other organizations in National Socialism. The results of the conference were published in an anthology and thus documented and made accessible for anyone. The title of this German volume is "Geschichte der Kaiser-Wilhelm-Gesellschaft im Nationalsozialismus. Bestandsaufnahme und Perspektiven der Forschung," which means "History of the Kaiser Wilhelm Society during National Socialism. Portrait and perspectives in research [*sic*]," edited by Doris Kaufmann, (Göttingen, 2000).

The commission chose to first focus its work on the field of biomedicine and the research into and practical application of racial biology. They made a correct and obvious choice, because this is where one can most clearly see in what way and to what extent German researchers at the time were involved with the Nazi regime. Furthermore, the field of biomedicine is where the largest number of people fell victim to science in the most horrible ways and where the rejection of science's moral boundaries due to the Nazis' racial mania becomes most directly obvious. For certain, there are many faces—and not just German ones—and deep roots—and by no means just German ones—to inhumane racism. There has been exploitation and enslavement, oppression and rape, as well as torture and mass murder to the point of genocide for reasons of racial arrogance and hatred. There were "master races" who subjected their "slave races" to agony and atrocities with a clear conscience and afterwards went unpunished. These are neither merely German nor modern depravities of a godlessly rootless society, and they are unfortunately also not ones that ceased to exist along with the Third Reich. We scientists, however, should consider one particular form of such malignant racism even worse than all the other atrocities in the catalog of humanity's sins. Because we think of science as one of mankind's greatest achievements—and rightfully so—we ought to shudder at the thought of scientifically justified racism and the allegedly scientifically justified practice of human extermination even more than at all other forms of torturous degradation and deprivation of a fellow human being's rights. For there is no crime worse than highly intelligent people with sound minds, cold hearts, and dead consciences with absolutely no compassion mistreating other people worse than animals and killing them while professing to be contributing to the search for scientific knowledge. Criminal acts of this kind are an inextinguishable shame, not only for those who perpetrated them, but also for all those who tolerated them, and in fact, for the life sciences themselves, in the name of which they were committed, and shame of this kind will continue to live as long as one remembers it.

Building upon the already weighty level of research, the commission has managed to collect extensive information during its work. First of all, it has been able to confirm some of what was suspected up to this point. Secondly, additional knowledge has been gained in some important areas. After two years now, there is scientific evidence historically proving beyond the shadow of a doubt that directors and employees at Kaiser Wilhelm Institutes co-masterminded and sometimes even actively participated in the crimes of the Nazi regime, thus allowing— indeed demanding—clear recognition of these facts. The Max Planck Society, as the Kaiser Wilhelm Society's "heir," must face up to these historical facts and, together with them, its moral responsibility. As President of the Max Planck Society, I would therefore like to make an assessment and publicly substantiate it here today.

As far as we know, the Kaiser Wilhelm Society as a whole did not pass any resolutions via its board of directors or other bodies to take an active part in criminal research work. Nevertheless, it did either knowingly or unknowingly tolerate directors and leading scientists at several Kaiser Wilhelm Institutes as they, by their own endeavor, promoted and took an active role in the racist policies of those in power at the time. The activities revolved especially (but not exclusively) around the Kaiser Wilhelm Institute for Anthropology, Human Genetics, and Eugenics in Berlin, the Kaiser Wilhelm Institute for Brain Research in the Berlin suburb of Buch, and the German Research Institute for Psychiatry in Munich. As far as we have been able to determine with a high degree of assurance, the activities transpired in three fields in particular.

1. Nazi racial legislation, including the revolting 1935 Nuremberg Laws, and its practical application for purposes of "racial hygiene" was supported and sometimes even initiated by a number of

directors and employees at Kaiser Wilhelm Institutes, such as Ernst Rüdin or Eugen Fischer.

2. Involvement in criminal euthanasia based on eugenics and "racial hygiene" or even the mere use of killed victims for scientific experiments by Kaiser Wilhelm scientists such as Hugo Spatz or Julius Hallervorden was a clear and indubitable violation of the boundaries of ethically responsible research.

3. This also holds for knowingly and willingly using without permission the allegedly scientific research facilities at Nazi coercive institutions, be they psychiatric clinics or concentration camps like Auschwitz. These especially included certain projects involving studies conducted on twins at the Kaiser Wilhelm Institute for Anthropology, under the administration of Otmar von Verschuer beginning in 1942. Although concentration camp doctor Josef Mengele was not working as an employee or on behalf of the Kaiser Wilhelm Society, he was a protege of Otmar von Verschuer's, under whom he had earned his doctorate in 1938 at the University of Frankfurt. Even after that, they maintained close contact with one another, as various documents clearly show. We may never be able to clear up all the details of their relationship, but today, it is safe to say that Verschuer knew that crimes were being committed at Auschwitz, that he and his employees used the victims for scientific purposes, and that he probably had an active influence on how these crimes were carried out. The results of the Presidential commission's research on this topic have been recorded and published. One title in particular by Doctors Carola Sachse and Benoit Massin would be in English "Life Science Research at Kaiser Wilhelm Institutes and the Crimes of the Nazi Regime. Information on the Current Level of Knowledge," (Berlin 2000). Among other things, the symposium taking place this afternoon and tomorrow will also be dealing with how these details are connected.

Verschuer and others attempted to justify actions violating every known human right by offering the excuse that they were serving the best interests of science. Leading German scientists—from within the Kaiser Wilhelm Society as well—cooperated in the preparation of Nazi crimes, and they used them to pursue their scientific goals beyond every moral boundary of humanity. They contributed to innocent people, many of them children, being torn away from their families, humiliated, tortured, and even murdered. The assessment of their guilt in legal terms is the responsibility of the courts in a society governed by the rule of law. Historians can only determine collaboration and responsibility. When viewing the past with human compassion, one should shudder at the thought of such inhumanity taking on the guise of scientific research.

What lessons and consequences can we draw from all this today? For one thing, we have to be aware that every realm of science has to have its moral bounds. We need to understand that scientists can become guilty of crime and how that happens. The history of the Kaiser Wilhelm Society during the period of National Socialism in Germany demonstrates how science can become involved in devising, preparing, and even actively participating in the most abominable crimes and the brutalization of scientific research that degrades human beings to mere objects of experimentation. For us as scientists, this is a warning to never forget there is no goal of research that can be viewed as so important and high-ranking that it justifies seriously restricting or completely disregarding another person's dignity or human rights against their [*sic*] will. The boundaries of freedom in science are delineated by the inalienable rights and inviolable dignity of human beings.

For another, I am forced by the findings of the research into the history of involvement and guilt of a number of scientists working at Kaiser Wilhelm Institutes at the time to both personally and as President of the Max Planck Society state my position on the events that took place. I feel it as a moral obligation that has been placed upon the Max Planck Society in accordance with its responsibility as the Kaiser Wilhelm Society's "heir," and I feel it as a German scientist—especially as a biologist—in the presence of victims of those inhumane experiments carried out at the time by German life scientists or on their orders.

A sincere confession of our historical responsibility must be expressed clearly, but it must equally include clear differentiation. In retrospect, I see three levels of guilt.

1. The guilt of German scientists:

> At the time, Germany was at the global forefront of many fields of science. The work done by the commission has made evident that even leading-edge research is not invulnerable to moral abysses. What took place then in the name of science for the purpose of promoting racism and allegedly "eugenic" human expurgation were crimes that will forever weigh heavily on German science.

2. The guilt of life scientists:

National Socialism's entire body of racist thought is an expression of a materialistic, Social Darwinist, dehumanized form of biology, for which Charles Darwin himself, however, in contrast to his racist disciples, is the last one who can be held responsible. For certain, the roots of this body of ideas were planted before 1933 and were even international and not just confined to Germany. But, here in Germany, doctors and biologists, having accepted that man descended from animals, went one step further: to treating human beings like animals. The guilt for utilizing human beings as laboratory animals can be specifically placed on biomedical science that was robbed of every moral boundary, a science whose racist theories do indeed not deserve to be called "scientific," but which cannot deny that it is also to blame for the terrible consequences to which they led.

3. The guilt of the Kaiser Wilhelm Society:

As I already outlined at the beginning, the Max Planck Society was intentionally founded after the war to be a new organization in order to enable science to have a fresh start in a new, democratic Germany. However, due to the fact that the Max Planck Society sees itself as the Kaiser Wilhelm Society's "heir," it has the obligation to admit its guilt as well. The Kaiser Wilhelm Society tolerated or even promoted within its ranks research that was not to be justified for any ethical or moral reasons. Thus, it placed itself—at least in a number of areas—in the service of a criminal regime, thereby taking upon itself the moral guilt for assisting in such crimes.

By confessing this three-fold historical responsibility, I, as a German scientist, life scientist, and President of the Max Planck Society, am fulfilling the obligation that has been placed upon us by the past. Therefore, I wish to apologize for the suffering inflicted upon the victims of these crimes in the name of science—to those who perished and have since passed away and the ones who have survived.

I do not make such an apology lightly. Though many people today are quite quick to think of demanding an apology and then give immediate expression to their thoughts, if one is to truly mean what is expressed by the English phrase "excuse me," namely the "removal of guilt," then one cannot remain silent concerning one's doubts. Most people apologize by saying, "Excuse me," or "I'm sorry," when they offend someone, say something wrong, or—either literally or figuratively—step one someone's toes. But can a perpetrator of heinous crimes against humanity really make an apology? Certainly, he can if he feels sincere remorse for his deeds. However, can another person feel that remorse in the offender's place, especially if the one who committed the crime perhaps felt none at all? Is there no such thing as an injustice so inexcusable that any apology seems to be shedding responsibility? As I stand here and apologize both personally and on behalf of the Max Planck Society in proxy for the Kaiser Wilhelm Society, I am referring to the sincere expression of deepest regret, compassion, and shame at the fact that crimes of this sort were committed, promoted, and not prevented within the ranks of German scientists.

There is something else I must add. The members of later generations may not be able to be held personally responsible for the events that took place back then, but they carry the responsibility for exposing and shedding light on the historical truth as a precondition for honest remembrance and learning. The fact that, for a long time, this did not take place to the desired extent within the Max Planck Society is for certain only partially due to classified documents having remained in the archives. It is certainly due to a lack of willingness on the part of some accessories or even accomplices inside and outside the Max Planck Society to face up to their historical responsibility. The Max Planck Society must also admit its fault in this area, for which I offer a very special apology, for it did not happen under the constraints of dictatorship, but in a free society which expressly guarantees and encourages freedom of research.

An admission of guilt is only concrete and complete once it has been spoken directly to those who have been injured, the ill-treated victims who suffered all these unimaginable atrocities with their very own minds and bodies. Therefore, both personally and on behalf of the Max Planck Society, allow me to express my deepest regrets to you, Mrs. Kor; to you, Mrs. Laks; and to the other victims in attendance, for today you are representing in a sense the victims in their entirety. I am very sorry.

It is a painful way to meet the past when one personally stands face to face with the victims of those crimes. At the same time, we feel growing in us a most enduring dedication to continue making every effort to unreservedly elucidate what happened back then, and it serves as a most permanent admonition to preserve the memory of it and, by teaching from what we remember, to learn together with others. Though truth does not set one free from guilt and shame, it releases one from repression and lying and opens the door to a future that can learn from the past.

The most honest form of apology is therefore exposing guilt; for scientists this ought to be perhaps the most appropriate form of apology. In actuality, the perpetrator is the only one who can ask for forgiveness. Nevertheless, I beg you, the surviving victims, from the bottom of my heart to forgive those who, no matter what their reasons, failed to ask you themselves.

CONTRIBUTORS

Garland E. Allen is Professor of Biology at Washington University in St. Louis. He is the author of *Life Science in the Twentieth Century* (Cambridge University Press, 1975), *Thomas Hunt Morgan, the Man and His Science* (Princeton University Press, 1978), and other works on the history of genetics, evolution, and eugenics.

Michael Burleigh is Distinguished Research Professor of History at Cardiff University in Wales. His books include *Death and Deliverance: "Euthanasia" in Germany, c. 1900–1945* (Cambridge University Press, 1994), *Ethics and Extermination: Reflections on Nazi Genocide* (Cambridge University Press, 1997), and *The Third Reich: A New History* (Hill and Wang, 2000).

Henry Friedlander is Professor of History in the Department of Judaic Studies, Brooklyn College, City University of New York. He is the author of *The Origins of Nazi Genocide: From Euthanasia to the Final Solution* (University of North Carolina Press, 1995), and the general coeditor with Sybil Milton of the multivolume *Archives of the Holocaust: An International Collection of Selected Documents* (Garland Publishers, 1990–1995).

Jonathan Huener is Assistant Professor of History at the University of Vermont, and is completing a book on the history of the Auschwitz memorial site and museum (Ohio University Press).

Michael H. Kater is Distinguished Research Professor of History and Social and Political Thought at the Canadian Centre for German and European Studies, York University, Toronto, Canada, and a Fellow of the Royal Society of Canada. His books include *The Nazi Party: A Social Profile of Members and Leaders, 1919–1945* (Blackwell, 1985);

Doctors Under Hitler (University of North Carolina Press, 1989), which won the Hannah Medal of the Royal Society of Canada; and *Composers of the Nazi Era: Eight Portraits* (Oxford University Press, 2000).

Francis R. Nicosia is Professor of History at Saint Michael's College in Vermont. He is author of *The Third Reich and the Palestine Question* (Transaction Publishers, 2000), coauthor with Donald Niewyk of *The Columbia Guide to the Holocaust* (Columbia University Press, 2000), and coeditor with Lawrence Stokes of *Germans Against Nazism: Non-Conformity, Opposition, and Resistance in the Third Reich* (Berg, 1990).

Robert N. Proctor is Distinguished Professor of the History of Science at Pennsylvania State University. His books include *Racial Hygiene: Medicine Under the Nazis* (Harvard University Press, 1988); *Cancer Wars: How Politics Shapes What We Know and Don't Know about Cancer* (Basic Books, 1995), and *The Nazi War on Cancer* (Princeton University Press, 1999).

William E. Seidelman is Professor of Family and Community Medicine at the University of Toronto and attending physician at the Baycrest Centre for Geriatric Care in Toronto. An internationally noted authority on the history of medicine in the Third Reich and the continuing legacy of that era, he has published papers on this subject in the *British Medical Journal, Journal of the American Medical Association,* the *Milbank Quarterly,* and most recently, *Perspectives in Biology and Medicine.*

SELECTED BIBLIOGRAPHY

Eugenics

Adams, Mark B., ed. *The Wellborn Science: Eugenics in Germany, France, Brazil and Russia.* New York: Oxford University Press, 1990.

Allen, Garland E. "The Eugenics Record Office at Cold Spring Harbor, 1910–1940: An Essay in Institutional History." *Osiris* (2nd Series) 2 (1986): 225–264.

Chase, Allan. *The Legacy of Malthus.* New York: Alfred A. Knopf, 1977.

Chesterton, G. K. *Eugenics and Other Evils.* London: Cassell, 1922.

Davenport, Charles B. *Eugenics.* New York: Henry Holt, 1910.

———. *Heredity in Relation to Eugenics.* New York: Henry Holt, 1911.

Dikoetter, Frank. *Imperfect Conceptions: Medical Knowledge, Birth Defects, and Eugenics in China.* New York: Columbia University Press, 1998.

Dowbiggin, Ian Robert. *Keeping America Sane: Psychiatry and Eugenics in the United States and Canada, 1880–1949.* Ithaca: Cornell University Press, 1997.

Duster, Troy. *Back Door to Eugenics.* New York: Routledge, 1990.

Gallagher, Nancy. *Breeding Better Vermonters: The Eugenics Project in the Green Mountain State.* Hanover and London: University Press of New England, 1999.

Haller, Mark. *Eugenics: Hereditarian Attitudes in American Thought.* New Brunswick, NJ: Rutgers University Press, 1963.

Harwood, Jonathan. *Styles of Scientific Thought: The German Genetics Community, 1900–1933.* Chicago: University of Chicago Press, 1993.

Kevles, Daniel J. *In the Name of Eugenics: Genetics and the Uses of Human Heredity.* Cambridge, MA: Harvard University Press, 1985.

Kimmelman, Barbara A. "The American Breeders' Association: Genetics and Eugenics in an Agricultural Context, 1903–1913." *Social Studies of Science* 13 (1983): 163–204.

Kühl, Stefan. *The Nazi Connection: Eugenics, American Racism and German National Socialism.* New York: Oxford University Press, 1994.

Larson, Edward J. *Sex, Race, and Science: Eugenics in the Deep South.* Baltimore: Johns Hopkins University Press, 1998.

Lens, Sydney. *The Labor Wars.* New York: Doubleday, 1973.

Mazumdar, Pauline M. H. *Eugenics, Human Genetics and Human Failings: The Eugenics Society, Its Sources and Its Critics in Britain.* London: Routledge, 1992.

McClaren, Angus. *Our Own Master Race: Eugenics in Canada, 1885–1945.* Toronto: McClelland and Stewart, 1990.

Morgan, Thomas Hunt. *Evolution and Genetics.* Princeton: Princeton University Press, 1925.

Paul, Diane. "Eugenics and the Left." *Journal of the History of Ideas* 45 (1984): 567–590.

———. *Controlling Heredity, 1865 to the Present.* Atlantic Highlands, NJ: Humanities Press International, 1995.

Rafter, Nicole Hahn, ed. *White Trash: The Eugenic Family Studies, 1877–1919.* Boston: Northeastern University Press, 1988.

Reilly, Philip. *The Surgical Solution: A History of Involuntary Sterilization in the United States.* Baltimore: Johns Hopkins University Press, 1992.

Robitscher, Jonas. *Eugenic Sterilization.* Springfield, IL: Charles C. Thomas, 1973.

Roll-Hansen, Nils. "Eugenic Sterilization: A Preliminary Comparison of the Scandinavian Experience to That of Germany." *Genome* 31 (1989): 890–895.

Schwartz, Michael. *Sozialistische Eugenik: Eugenische Sozialtechnologien in Debatten und Politik der deutschen Sozialdemokratie 1890–1933.* Bonn: J.H.W. Dietz, 1995.

Selden, Steven. *Inheriting Shame: The Story of Eugenics and Racism in America.* New York: Teachers College Press, 1999.

Shevell, Michael. "Racial Hygiene, Active Euthanasia, and Julius Hallervorden." *Neurology* 42 (1992): 2214–2219.

Stepan, Nancy L. *'The Hour of Eugenics': Race, Gender, and Eugenics in Latin America.* Ithaca: Cornell University Press, 1991.

Turney, Jon. *Frankenstein's Footsteps: Science, Genetics, and Popular Culture.* New Haven: Yale University Press, 1998.

Weindling, Paul. *Health, Race and German Politics between National Unification and Nazism, 1870–1945.* Cambridge: Cambridge University Press, 1989.

Weingart, P. "German Eugenics between Science and Politics." *Osiris* (2nd Series) 5 (1989): 260–282.

———. "Weimar Eugenics: The Kaiser Wilhelm Institute for Anthropology, Human Heredity and Eugenics in Social Context." *Annals of Science* 42 (1985): 303–318.

Weiss, Sheila. *Race Hygiene and National Efficiency: The Eugenics of William Schallmayer.* Berkeley: University of California Press, 1987.

———. "The Race Hygiene Movement in Germany." *Osiris* 3 (1987): 193–236.

Selected Bibliography

Racism and Anti-Semitism

Arendt, Hannah. *The Origins of Totalitarianism.* Part I: *Antisemitism.* New York: Harcourt Brace Jovanovich, 1973.

Bankier, David, ed. *Probing the Depths of German Antisemitism: German Society and the Persecution of the Jews, 1933–1941.* New York: Berghahn Books, 2000.

Barkan, Elazar. *The Retreat of Scientific Racism: Changing Concepts of Race in Britain and the United States between the World Wars.* Cambridge: Cambridge University Press, 1992.

Efron, John. *Defenders of Race: Jewish Doctors and Race Science in Fin de Siècle Europe.* New Haven: Yale University Press, 1994.

Field, Geoffrey. *Evangelist of Race: The Germanic Vision of Houston Stewart Chamberlain.* New York: Columbia University Press, 1981.

Hertzberg, Arthur. *The French Enlightenment and the Jews: The Origins of Modern Antisemitism.* New York: Columbia University Press, 1990.

Massing, Paul. *Rehearsal for Destruction: A Study of Political Antisemitism in Imperial Germany.* New York: Harper, 1949.

Mosse, George. *Toward the Final Solution: A History of European Racism.* New York: Harper & Row, 1978.

———. *The Crisis of German Ideology: Intellectual Origins of the Third Reich.* New York: Schocken, 1981.

Poliakov, Leon. *The Aryan Myth: A History of Racist and Nationalist Ideas in Europe.* New York: Basic Books, 1971.

Pulzer, Peter. *The Rise of Political Antisemitism in Germany and Austria.* Cambridge, MA.: Harvard University Press, 1988.

Rose, Paul Lawrence. *German Question—Jewish Question: Revolutionary Antisemitism from Kant to Wagner.* Princeton: Princeton University Press, 1992.

Stern, Fritz. *The Politics of Cultural Despair: A Study of the Rise of Germanic Ideology.* Berkeley: University of California Press, 1961.

Zimmermann, Moshe. *Wilhelm Marr: The Patriarch of Antisemitism.* New York: Oxford University Press, 1986.

Physicians and the Crimes of the German Medical Establishment

Annas, George, and Michael Grodin. *The Nazi Doctors and the Nuremberg Code: Human Rights in Human Experimentation.* New York: Oxford University Press, 1992.

Boehncke, Georg. *Die gesetzlichen Grundlagen der Bekämpfung des Tabakmissbrauches in Deutschland.* Berlin: Wacht Verlag, 1937.

———. *Die Bedeutung der Tabakfrage für das deutsche Volk.* Berlin: Reichsausschuss für Volksgesundheitsdienst, 1939.

Breggin, Peter. *Toxic Psychiatry.* New York: St. Martin's Press, 1991.

Burleigh, Michael. *Death and Deliverance: "Euthanasia" in Germany, c. 1900–1945.* Cambridge: Cambridge University Press, 1994.

Caplan, Arthur L., ed. *When Medicine Went Mad: Bioethics and the Holocaust.* Totowa, NJ: Humana Press, 1992.

Ebbinghaus, Angelika. "Dokumentation: Die Ärztin Herta Oberheuser und die kriegschirurgischen Experimente im Frauen-Konzentrationslager Ravensbrück." In *Opfer und Täterinnen: Frauenbiographien des National-sozialismus,* edited by idem, 313–343. Frankfurt am Main: Fischer Taschenbuch Verlag, 1996.

"Erkennung und Bekämpfung der Tabakgefahren." *Deutsches Ärzteblatt* 71 (1941): 183–185.

Faulstich, Heinz. *Von der Irrenfürsorge zur "Euthanasie". Geschichte der badis-che Psychiatrie bis 1945.* Freiburg im Breisgau: Lambertus, 1993.

Friedlander, Henry. *The Origins of Nazi Genocide: From Euthanasia to the Final Solution.* Chapel Hill: University of North Carolina Press, 1995.

———. "Step by Step: The Expansion of Murder, 1939–1941." *German Studies Review* 17 (1994): 495–507.

———. "Die Entwicklung der Mordtechnik: Von der 'Euthanasie' zu den Vernichtungslagern der 'Endlösung.'" In *Die nationalsozialistischen Konzentrationslager: Entwicklung und Struktur,* edited by Ulrich Herbert, Karin Orth, and Christoph Dieckmann. 2 vols. Vol. 1, 493–507. Göttingen: Wallstein Verlag, 1998.

———. "Motive, Formen und Konsequenzen der NS-Euthanasie." In *NS-Euthanasie in Wien,* edited by Eberhard Gabriel and Wolfgang Neugebauer, 47–59. Vienna: Böhlau Verlag, 2000,

Gabriel, Eberhard, and Wolfgang Neugebauer, eds. *NS-Euthanasie in Wien.* Vienna: Böhlau Verlag, 2000.

Gallagher, Hugh. *By Trust Betrayed: Patients, Physicians, and the License to Kill in the Third Reich.* New York: Henry Holt, 1990.

Hüttig, Werner. "Der Einfluss der Genussgifte auf das Erbgut und seine Entwicklung (Alkohol und Nikotin)." *Öffentlicher Gesundheitsdienst* 1 (1935): 169–171.

Israel, Howard, and William Seidelman. "Nazi Origins of an Anatomy Text: The Pernkopf Atlas." *Journal of the American Medical Association* 276 (1996): 1633.

Kater, Michael. *Doctors Under Hitler.* Chapel Hill: University of North Carolina Press, 1989.

———. *Das "Ahnenerbe" der SS, 1935–1945: Ein Beitrag zur Kulturpolitik des Dritten Reiches.* 2nd ed. Munich: R. Oldenbourg, 1997.

———. "Dr. Leonardo Conti and His Nemesis: The Failure of Centralized Medicine in the Third Reich." *Central European History* 18 (1985): 299–325.

———. "Hitler's Early Doctors: Nazi Physicians in Pre-Depression Germany." *Journal of Modern History* 59 (1987): 25–52.

————. "Medizin und Mediziner im Dritten Reich: Eine Bestandsaufnahme." *Historische Zeitschrift* 244 (1987): 299–352.

Kersting, Franz-Werner. *Anstaltsärzte zwischen Kaiserreich und Bundesrepublik: das Beispiel Westfalen.* Paderborn: F. Schöningh, 1996.

Kittel, Walther. "Hygiene des Rauchens." In *Wehrhygiene,* edited by Siegfried Handloser and Wilhelm Hoffmann, 242–248. Berlin: Springer, 1944.

Klarner, Wolfgang. *Vom Rauchen: Eine Sucht und ihre Bekämpfung.* Nürnberg: Kern, 1940.

Klee, Ernst. *"Euthanasie" im NS-Staat: Die "Vernichtung lebensunwerten Lebens."* Frankfurt am Main: S. Fischer Verlag, 1983.

————. *Auschwitz, die NS-Medizin und ihre Opfer.* Frankfurt am Main: S. Fischer Verlag, 1997.

Kubica, Helena. "The Crimes of Josef Mengele." In *Anatomy of the Auschwitz Death Camp,* edited by Yisrael Gutman and Michael Berenbaum, 317–337. Bloomington: Indiana University Press, 1998.

Lickint, Fritz. *Tabak und Organismus.* Stuttgart: Hippokrates Verlag, 1939.

Lifton, Robert Jay. *The Nazi Doctors: Medical Killing and the Psychology of Genocide.* New York: Basic Books, 1986.

————. "Medicalized Killing in Auschwitz." *Psychiatry* 45 (1982): 383–397.

Lifton, Robert Jay, and Amy Hackett. "Nazi Doctors." In *Anatomy of the Auschwitz Death Camp,* edited by Yisrael Gutman and Michael Berenbaum, 301–316. Bloomington: Indiana University Press, 1998.

McFarland-Icke, Bronwyn Rebekah. *Nurses in Nazi Germany: Moral Choice in History.* Princeton: Princeton University Press, 1999.

Müller-Hill, Benno. *Murderous Science: Elimination by Scientific Selection of Jews, Gypsies and Others, Germany 1933–1945.* New York: Oxford University Press, 1988.

Nyiszli, Miklos. *Auschwitz: A Doctor's Eyewitness Account of Mengele's Infamous Death Camp.* New York: Arcade, 1993.

Peiffer, J. "Neuropathology in the Third Reich: Memorial to Those Victims of National Socialist Atrocities in Germany Who Were Used by Medical Science." *Brain Pathology* 1 (1991): 125–131.

————. "Assessing Neuropathological Research Carried out on Victims of the 'Euthanasia' Program." *Medical History Journal* 34 (1999): 339–356.

Platen-Hallermund, Alice. *Die Tötung Geisteskranker in Deutschland.* Bonn: Psychiatrie Verlag, 1998.

Platzer, Werner, ed. *Pernkopf Anatomy: Atlas of Topographic and Applied Human Anatomy.* 3rd ed. Baltimore and Munich: Urban & Schwarzenberg, 1989.

Proctor, Robert. *Racial Hygiene: Medicine Under the Nazis.* Cambridge, MA: Harvard University Press, 1988.

————. *The Nazi War on Cancer.* Princeton: Princeton University Press, 1999.

Richarz, Bernhard. *Heilen-Pflegen-Töten: Zur Alltagsgeschichte einer Heil- und Pflegeanstalt bis zum Ende des Nationalsozialismus*. Göttingen: Vandenhoeck & Ruprecht, 1987.

Roland, Charles, Benno Müller-Hill, and Henry Friedlander, eds. *Medical Science Without Compassion, Past and Present*. Hamburg: Hamburger Stiftung für Sozialgeschichte des 20. Jahrhunderts, 1992.

Schmidt, Gerhard. *Selektion in der Heilanstalt, 1939–1945*. 2nd ed. Frankfurt am Main: Edition Suhrkamp, 1983.

Schwarberg, Günther. *Der SS-Artz und die Kinder: Bericht über den Mord vom Bullenhuser Damm*. Hamburg: Gruner und Jahr, 1979.

Seidelman, William. "Medical Selection: Auschwitz Antecedents and Effluent." *Holocaust and Genocide Studies* 4 (1989): 435–448.

———. "Medicine and Murder in the Third Reich." *Dimensions: A Journal of Holocaust Studies* 13 (1999): 9–13.

———. "Medicine and the Holocaust: Physician Involvement in Genocide." In *Encyclopedia of Genocide*, edited by Israel Charney, 412–415. Santa Barbara: ABC-CLIO, 2000.

Sieman, Hans Ludwig. *Menschen blieben auf der Strecke…: Psychiatrie zwischen Reform und Nationalsozialismus*. Gütersloh: J. van Haddis, 1987.

Spann, Gustav. "Untersuchungen zur anatomischen Wissenschaft in Wien 1938–1945: Senatsprojekt der Universität Wien: Eine Zusammenfassung." *Dokumentationsarchiv des Österreichischen Widerstandes Jahrbuch 1999*, 43–52.

Steppe, Hildegard, ed. *Krankenpflege im Nationalsozialismus*. Frankfurt am Main: Mabuse Verlag, 1989.

Thom, Achim, and Genadij Ivanovic Caregorodcev, eds. *Medizin unterm Hakenkreuz*. Berlin: Verlag Volk und Geschichte, 1989.

Walter, Bernd. *Psychiatrie und Gesellschaft in der Moderne: Geisteskrankenfürsorge in der Provinz Westfalen zwischen Kaiserreich und NS-Regime*. Paderborn: F. Schöningh, 1996.

Weber, Mathias. "Ernst Rüdin, 1874–1952: A German Psychiatrist and Geneticist." *American Journal of Medical Genetics (Neuropsychiatric Genetics)* 67 (1996): 323–331.

Zerbin-Rudin, Edith, and Kenneth S. Kendler, "Ernst Rüdin (1874–1952) and His Geneologic Department in Munich (1917–1986): An Introduction to their Family Studies of Schizophrenia." *American Journal of Medical Genetics (Neuropsychiatric Genetics)* 67 (1996): 332–337.

Legacy

Gottesman, I., and A. Bertelsen, "A Legacy of German Psychiatric Genetics: Hindsight Is 20/20." *American Journal of Medical Genetics (Neuropsychiatric Genetics)* 67 (1996): 317–322.

———. "Unresolved Questions of German Medicine and Medical History in the Past and Present." *Central European History* 25 (1992): 407–423.

Kolb, Stephan, and Horst Seithe, eds. *Medizin und Gewissen: 50 Jahre nach dem Nürnberger Ärzteprozess – Kongressdokumentation.* Frankfurt am Main: Mabuse Verlag, 1998.

Ludmerer, Kenneth. *Genetics and American Society: A Historical Appraisal.* Baltimore: Johns Hopkins University Press, 1972.

Malina, Peter. "Eduard Pernkopfs Anatomie oder: Die Fiktion einer 'reinen' Wissenschaft." *Wiener Klinische Wochenschrift* 109 (1997): 935–943.

Neugebauer, Wolfgang, and Georg Stacher. "Nazi Child 'Euthanasia' in Vienna and the Scientific Exploitation of Its Victims before and after 1945." *Digestive Diseases* 17 (1999): 279–285.

Seidelman, William. "The Legacy of Academic Medicine and Human Exploitation in the Third Reich." *Perspectives in Biology and Medicine* 43 (2000): 325–334.

———. "Erinnerung, Medizin und Moral. Die Bedeutung der Ausbeutung des menschlichen Körpers im Dritten Reich." In *NS-Euthanasie in Wien,* edited by Eberhard Gabriel and Wolfgang Neugebauer, 27–46. Vienna: Böhlau Verlag, 2000.

———. "Mengele Medicus: Medicine's Nazi Heritage." *Milbank Quarterly* 66 (1988): 221–239.

Tröhler, Ulrich. "Graduate Education in the History of Medicine: Federal Republic of Germany." *Bulletin of the History of Medicine* 63 (1989): 435–443.

Wade, Nicholas. "Doctors Question Use of Nazis' Medical Atlas." *New York Times,* 26 November 1996.

Other Professions

Beyerchen, Alan. *Scientists under Hitler: Politics and the Physics Community in the Third Reich.* New Haven: Yale University Press, 1977.

Billstein, Reinhold, Karola Fings, Anita Kugler, and Nicholas Levis, eds. *Working for the Enemy: Ford, General Motors and Forced Labor in Germany During the Second World War.* New York: Berghahn Books, 2000.

Borkin, Joseph. *The Crime and Punishment of IG Farben: The Unholy Alliance of Adolf Hitler and Germany's Great Chemical Combine.* New York: Free Press, 1978.

Deichmann, Uta. *Biologists Under Hitler.* Cambridge, MA: Harvard University Press, 1996.

Friedlander, Henry, and Sybil Milton, eds. *The Holocaust: Ideology, Bureaucracy, and Genocide.* New York: Kraus International Publications, 1980.

Gregor, Neil. *Daimler Benz in the Third Reich.* New Haven: Yale University Press, 1998.

Hayes, Peter. *Industry and Ideology: IG Farben in the Nazi Era*. Cambridge: Cambridge University Press, 1987.

Kater, Michael. *The Twisted Muse: Musicians and Their Music in the Third Reich*. New York: Oxford University Press, 1997.

Macrakis, Kristie. *Surviving the Swastika: Scientific Research in Nazi Germany*. New York: Oxford University Press, 1993.

———. "The Rockefeller Foundation and German Physics under National Socialism." *Minerva* 27 (1989): 33–57.

Schulze, Winfried, and Otto Gerhard Oexle, eds. *Deutsche Historiker im Nationalsozialismus*. Frankfurt am Main: Fischer Taschenbuch Verlag, 1999.

Steinweis, Alan. *Art, Ideology, and Economics in Nazi Germany: The Reich Chambers of Music, Theater and the Visual Arts*. Chapel Hill: University of North Carolina Press, 1996.

Weale, Adrian. *Science under the Swastika*. London: Channel 4 Books, 2001.

Weinreich, Max. *Hitler's Professors: The Part of Scholarship in Germany's Crimes against the Jewish People*. New Haven: Yale University Press, 1999.

Holocaust, "Final Solution," the German People

Arendt, Hannah. *Eichmann in Jerusalem: A Report on the Banality of Evil*. New York: Penguin, 1994.

Bankier, David. *The Germans and the Final Solution: Public Opinion under Nazism*. Oxford: Basil Blackwell, 1992.

Bartov, Omer. *Hitler's Army: Soldiers, Nazis and War in the Third Reich*. New York: Oxford University Press, 1991.

———, ed. *The Holocaust: Origins, Implementation, Aftermath*. New York: Routledge, 2000.

Browder, George. *Hitler's Enforcers: The Gestapo and the SS Security Service in the Nazi Revolution*. New York: Oxford University Press, 1996.

Browning, Christopher. *Ordinary Men: Reserve Police Battalion 101 and the Final Solution in Poland*. New York: HarperCollins, 1992.

———. *The Path to Genocide: Essays on Launching the Final Solution*. New York: Cambridge University Press, 1992.

———. *Nazi Policy, Jewish Workers, German Killers*. New York: Cambridge University Press, 2000.

Burleigh, Michael. *Ethics and Extermination: Reflections on Nazi Genocide*. Cambridge: Cambridge University Press, 1997.

———, ed. *Confronting the Nazi Past: New Debates on Modern German History*. New York: St. Martin's Press, 1996.

Burleigh, Michael, and Wolfgang Wippermann. *The Racial State: Germany 1933–1945*. Cambridge: Cambridge University Press, 1991.

Cesarani, David, ed. *The Final Solution: Origins and Implementation*. London and New York: Routledge, 1994.

Friedländer, Saul. *Nazi Germany and the Jews: The Years of Persecution, 1933–1939.* New York: HarperCollins, 1997.

Gellately, Robert. *The Gestapo and German Society: Enforcing Racial Policy, 1933–1945.* Oxford: Oxford University Press, 1990.

Goldhagen, Daniel. *Hitler's Willing Executioners: Ordinary Germans and the Holocaust.* New York: Alfred A. Knopf, 1996.

Gordon, Sarah. *Hitler, Germans and the Jewish Question.* Princeton: Princeton University Press, 1984.

Hamburg Institute for Social Research, ed. *The German Army and Genocide: Crimes against War Prisoners, Jews, and Other Civilians in the East, 1939–1944,* translated by Scott Abbott. New York: New Press, 1999.

Hilberg, Raul. *The Destruction of the European Jews.* 3 vols. New York: Holmes and Meier, 1985.

————. *Perpetrators Victims Bystanders: The Jewish Catastrophe, 1933–1945.* New York: HarperCollins, 1992.

Höhne, Heinz. *The Order of the Death's Head: The Story of Hitler's SS.* Trans. Richard Barry. London: Penguin, 1969.

Kershaw, Ian. *Popular Opinion and Political Dissent in the Third Reich: Bavaria.* Oxford: Clarendon Press, 1984.

Langbein, Hermann. *Menschen in Auschwitz.* Vienna and Munich: Europa Verlag, 1995.

Lewy, Guenther. *The Nazi Persecution of the Gypsies.* New York: Oxford University Press, 2000.

Peukert, Detlev. *Inside Nazi Germany: Conformity, Opposition, and Racism in Everyday Life.* New Haven: Yale University Press, 1987.

Reitlinger, Gerald. *The Final Solution: The Attempt to Exterminate the Jews of Europe, 1939–1945.* New York: A.S. Barnes, 1961.

Rückerl, Adalbert. *NS-Vernichtungslager im Spiegel deutscher Strafprozesse: Belzec, Sobibor, Treblinka, Chelmno.* Munich: Deutscher Taschenbuch Verlag, 1977.

Steinert, Marlis. *Hitler's War and the Germans: Public Mood and Attitude during the Second World War.* Athens, OH: Ohio University Press, 1977.

Yahil, Leni. *The Holocaust: The Fate of European Jewry.* New York: Oxford University Press, 1990.

INDEX

abortion, selective, 36
Adams, Mark, 16
Adler, Isaac, 43
Adorno, Theodor W., 55
Ahnenerbe, 97
alcoholism, 35
    corrupting German bodies, 42
    and eugenics movement, 22
    hereditary basis, 14, 16, 36
    registered addicts, 45
    sterilization laws in Nazi Germany, 32
Allen, Garland E., 6, 13–39, 113–14, 117
Alt-Rehse, 79
Alzheimer, Alois, 93, 94, 96
Alzheimer's disease, 9, 103, 125
American Eugenics Society, 22, 31
American Neurological Association, 28
Am Spiegelgrund, 61
Anschluss, 65
anti-Semitism:
    agenda in party groups, 78
    annihilationist, 3
    definition of perpetrators, 2
    post–World War I Germany, 34
Arendt, Hannah, 1
Argentina, 45
Art, Ideology and Economics in Nazi Germany: The Reich Chambers of Music Theater and the Visual Arts (Steinweis), 4
Aryans, 82
asbestos, 42
Ashes to Ashes (Kluger), 41
Askanazy, Max, 48
Askaris, 65
"asocials," 45
Astel, Karl, 50, 54, 55
Auschwitz, 7, 62
    assembly line murder, 68
    Auschwitz I,II, and III, 67
    extermination camp, 66–71
    "final solution," 66
    gassings, 66
    human histological specimens, 85
    Mengele, Josef, 71, 86–87, 88, 113

selections at the ramp, 8, 95
slave labor, 67
SS Hygiene Institute, 69
SS perpetrators, 1
sterilization, 65
unethical human experiments, 70
Austria, 65, 123
    academic psychiatry, 94
    Anschluss, 53, 65
    desirables/undesirables, 94–95
    killing center, 65
    medicine and medical ethics in Third Reich, 9, 96

Bankier, David, 2
Bartov, Omer, 2, 3
Baycrest Centre for Geriatric Care, Toronto, 95
Bell, Alexander Graham, 22
Bell, W. Blair, 48
Belzec, 64
Berblinger, Walther, 48
Bergen-Belsen, 88
Berlin, University of, 100
Bernburg, 65, 66
Bernotat, Fritz, 122
Beyerchen, Alan, 4
Binding, Karl, 120
biological psychiatry, 14
Biologists under Hitler (Deichmann), 4
"Biomedical Sciences and Human Experimentation at Kaiser Wilhelm Institutes—The Auschwitz Connection," 107, 128–39
Birkenau:
    "Canada" camp, 67
    extermination camp, 66–71
    gassings, 67
    Gypsy camp, 71
    Theresienstadt, 69
Black Stork, The, 24
Bluhm, Agnes, 44
Blumer, Alfred, 116
Borkin, Joseph, 3
Borm, Kurt, 62
Brandenburg, 65, 98, 99

Britain:
eugenics movement, 16, 114
tobacco as lung cancer hazard, 41
Brocke, Bernhard vom, 130
Browning, Christopher, 2, 3
Brown Shirts, 80
Buchenwald, 84
Buna camp, 67
Bunke, Heinrich, 62
Burleigh, Michael, vii, 4, 5, 9–10, 112–27
Burnham, John, 51–52
Butenandt, Adolf, 106
By Trust Betrayed: Patients, Physicians, and the License to Kill in the Third Reich (Gallagher), 4

Cameron, Ewen, 89
Campbell, Clarence C., 32
Canada, medical crimes in Canadian curricula, 89
cancer, metaphors in Nazi Germany, 40
Caplan, Arthur, 55
Cardiff University, vii
Carnegie Foundation, 19, 31, 35, 117
Casti connubi, 29
Castle, W. E., 19
castration, 83
Catel, Werner, 82
Catholic Center Party, 118
Chancellery of the Führer (*Kanzlei des Führers*, KDF), 60
Chase, Allan, 30
Chelmno, 64
Chesterton, G. K., 116, 118
China:
eugenic strategies, 114, 124
income from tobacco taxes, 53
tobacco and cancer death, 43
chronic granulomatous disease, 13
Clauberg, Carl, 70
Cold Spring Harbor, 18, 19, 34
Cologne, University of, 46, 47, 131
Cologne Bürgerhospital, 46
Columbia University, 89
Combat League for German Culture, 78–79
concentration camps, 66
Conti, Leonardo, 45, 54, 84, 88
Coolidge, Calvin, 25
Crime and Punishment of IG Farben: The Unholy Alliance of Adolf Hitler and Germany's Great Chemical Combine, The (Borkin), 3
criminality, 35
compulsory sterilization laws in U.S., 28
and eugenics movement, 22
hereditary basis, 14, 16, 36
criminal physicians in the Third Reich:
ambition and sadism, 88
"Aryans," 82
bone transplants, 85–86

Brown Shirts, 80
Combat League for German Culture, 78–79
criminal, defined, 77
curricula of Third Reich schools, 88–90
death factor in SS value system, 81–82
female Nazi physicians, 88
gas gangrene experiments, 85
gender bias, 88
group profile of medical criminals, 87–88
hereditary health courts, 83
human experiments and mass killings, 84
Leadership School at Alt-Rehse, 79
medical crimes in U.S. and Canadian curricula, 89
"mind patterning" experiments, 89
National Socialist Physicians' League, 78
National Socialist Students League, 83
Nazi Physicians' League, 78, 84, 88
Nuremberg Racial Laws, 81
Physicians' League, 78, 79
political association, 77–82
professional and financial security, 81
professional-ethical conduct, 82–87
Red Front, 80
Reich Physician's Chamber, 80
SA physicians in street brawls, 80, 83
viability of Nazi medical experiments, 89
Cruzan, Nancy, 125
Crystal Night pogrom, 80
cystic fibrosis, 13, 37

Dachau, 55, 67, 82, 84, 88
Daimler Benz in the Third Reich (Gregor), 3
Darwin, Charles, 5, 17, 119
Das Standardwerk, 43
Davenport, Charles B., 17–18
Eugenics Record Office (ERO), 19
old-style eugenics platform, 34
Death and Deliverance: "Euthanasia" in Germany, c. 1900–1945 (Burleigh), 4
Deichmann, Ute, 4
DeJarnette, Joseph S., 33
dementia, Alzheimer's, 103
Denmark, eugenics movement, 114
Destruction of the European Jews, The (Hilberg), 1
Deussen, Julius, 106
Deutsche Forschungsgemeinschaft (DFG), 71, 130
Deutsche Historiker im Nationalsozialismus (Schulze and Oexle), 4
Dewey, John, 52
Dickens, Charles, 115
disabled, T4 killing wards, 60
Disraeli, Benjamin, 115
Doctors under Hitler (Kater), 4
Doll, Richard, 41, 49, 51, 112, 113
Draper, W. P., 19
Düsseldorf, University of, 100

Duster, Troy, 37
dysgenics, 22

Eberl, Irmfried, 7, 62, 65–66, 72
Eglfing-Haar, 98
Eichberg Hospital, 64
Eichmann, Adolf, 1, 119
Eichmann in Jerusalem (Arendt), 1
Eickhoff, Clemens, 119
Einstein, Albert, 130
Ellen institution, 82, 83
Endlösung der Brotfrage (final solution to
    the bread question), 50
Endruweit, Klaus, 62
Engels, Friedrich, 115
Entress, Friedrich, 68
epilepsy:
    compulsory sterilization laws in U.S.,
        28, 34
    sterilization laws in Nazi Germany, 32
Erlangen, 121, 122
*Ethics and Extermination: Reflections on
    Nazi Genocide* (Burleigh), 5
eugenics, vi–vii, 5
    agricultural breeding, 17
    "back door eugenics," 37
    blank spaces in, 10
    decline in United States, 34–35
    dysgenics, 22
    "eugenic tree," 18
    feeblemindedness, 19
    genetic determinist explanations for
        social problems, 15–17
    hereditary degeneracy, 19, 23
    and immigration laws in United States,
        25, 26, 27, 28
    Juke family studies, 19
    Kallikak family study, 19, 23, 35, 114
    "Model Sterilization Law," 28, 32
    movement in U.S. and Germany, 113–14
    national breeding program, 5
    national efficiency, 30
    Nazi connection, 32–34
    in Nazi Germany, 5
    negative eugenics, 17
    in North America, 5
    opposition to, 28–29
    overview of ideology of elimination, 15–17
    philanthropic funding in U.S., 31
    political action programs, 25–28
    position in Third Reich policies, 34
    positive eugenics, 17
    research program, 1900–1940, 17–24
    residuum, 22
    social action, 22, 23, 24
    in social context, 29–31
    social versus biological transmission, 19
    "Taylorism," 30
    turning genes on and off, 16
Eugenics Committee of American Breeders'
    Association, 19

Eugenics Record Office (ERO), 19
Eugenics Research Association, 25, 31, 32
euthanasia:
    brain preparations from victims, 102, 103
    child killing at Vienna Psychiatric Hospi-
        tal, 101–4
    euthanasia physicians, 82–83, 87–88
    killing centers, 65
    negative selection, 82
    at T4, 7
    voluntary, 10
Evolution and Genetics (Morgan), 29
evolutionary psychology, 13

Fabians, 117
Faltlhauser, Valentin, 121–22
Faulstich, Heinz, 123
feeblemindedness, 19
    compulsory sterilization laws in U.S., 28
    sterilization laws in Nazi Germany, 32
    undesirable and hereditary, 94–95
Ferrari, Enrico:
    cigarettes and lung cancer, 45, 46,
        57n.15
"final solution," 50
    in Nazi Germany rhetoric, 40
    and "ordinary Germans," 2
*Final Solution: The Attempt to Exterminate
    the Jews of Europe, 1939–1945, The*
    (Reitlinger), 1
Fischer, Eugen, 105, 134
Fisher, Irving:
    eugenics movement, 19
Fleckseder, Rudolf, 45–46
Flexner, Abraham, 104, 105
Flossenbürg, 68
forced sterilization, 4, 5
Forest Cemetery, Munich, 99, 100
France, smoking and cancer link, 112
Frankfurt Institute for Hereditary Biology
    and Race Hygiene, 71
Frankfurt, University of, 98, 135
Frankfurt trials, 1
Frewer, Andreas, 119
Friedlander, Henry, 4, 7, 59–76, 113,
    115, 120
Friedländer, Saul, 11
Frowein, Jochen, 131
Funk, Walter, 53

Gallagher, Hugh, 4
Gallagher, Nancy, vii
Galton, Francis, 5, 118
    "eugenics" term, 17
Galton Society, 31
gas gangrene experiments, 85
gassings:
    of disabled patients, 61
    physician initiated, 66, 69, 95
    at Treblinka, 7
Gebhart, Karl, 84, 85

gender bias, 88
genetic blindness and deafness, sterilization
    laws in Nazi Germany, 32
geneticization, description of, 6, 36
genetics:
    absolving responsibility, 36
    basis for mental and social behaviors,
        13–16
    genetically "informed" solutions, 14
    genetic explanations in current society, 36
    "Holy Grail" of modern medicine, 14, 35
    medicalization and geneticization, 6
    Mendelian genetics, 17
    reproductive decisions based on, 37
    selective abortion, 36
German Army, 101
German Institute for Psychiatric Research,
    94
German Research Institute for Psychiatry,
    134
*Germans and the Final Solution: Public
    Opinion under Nazism, The*
    (Bankier), 2
Germany, 123
    academic psychiatry, 94
    defeat in World War I, 33, 38
    desirables/undesirables, 94–95
    eugenics movement, 16, 17, 32–34,
        113–14, 114, 116
    Gessellschaft für Rassenhygiene (Society
        for Racial Hygiene), 32
    growth of eugenics movement, 29–31
    history of medicine and medical ethics in
        Third Reich, 96
    medical establishment, 9
    National Cancer Institute, 54
    Thuringia, 50, 54
    Treaty of Versailles, 33, 38
    Weimar Germany, 32, 33, 34, 38, 48,
        80, 115, 118
germline gene replacement, 13
Gershon, Elliott, 100
Gestapo, 65
Gesundheitsführung (leadership in health),
    7, 41
Giessen, 99
Gilbert, Walter, 14
Globocnik, Odilo, 64, 66
Glücks, Richard, 66
Goddard, Henry H., 23
Goebel, Margaret, 122
Goethe, Charles M., 32
Goldhagen, Daniel Jonah, 2, 3
Goldschmidt, Richard, 32
Görden, 98, 99, 101
Gordon, Sarah, 2
Gorgaß, Hans-Bodo, 63
Gregor, Neil, 3
Groß-Rosen, 68
Gross, Heinrich, 101–4
guinea pigs, TB experimentation, 85

Gypsies, 87
    camp at Auschwitz, 69
    corrupting German bodies, 42
    experimentation and mass killings of,
        82, 83
    genetic research, 105
    mass murder of, 4, 5, 6, 64
    twins used for studies, 71

Hadamar, 7
Haeckel, Ernst, 120
Haiselden, Harry, 24
Haldane, J. B. S., 116
Hallervorden, Julius, 98, 99, 100, 105, 134
    brain specimens from euthanasia pro-
        grams, 113
Hallervorden-Spatz disease, 98
Hamburg Institute for Social Research, 3
handicapped:
    mass murder of, 4, 6
    and national breeding programs, 5
Harms, Juliane, 79
Harmsen, Hans, 117
Harnack, Adolf von, 130
Harriman Foundation, 19, 31, 117
Hartheim, 65
Hayes, Peter, 3
Hebold, Otto, 63
Heidelberg, University of, 32, 94, 98
    anatomical and pathological specimens, 95
    Department of Psychiatry, 94, 95
Heilstaetten, 100
Heissmeyer, Kurt, 84–85, 88
Hermann von Helmholtz Association, 130
Hess, Rudolf, 78
Heyde, Werner, 63, 82
Hilberg, Raul, vi, 1
Hilfswillige or *Hiwis*, 64
Himmler, Heinrich, 66, 84, 85, 119
    ban on smoking, 49
    black shirts, 8
    SS, 81
Hitler, Adolf, 78, 79
    anti-tobacco effort/funding, 42, 46, 50,
        51, 53
    gassing of disabled, 61
    racial hygiene policies, 96–97
    social Darwinism, 82
Hitler, Germans and the "Jewish Question"
    (Gordon), 2
*Hitler's Army: Soldiers, Nazis and War in the
    Third Reich* (Bartov), 2
*Hitler's Professors: The Part of Scholarship in
    Germany's Crimes against the Jewish
    People* (Weinreich), 3
*Hitler's War and the Germans: Public Mood
    and Attitude during the Second World
    War* (Steinert), 2
*Hitler's Willing Executioners: Ordinary Ger-
    mans and the Holocaust* (Goldhagen), 2
Hitler Youth, 79, 83

Index

Hoche, Alfred, 120
Hoehe, Margaret, 100
Hohenlychen, 84, 88
homeless, registries for, 45
homosexuality, hereditary basis, 36
Horkheimer, Max, 55
Hospital for Curative Paedogogics am
    Spiegelgrund, the, 101
Höss, Rudolf, 66, 67
Huener, Jonathan, 1–12, 117
Human Betterment Foundation, 22
Human Genetics and Eugenics, Berlin, 134
Human Genome Project, 13
Humphreys of Whitehall, Sir, 118
"hunger houses," 98
Huntington's chorea, 32, 36

I.G. Farben, 3, 85
    *The Crime and Punishment of IG Farben:
        The Unholy Alliance of Adolf Hitler
        and Germany's Great Chemical Com-
        bine* (Borkin), 3
    *Industry and Ideology: IG Farben in the
        Nazi Era* (Hayes), 3
    Monowitz camp, 67
ignorance, social production of, 40
Illing, Ernst, 61, 101, 102
industrialization, growth of eugenics
    movement, 29
inmate bands, 87
Innsbruck, University of, 65
*Inside Nazi Germany: Conformity, Opposi-
    tion and Racism in Everyday Life*
    (Peukert), 2
Inspectorate of the Concentration Camps, 63
Institute for the Study of Genius, 98
Institute for Tobacco Hazards Research, 54
Intelligence Quotient (IQ), and eugenics
    movement, 25, 26, 27, 28, 29, 35
International Physicians for Peace and
    against Nuclear War, 89
Israel, 130
Israel, Howard, 89–90

Jekelius, Erwin, 61, 101
Jena, University of, 50
Jena Institute for Tobacco Hazards
    Research, 7, 46, 50
Jennings, Herbert Spencer, 28
Jews, 11
    and cancer metaphors used by Nazi Ger-
        many, 40, 113
    corrupting German bodies, 42
    experimentation and mass killings of, 83
    gas chambers at Auschwitz, 86
    genetic research, 105
    "Jewish question," 79
    Jewish scientists cited, 48
    mass murder campaign, 64
    mass murder of, 4, 5, 6
    Nuremberg Racial Laws, 78

physical elimination of, 82
practicing physicians in Germany, 79
prohibited marriages in Germany, 33
selection in Operation 14f13, 64
tobacco association with, 42
twins used for studies, 71
Johnson, Albert, 25
Johnson, Kathy, vii
Johnson Act of 1924, 25, 27, 28
Jordan, David Starr, 19
Jost, Adolf, 120
Juke family, 19, 35

Kaiser Wilhelm Institute for Anthropology,
    134, 135
    genetic research on Jews and Gypsies, 105
    Mengele and Verschuer connection, 108
Kaiser Wilhelm Institute for Brain
    Research, 95, 98, 105, 134
Kaiser Wilhelm Institute for Genetics, 32
Kaiser Wilhelm Institute of Psychiatry,
    brains from euthanasia killings, 94,
    95, 105
Kaiser Wilhelm Society, 9, 71, 73, 86
    brain research, 97
    eugenic and racial programs, 105–7
    funding by Rockefeller Foundation, 104
    genealogical/demographic research, 96, 97
    institutional disorder, 104–7
    levels of guilt, 136–37
    as predecessor of Max Planck Society,
        128–39
    psychiatric research, 94
    research materials from euthanasia pro-
        grams, 113
    study of neuropathology, 99
Kallikak family, 19, 23, 35, 114
Kant, Immanuel, 119
Katcher, Brian, 52
Kater, Michael, 4, 8–9, 77–92, 116, 121
Kaufmann, Doris, 131, 133
Kellogg family, 22, 31, 117
Kershaw, Ian, 2
Kevles, Daniel J., 16, 41, 113
Kimmelman, Barbara, 19
Kinderfachabteilungen (pediatric depart-
    ments), 98
Kirchert, Werner, 62
Kitcher, Philip, 37
Klee, Ernst, 113, 121
Klein, Fritz, 69
Kluger, Richard, 41
Koch, Robert, 84
Kommandos, 87
Koplewitz, Martin, vii
Kopp, Marie E., 32
Korson, Roy, vii
Kraepelin, Emil, 93, 94, 96, 97
Kremer, Johann, 7, 69–70, 72, 85
Krupp family, 97, 100

Kühl, Stefan, 17, 32, 117
Kunin, Arthur, vi, vii

Labour Party, 118
Langbein, Hermann, 67
Laue, Max von, 130
Laughlin, Harry H., 25, 26, 27, 30, 117
    eugenics movement, 19
    honorary MD from Heidelberg University, 32
    late-onset epilepsy, 34–35
    old-style eugenics platform, 34
Law for the Prevention of Progeny of Sufferers from Hereditary Diseases, 32
lead, corrupting German bodies, 42
Leadership in Health, 7, 41
Leadership School, 79
Lehmann, Hartmut, 131
Lehner, Ludwig, 60–61
Leichenfledderei (looting the corpses), 62, 63
Lenin, Vladimir, 97, 98
Lens, Sidney, 29
Lenz, Fritz, 105, 118
Lickint, Fritz, 44, 45, 46, 56n.13, 57n.19, 112
Liebehenschel, Arthur, 67
Lifton, Robert Jay, 4, 81, 87
Lippmann, Walter, 29
Lipschitz, Marx, 48
Loeb, James, 94, 96, 97, 104, 117
Lonauer, Rudolf, 62, 63, 65
London, Jack, 115
London School of Economics and Political Science, 117
Lübeck, University of, 106
Lublin, 64
Ludwig Boltzmann Institute for Research on Malformations of the Nervous System, 103
Ludwig Boltzmann Society, 103
Ludwigsburg, 123
Luftwaffe, smoking ban, 49
Luminal, 60, 122
Lüst, Reimar, 130

Macrakis, Kristie, 4
Madlung, Inga, 86, 88
Madlung, Jutta, 86
Magnussen, Karin, 71
Majdanek, 66
manic-depressive disorder, 35
    anecdotal information for diagnosis, 28
    and eugenic movement, 19, 20
    sterilization laws in Nazi Germany, 32
    undesirable and hereditary, 14, 94–95
Markl, Hubert, 107–8, 128–39
Marshall Plan, 54
Marx, Karl, 115
Massin, Benoit, 135
Mauthausen, 65, 84
Max Planck Institute for Brain Research, 98, 99

Max Planck Society, 9
    "Biomedical Sciences and Human Experimentation at Kaiser Wilhelm Institutes—The Auschwitz Connection," 107, 128–39
    confronting legacy of Kaiser Wilhelm Society, 104, 105–7, 113, 128–39
    origins of brain specimens, 99
    Presidential Commission ("History of the Kaiser Wilhelm Society in the National Socialist Era"), 106–7
Mazumdar, Pauline, 16
McFarland-Icke, Bronwyn, 122
medicalization, description of, 36
Meitner, Lise, 130
memory, pathology of, 93–111
    acquisition of brain specimens, 98–100
    case of Dr. Heinrich Gross, 101–4
    Cecile and Oscar Vogt Institute for Brain Research, 100
    child killing at Vienna Psychiatric Hospital, 101–4
    dementia, description of, 93
    euthanasia of mentally handicapped, 95
    German Institute for Psychiatric Research, 94
    Institute for the Study of Genius, 98
    Kaiser Wilhelm Institute for Brain Research, 98, 99
    Kaiser Wilhelm/Max Planck Institute of Psychiatry, 94
    Kaiser Wilhelm Society, 100
    Kinderfachabteilungen (pediatric departments), 98
    Ludwig Boltzmann Institute for Research on Malformations of the Nervous System, 103
    Nervenklinik für Kinder, 101
    Neurohistology Laboratory of the Vienna Psychiatric Hospital, 103
    neuropathology: brains of the dead, 97–100
    Nuremberg Racial Laws, 95
    pathology of institutional memory, 104–7
    pneumoencephalograms, 101–2
    psychiatry, eugenics, and sterilization, 96–97
    psychological studies on doomed to die, 98
    Second Psychiatric Department and the Neurohistology Laboratory, 102
    Vienna Psychiatric Hospital, 103
memory disorders, German and Austrian research, 9
Mengele, Josef, 8, 55, 113
    connection with Verschuer, 108, 135
    genetic research on Jews and Gypsies, 105, 106
    medical criminality at Auschwitz, 82, 84, 86–87, 88
    physician killer, 70–71, 73
Mennecke, Eva, 63
Mennecke, Friedrich, 63–64, 72

mental and social behaviors, genetic basis
for, 13–16
Meseritz-Obrawalde, 61
Mieder, Wolfgang, vii
Miller Symposium, vi
"Model Sterilization Law," 28, 32
Mollison, Theodor, 70
Monowitz camp, 67
Morgan, Thomas Hunt, 19, 28, 29
Muckermann, Hermann, 117
Müller, Franz, 46–49, 112
Muller, H. J., 28
Müller, Robert, 63
Müller-Hill, Benno, 4, 105
Münch, Hans, 70
Münster, University of, 69, 85
*Murderous Science: Elimination by Scientific
Selection of Jews, Gypsies and Others,
Germany 1933–1945* (Müller-Hill), 4
Myerson, Abraham, 28

National Institutes of Health (NIH), 100
National Socialism, vi, vii, 6, 123
Darwinism, 82
exploitative research, 9
in history of science and medicine, 55
Kaiser Wilhelm Society activities, 128–39
medicalized crimes, 118
physician political association, 77–78
public health initiatives, 7, 41
tobacco and alcohol temperance, 52
tobacco research, 7
National Socialist German Workers Party,
10, 119
National Socialist Physicians' League (Nazi
Physicians' League), 8, 78, 79, 80, 84
National Socialist Students League, 83
National Union of Scientific Workers, 117
*Nazi Doctors: Medical Killing and the Psy-
chology of Genocide, The* (Lifton), 4
Nazi Germany:
anticancer campaign, 40
"Aryan" racial superiority, 5
campaign against tobacco, 40–58
"eugenics courts," 32
eugenics movement, 5, 17
field of ethics, 120
historical responsibility, 136–37
Inspectorate of the Concentration
Camps, 63
Kaiser Wilhelm Institute for Genetics, 32
Law for the Prevention of Progeny of
Sufferers from Hereditary Diseases, 32
levels of guilt, 136–37
"Model Sterilization Law," 32
"Nazi beans," 40
Nuremberg Laws of 1935, 33
Office of Racial Affairs, 50
physicians as killers in, 59–76
racial ideology, 17
refugees from, 25, 28

rise of "national efficiency," 34
science and Nazi past, 126
SS *St. Louis*, 25, 28
Nazi medicine:
ethical context, 119–20
in historiographical context, 1–12
Nazi Motor League, 79
Nazi Party:
anti-Semitism, 78
Nazi Physicians' League, 78, 79, 80, 84, 88
physician membership and motives, 8,
72, 78–82
Nazi Party Office of Racial Policy, on
smoking, 44
Nazi War on Cancer, The (Proctor), 4, 40
negative eugenics, 17
Netherlands, practice of euthanasia,
124–25
Neuengamme, 67, 85, 88
Neurohistology Laboratory of the Vienna
Psychiatric Hospital, 103
neuropathology, acquisition of brain speci-
mens, 98–100
neuropsychiatric disorders, pathology of
memory, 93–111
Nicosia, Francis R., 1–12, 117
Niedernhard, 65
Nietzsche, Friedrich, 115, 119
Nissl, Franz, 94, 98
Nitsche, Paul, 63
Nuremberg:
International Physicians for Peace and
against Nuclear War, 89
trials by Allies, 1, 78
U.S. Military Tribunal, 60
Nuremberg Racial Laws, 78, 81, 95
nurses, in the Third Reich, 122

Oberheuser, Herta, 85–86, 88
Oexle, Otto Gerhard, 4
Office of Racial Affairs, 50
Operation 14f13, 63–64, 73
Operation Reinhard, 64, 66
Order Police, 3
"ordinary Germans," 11
expanded definition of perpetrators, 2
in the Order Police, 3
professionals as perpetrators, 3
*Ordinary Men: Reserve Police Battalion 101
and the Final Solution in Poland*
(Browning), 2
*Origins of Nazi Genocide: From Euthanasia
to the Final Solution, The* (Fried-
lander), 4
Ostertag, Berthold, 100
Oxford, University of, 112

Paul, Diane, 16, 30
Pauly, Philip J., 52
Pearl, Raymond, 28, 35
pellagra, 19, 21

Index

Permission for the Destruction of Life Unworthy of Life (Binding and Hoche), 120
Peukert, Detlev, 2
Pfannmüller, Hermann, 7, 60–61, 72
phenol, 68
physicians as killers in Nazi Germany:
  camp hygienic conditions, 68
  corporal punishments, 68
  criminal physicians in the Third Reich, 5, 77–92
  "death through natural causes," 60
  extermination camp Auschwitz-Birkenau, 66–71
  intentional starvation, 60
  killing center at Treblinka, 64–66
  looting of the corpses, 63
  loyalty to the SS, 72
  membership in Nazi Party, 72
  motives of physician perpetrators, 72–73
  Operation 14f13, 63–64, 73
  Operation Reinhard, 64
  overdoses, 60
  phenol injections, 68
  political association with Nazi state, 8
  professional-ethical conduct, 8
  Rampe selections, 68, 69
  Revier or *Krankenbau*, 68
  situational killers, 72
  "Special Treatment 14f13," 63
  tattoos of prisoners, 68
  T4 killing centers, 62–63
  T4 killing wards, 59–62
  turning on the gas, 66, 69
  twin studies, 71
  unethical human experiments, 70
  using inmate physicians, 70, 71
  "wild euthanasia," 60, 61, 62
Pius XI, Pope, opposition of eugenics, 29
Planck, Max, 98, 104, 130
Platen-Hallermund, Alice, 113
Plauzoles, Sicard de, 115
Ploetz, Alfred, 118
pneumoencephalogram, 101–2
Pohl, Oswald, 84
poor/pauperism, 5, 19, 22
Popular Opinions and Political Dissent in the Third Reich: Bavaria (Kershaw), 2
positive eugenics, 17
positive health activism, 4–5
prisoners of war, Soviet, 66
Proctor, Robert, 4, 6–7, 17, 40–58, 95, 106, 112–13
professionals, role in crimes during Third Reich, 3, 4
Prohibition, 52, 53
Protestant Inner Mission, 117
psychiatry, pathology of memory, 93–111

Race Betterment Foundation, 22, 31
Racial Hygiene: Medicine under the Nazis (Proctor), 4

racial ideology, vii
racial purification, 5
racism, in Nazi Germany, 34
Rascher, Sigmund, 82, 88
Ratka, Viktor, 63
Ravensbrück, 62
  human experiments, 88
  Operation 14f13, 63
  women's camp at, 85, 86
Red Front, 80
Rehm, Ruth, 65, 72
Reich Bureau for the Struggle against Addictive Drugs, 44
Reich Health Führer, 84
Reich Health Office, 54
Reich Institute for Tobacco Research, 49
Reich Ministry of the Interior, 60
Reich Physician's Chamber, 80
Reiter, Hans, 54
Reitlinger, Gerald, 1
Renn, Jürgen, 131
residuum, 22
Rheinberger, Hans-Jörg, 131
Richarz, Bernhard, 123
Rockefeller, John D., Jr., 19, 31
Rockefeller Foundation, 94, 117
  funding for psychiatric research in Munich, 96, 97
  funding of Kaiser Wilhelm Society, 104
Roelcke, Volker, 106
Roffo, Angel H., 45, 46, 56n.12
Röhm, Ernst, 80, 81
Roll-Hanson, Nils, 17
Rosenberg, Alfred, 78
Rüdin, Ernst, 96–97, 98, 105, 106, 134
Rudolf Virchow Hospital, 100
Rürup, Reinhard, 131
Russia, Bolshevik revolution, 29–30

Sachse, Carola, 131, 135
Sachsenhausen, human experiments, 84
Sarton, George, 16
SA (Sturmabteilungen):
  criminal physicians in the Third Reich, 80–81
  Hitler's purging, 81
  physician political association, 8, 78
  "Röhm purge," 81
Sauckel, Fritz, 50, 54
Sauerbruch, Ferdinand, 85
Schairer, Eberhard, 46, 49, 50, 51
Schenck, Ernst Günther, 83–84
Schieder, Wolfgang, 131
schizophrenia, 35, 100
  genetic basis for, 14
  sterilization laws in Nazi Germany, 32
  undesirable and hereditary, 94–95
Schmalenbach, Kurt, 63
Schmitz, Heinrich, 68
Schneider, Carl, 82, 98
Schöniger, Erich, 46, 49, 50, 51

Schreibtischtäter (desk killers), 59
Schultze, Walter, 122
Schulze, Winfried, 4
Schumann, Coco, 86–87
Schumann, Horst, 62, 63, 65, 70
Schwarz, Michael, 118
scientific amnesia, 9, 58n.33
scientism, 14, 115
Scientists under Hitler: Politics and the
    Physics Community in the Third Reich
    (Beyerchen), 4
scopolamine, 60, 122
Scrase, David, vii
Seattle, general strike, 30
Second Psychiatric Department and the
    Neurohistology Laboratory, 102
Seidelman, William, 9, 90, 113
Sengenhoff, Werner, 83, 87
sexual perversion, compulsory sterilization
    laws in U.S., 28
Seyfarth, Carly, 48
Shaw, George Bernard, 115
Shorter, Edward, 94
Singapore, eugenic strategies, 114
Slavs, experiments on and mass killings
    of, 83
Sobibor, 64
social Darwinism, 120, 124
Social Democratic Party, 10, 79, 116,
    118, 119
Socialist Party, 102
sociobiology, 13
somatic gene therapy, 13
Spatz, Hugo, 98, 134
Spiegelgrund, child killing at, 101–4
Spielmeyer, Walther, 98
SS (Schutzstaffel):
    Ahnenerbe, 97
    ban on smoking, 49
    criminal physicians in the Third Reich,
        8, 81
    death factor in SS value system, 81–82
    defined as criminal organization, 78
    Hygiene Institute, 69
    officials as perpetrators, 1
    physician association with, 8
    "Special Treatment 14f13," 63
Staab, Heinz, 130
Stanford University, 19
starvation, intentional, 98, 100
Stasi, 103
Steinert, Marlis, 2
Steinmeyer, Theodor, 63, 82–83, 87
Steinweis, Alan, 4
Steppe, Hildegard, 122
sterilization, 83
    diagnostic categories for, 97
    involuntary victims in U.S., 114
    Law for the Prevention of Progeny of
        Sufferers from Hereditary Diseases in
        Germany, 32

laws in United States, 28
    "Model Sterilization Law," 28, 32
    by Nazi Party physicians, 83
Stern, Fritz, 131
Stoddard, Lothrop, 32–33
Stolleis, Michael, 131
substance abuse, genetic basis for, 14
Surviving the Swastika: Scientific Research in
    Nazi Germany (Macrakis), 4
Sweden:
    compulsory sterilization laws, 28
    eugenics movement, 114

T4, 7, 65, 66, 69
    Berlin office, 60
    killing centers, 62–63
    killing wards, 59–62
    neuropathological brain specimens, 98
    "wild euthanasia," 60, 61, 62
Tabacologia medicinalis, 53
Tabak und Organismus (Lickint), 44
"Taylorism," 30
Technical University of Berlin, 131
thalassemia, 13
thalassophilia, 19
Theresienstadt, 69
Third Reich:
    criminal physicians in, 77–92
    history of medicine and medical ethics, 96
    legacy of Nazi medicine, 112–27
    professions and role of crimes, 3, 4
Thom, Achim, 123
Tille, Alexander, 120
tobacco, Nazi campaign against, 6–7, 40–58
    Astel and Jena's Institute for Tobacco
        Hazards Research, 50–51
    fascist anti-tobacco campaign, 55
    female smokers, 49
    first epidemiological study, 46–49
    interpreting Nazi Germany's tobacco
        research, 51–52
    legal sanctions and ban of smoking, 49–50
    "lung masturbation," 42
    medical moralism, 42–45
    Müller's 1939 case-control study, 45–49
    "nico-Nazis," 55
    "passive smoking," 44
    "plague" or "dry drunkenness," 42
    possible causes of lung cancer, 43, 48
    postwar anti-tobacco campaign, 54–55
    quit smoking techniques/preparations,
        49–50
    Rauchstrasse ("smoking street"), 44
    smoking as passive resistance, 52
    Stunde Null, 41–42
    Tabacologia medicinalis, 53
    tobacco collapse, 52–54
    tobacco taxes, 53
    U.S. shipments of tobacco to Germany, 54
Tobacco Institute, 53
Toronto, University of, 89

Trawniki, *Hilfswillige* or *Hiwis,* 64
Treblinka, 7, 66, 72
  killing center at, 64–66
  Operation Reinhard, 64
  selections for gas chambers, 69
  tuberculosis, human experiments with,
    84–85
Tübingen, University of, 100
Türk, Marianne, 101, 102
twin studies, 71, 100
*Twisted Muse: Musicians and Their Music in
  the Third Reich, The* (Kater), 4

Ullrich, Aquilin, 62
Union of Socialist Scholars, 102
United States:
  African-American population, 115
  American Eugenics Society, 22, 31
  American Neurological Association, 28
  Army IQ testing, 27
  attitudes toward tobacco, 51–52
  compulsory sterilization, 28, 30
  the Depression, 30, 38
  eugenics and immigration laws, 25, 26,
    27, 28
  eugenics and ruling class, 30–31
  Eugenics Committee of American Breed-
    ers' Association, 19
  eugenics movement, 16, 17, 113–14, 114
  Eugenics Record Office (ERO), 19
  Eugenics Research Association, 25, 31, 32
  Galton Society, 31
  growth of eugenics movement, 29–31
  House Committee on Immigration and
    Naturalization, 19, 25
  Human Betterment Foundation, 22
  Johnson Act of 1924, 25, 28
  Juke family study, 35
  Kallikak family study, 19, 23, 35, 114
  medical crimes in U.S. curricula, 89
  Prohibition, 52, 53
  Race Betterment Foundation, 22, 31
  Sacco-Vanzetti case, 30
  shipments of tobacco to Germany, 54
  tobacco and cancer death, 41, 43
  Tobacco Institute, 53
University Hospital of Neurology and Psy-
  chiatry, Basel, 96
urbanization, growth of eugenics move-
  ment, 29
U.S. Military Tribunal, 60

Vermont, University of, vi
  Center for Holocaust Studies, vi
  College of Medicine, vi, vii
Verschuer, Otmar Freiherr von, 71, 84, 86
  brain specimens from euthanasia pro-
    grams, 113
  connection with Mengele, 105, 107–8
  twin studies, 134

Vienna:
  funding brain research, 103
  Heilpädagogische Klinik am Spiegel-
    grund (Hospital for Curative Paedo-
    gogics am Spiegelgrund), 101
  Wiener Städtische Erziehungsheim am
    Spiegelgrund (City of Vienna Educa-
    tional Establishment am Spiegel-
    grund), 101
  Wiener Städtische Jugenfürsorgeanstalt
    am Spiegelgrund (City of Vienna
    Young People's Welfare Institution am
    Spiegelgrund), 101
  Wiener Städtische Nervenklinik für
    Kinder (City of Vienna Psychiatric-
    Neurological Hospital for Children), 101
Vienna, University of, 90, 102, 103
Vienna Medical Society, 102
Vienna Psychiatric Hospital, 101–4, 103
Vierhaus, Rudolf, 130
Vineland Training School, 23
Vogt, Cecile, 97–98, 100
Vogt Institute for Brain Research, Cecile
  and Oscar , 100
Vogt, Oskar, 97–98, 100
Vogt, Werner, 103

Waffen-SS, 71, 84
Wagner, Gerhard, 78, 88
Ward, Harold, 31
Watson, James D., genetic fate, 14–15
Webb, Beatrice, 117
Webb, Sidney, 117
Weber, Bruno, 70
Wehrmacht, 101
Weindling, Paul, 17, 131
Weinert, Franz Emanuel, 131
Weinreich, Max, 3
Weiss, Sheila, 17, 34
Weizmann Institute, 130
Wender, Neumann, 45, 46
"wild euthanasia," 60, 61, 62
Wirths, Eduard, 67, 72
Wirtinger, Dozent, 102
Wischer, Gerhard, 63
Wittenau, 100
World War II, vii, 1–2
Worthmann, Ewald, 62

X-rays:
  impact on lung cancer diagnoses, 43
  as "Nazi Stormtroopers," 113

Zacher, Hans, 131
Zyklon B, 66, 69